# HOLISTIC INVESTING
## IN A RISK-AVERSE WORLD

JOSEPH F. IPPOLITO

Copyright © 2012 Joseph F. Ippolito
All rights reserved.

ISBN: 1475121199
ISBN-13: 9781475121193

# Contents

INTRODUCTION . . . . . . . . . . . . . . . . . . . . . . . . . . . . . 1

PART A: THE 5 MYTH BUSTERS. . . . . . . . . . . . . . . . . . . 15
   The Earnings Myth. . . . . . . . . . . . . . . . . . . . . . . . . . 17
   Beware the White Noise in our Embroidered Society . . . . . . . . . . 25
   Beware the Name Brand Myth: Smaller is Better . . . . . . . . . . . . 31
   Beware of Wall Street Bearing Gifts: Yesterday's Darling
      Can Be Today's Dunce . . . . . . . . . . . . . . . . . . . . . . 37
   Why Chase Price? Let it Come to You . . . . . . . . . . . . . . . . 43

PART B: THE ANTIDOTE. . . . . . . . . . . . . . . . . . . . . . . . 47
   The Big Picture: What Time is it? . . . . . . . . . . . . . . . . . . 49
   A Picture in Time: Personal Revelation of the 1980s . . . . . . . . . . 55
   Follow the Money: The haystack is more important than the needle . . . . . 61
   New Tools of the Trade Technical and Fundamental Tools . . . . . . 67
   Buying Pattern Signals: The Cosmos Moves in Patterns . . . . . . . 73
   Selling Pattern Signals . . . . . . . . . . . . . . . . . . . . . . . . 79

PART C: HOLISTIC PORTFOLIO THEORY . . . . . . . . . . . . . 83
   The Value 3 Portfolio: Micro View: Positioning Your Money
      in a Risk/Reward World. . . . . . . . . . . . . . . . . . . . . . 85
   The Value 3 Portfolio: Macro View: Positioning Your Money
      in a Risk/Reward World. . . . . . . . . . . . . . . . . . . . . . 91
   Core Value Stocks: The Driver . . . . . . . . . . . . . . . . . . . 97
   Holistic Portfolio Principles. . . . . . . . . . . . . . . . . . . . . 103
   A Cubby Bear Correction . . . . . . . . . . . . . . . . . . . . . 113
   Navigating Home in a Multi-Year Bear Market: The Basics . . . . . 119

PART D: HOLISTIC INVESTMENT R & D . . . . . . . . . . . . . 129
   Researching Common Stocks . . . . . . . . . . . . . . . . . . . 131
   Researching Trends: Again: Follow the Money . . . . . . . . . . . 141
   Leave the Market to the Media: The Glory of Cash/Bonds. . . . . . 145

## PART E: WHY MACROECONOMIC TRENDS MATTER ...151
The Big Picture: And Why it makes all the difference. . . . . . . . . 153
A Time to Sow, A Time to Reap: Why Economic Cycles Matter . . . . 161
Suspending the Law of Probability - At least for awhile . . . . . . . . 165
The Power of Precious Metals -Heaven's Answer to a Weak Dollar. . . . . 173
Managing Your Money in a Financial Crisis -Don't Buy: Wait . . . 179
Navigating Home in a Multi-year Bear Market and Surviving Deflation: Part 2 It's all about Demand. . . . . . . . . . . . . . . . . 183
The Rebirth of Economic Recovery -The Longer the Bottom, the Bigger the Rise. . . . . . . . . . . . . . . . . . . . . . . . . . . . . . 191

## PART F: FINAL THOUGHTS: THE FUTURE OF HOLISTIC INVESTING. . . . . . . . . . . . . . . . . . . . . . . .197
Time Value of Money The Great Grimm Reaper. . . . . . . . . . . . . 199
The Fall of Trickle Down Economics: Return of the Purple Decade . . . .205
The Rebirth of Bonds: - A Recession's Best Friend . . . . . . . . . . . . 211
The Tangible Common Stock -A sober friend or an imposter?. . . . 215
A Second Look at Sector Funds -Add value to Your Portfolio . . . . 225
Piquing the Apocryphal Pale - Beware the New Pharisees . . . . . . 233
Avoid Commodity Products "A never ending Greek Tragedy" . . . 241
The Future of Holistic Investing Israel: A Powerhouse of Value . . 247
Wrapping it all up: Part 1: The Value 3 Portfolio: Content Drives Value. . . . . . . . . . . . . . . . . . . . . . . . . . . . . . . . . . 259
Wrapping It All Up: Part 2  15 Lessons Learned. . . . . . . . . . . . . 273

## APPENDIX: HOLISTIC INVESTING . . . . . . . . . . . . . . . . .295

## SUBJECT INDEX. . . . . . . . . . . . . . . . . . . . . . . . . . . . . . .307

## BIOGRAPHY. . . . . . . . . . . . . . . . . . . . . . . . . . . . . . . . . .313

# Dedication

–This book is dedicated to my parents:
Charlett B. and Clifford G. Long
And

Frank P. Ippolito

Their constant love, encouragement and example gave me the confidence and help cultivate my passion to continue even after failure.

# ACKNOWLEDGMENTS

*To my wife Ellie who would call me to dinner on Sunday only to wait for me to finish that thought. I admire her for giving me that freedom.*

Createspace           For their Vision and Creative suggestions
North Charleston, SC   strewed with patience.
Team 6

HELP! Computer Repair
St. Augustine Beach, FL   Cole Pelzer, Matt Huss and Carlos Calixtro, Proprietor

Alpha Computer        Michael and staff
Frazer, PA

Power Breakfast Group:   Steve Friedlander and the late Ed Woelfel
We often tried the patience of waitresses at Mom's on Saturdays in Ringos NJ.

To my Rider professors long ago:
   Dr. Harry S. Sprouls, English Department
   Gerald Crowningshield, Accounting Department
   Dr. Derrill McGuiggan, Psychology Department
To this day I cherish their toughness, integrity in the pursuit of truth.

HOLISTIC INVESTING IN A RISK-AVERSE WORLD

Phi Sigma Epsilon(Kappa): We Bearcats ruled the road in those spirited Kennedy years, the best years of our lives.

The New School, Graduate Faculty, Economics
        The late Dr. Robert Heilbroner, Economics Chair
        *The Worldly Philosophers*
        Prof. Heilbroner would have me write, rewrite, et.

Dr. David Schwartzman, Economics
        I remember arriving late for Micro Eco.
        I blamed the subways. You smiled. Sept., 1977

New York University: Stanley Cohen, CEF
        Your charts opened our eyes. Forever grateful.

# INTRODUCTION:

If you can't beat the market with half of your money then you have no business losing the rest of it. And the most important way to beat the market is to get on base, it's everything. Getting on base, from a hit or walk puts you in a position to score. Stealing second by getting a jump on the pitcher is another confidence booster. This takes the double-play option off the table enabling you to score. Forget about swinging for the fences, just meet the ball squarely.

Why do I prefer the baseball analogy of singles and doubles over potential home runs? Because a good offense gets on base. This results in more runs. And winning is better. Baseball tactics and investment strategy agree. Overconfidence can cost you, asleep at the switch or being unfocused. Not doing your homework is like throwing a dart at the Wall Street Journal. You may get lucky but it won't hold. Beware of that hot tip.

Holistic Investing is Risk-Averse Investing. It protects your portfolio in tough times, and it will enable you to grow in the next bull market. It will allow you to transcend business as usual, by exposing some of the fallacies of the received wisdom. Holistic Investing will provide you with better tools, better ways to sense the dangers of runaway emotions. The proprietary **PVG Momentum Rank is presented in the Appendix.** This novel system will steer you to growth companies of the Russell 2000, today's innovators and tomorrow's winners.

KNOW WHY you are winning or losing. Having no system courts disaster. Holistic Investing will provide you with a coherent system, both technical and fundamental. Poverty needs no plan. Our steady-as-you-go approach builds momentum while you will win the battle of confidence for investment survival. You will not only survive, but in time you'll grow your portfolio—adding more years for quality time.

This book is for those who have given up on Wall Street, its firms, and for those who mistrust the market. As an individual investor for nearly forty years, I've experienced your pains and frustrations. I lived though the vicious bear markets of yesterday, the debacle of 1973-4, the Rust Belt Recession of 1981-2, the Crash of 1987 and the Chinese water torture "Dot-Com" bust of 2000-2002. However, the mother of all modern bear markets was the recent Real Estate Bust of 2008. Most investors remain in the red as I write this. If I can add one more important analogy, from the world of horse racing: If you're going to win, you win at the turns.

Consultants at McKinsey & Co. recently estimated that the average couple will fall $250,000 short in closing their retirement gap according to an article in Yahoo Finance, Kiplinger.com, 6/15/11. Maintaining a life style nurtured over years indeed may prove difficult. The article cautioned against "living too high on the hog" early into retirement.

However, the principles laid out in Holistic Investing can help you close a perceived retirement gap. Approximately forty to sixty percent of your funds will reside in a cash/bond mutual fund at all times. The remainder of your investments will grow with higher than market dividend value stocks and a lesser amount in small to mid-cap growth stocks and Sector Growth Funds.

Interest rates will remain low for an indefinite future. Savers like me twenty years ago made good money at double-digit rates. Those days are gone. Sound investments are your only hope.

The wreckage of Wall Street is an old story. The "best and the brightest," along with old institutions like Lehman Brothers,

# INTRODUCTION

Citigroup and Bernie Madoff have triggered countless business failures. We know the pain, and there's no use dwelling on it. While the bulk of this book contains the antidote to the manipulations of rogue Wall Street investors, its origins began before the meltdown of September, 2008. Listed below is a sample of Holistic Investing:

(1) We invest in well-capitalized domestic Value Stocks capable of growth paying above market dividends: Core stocks.

(2) We buy special situation small-cap growth stocks from the Russell 2000. The Russell 2000 is among the fastest growth indices in America. We buy rapid growth American companies analyzed from our proprietary **PVG Momentum System,** explained in the Appendix. We consider these Cyclical Stocks or shorter-term holdings. We also track Market Sectors and will buy Sector Funds capable of adding value

(3) **MOST IMPORTANT,** we maintain a FUSION of cash and Strong Currency bond funds and ETF's which comprise 40-60% of our portfolio. This provides ballast.

This is our plan, called THE VALUE 3 PORTFOLIO, simple and direct, no uncertainty or confusion required. CONTENT DRIVES VALUE. Traditional portfolio theory had some good points, such as diversification, risk/reward and value. However, this doesn't really address the questions of market sector risk, or when to buy or sell.

Holistic Investing helps the investor to follow an easy, no nonsense risk-averse discipline, while keeping an eye on the "big picture." We invest in selected (ETFs) which access strong currency bonds (Sweden and Switzerland). We'll avoid treasuries as the dollar weakens. Holistic Investing helps you create an Alpha Portfolio, capable of OUTPERFORMING THE MARKET BY FALLING LESS IN A DOWN MARKET.

At present, my Core stocks are the following: American Equity Life Investors, Fidelity National Financial, Gilead Sciences and Vector Group (12/23/13). Some of these companies pay a higher than average dividend. AEL is a retirement life insurer; FNF is a bank holding company active in growth sectors; Gilead Sciences is a leading developer of hepatitis C vaccines with recent FDA approval and Vector Group a holding company in electronic cigarettes and commercial New York City real estate. Of course these may change over time. Our goal is to buy mid cap value stocks paying above average dividends capable of growth. No more than five of your holdings should fit into the Core stock category. The remainder of your portfolio should contain a mix of small to mid-cap special situation growth stocks.

In market downturns, I'll keep a greater percentage of funds in cash, sometimes exceeding sixty percent and in upturns keeping nearly thirty-five percent, averaging around fifty percent over the market cycle: a three to five year period. Most important, I keep an eye for windows of reinvestment, adding to my core stocks, buying additional shares in market downturns. Believe it or not, most of your profits grow out of the many small or cubby bear corrections, discussed later, than from a boring bull market with seemingly no correction.

The passages of time will bring opportunity to you, on your terms. Cash, once an orphan in portfolio theory, will once again be your friend. It will shield you in market downturns because your risk will be cut in half, and will provide you with investment capital when it's time to buy.

No more that 50% of your assets will be invested most of the time. No gimmicks or leverage required. The Holistic Investor shuns margin accounts or short selling. **WE JUST ZERO IN ON STRAIGHT-FORWARD SMART INVESTING.** Holistic Investing will allow you to take advantage of market sectors that beat the market in up or down markets.

You will learn that Holistic Investing is more than investing as the name implies.

Holistic Investing can, if you will, become a boot camp of sorts helping beginners as well as professionals. It will help you focus in a different light. Emotions can ruin investment as well as lose baseball games. We aim to remain focused.. Don't sweat the small things as a friend from Santa Clara College told me years ago.

# INTRODUCTION

Investors can make money from most systems over time. But a Holistic Investor will understand why, along with his or her capacity to retain more of it. Let's take the first step.

Markets consist of three dynamic forces: geopolitical, economics (growth, interest rates) and currency flows, spawning liquidity inbalances or surpluses during speculative excesses.

Understanding their origins will add to your returns, such as the Asian-driven commodity boom recently. For example, in this time of economic crisis, April, 2009, I was invested in mutual funds and global bonds because of the global recession and weaker dollar. When the dollar strengthens, I will exit this trade in favor of cyclical equities, buying American growth companies.

Also, I'll consider companies of the following sectors as the economy expands: technology, industrial and resource companies. The financials had experienced headwinds because of coming regulations. But a whole generation of Boomers will retire and require financial services. This book will show you how to evaluate new market opportunities as they arise. More importantly, I'll outline a big picture, top-down investing or market sectors and bottom-up investing for individual stock analysis. You will learn to anticipate the next sea change in your home port before the coming storm. Remember, investing is all about information, anticipation, trimming your sails before the big blow. At this point it may be helpful if I provide some background.

The crash of 2008 occurred in September, unusual in an election year. All stocks went down, but my Holistic Portfolio was down less than ten percent, yes, a small comfort but a paper loss nonetheless. Trillions of savings were swept away from the credit bust. Financial and real estate stocks suffered the most. Money center banks and brokers were bailed out. Hundreds of smaller banks failed in the Great Recession.

As in 1929, the free market system failed, followed by systemic de-leveraging of debt and unemployment. All stocks crashed as in the fall of 1929. Many professional investors had fallen into the same morass. Hedge funds went bankrupt. Billionaire scams were uncovered. A German billionaire committed suicide. Millions of investors were caught in the vortex of investment bank derivative losses, interest only loans, etc. from arcane real estate schemes. Once honored names like Lehman Brothers and Merrill Lynch failed.

The epic market crashes of September and October, 2008 including the biggest point drop ever of 770 points on September 23rd. This changed everything. And perceptions of financial security for millions vanished overnight. And once again, another generation was baptized in the waters of reality. As taught, even preached by an earlier generation of enlightened figures from the past: Gerald Loeb, Graham and Dodd and today's investors like George Soros and Warren Buffett: investing is serious business, no game to be taken lightly. Gerald Loeb had written over a half century ago in "The Battle for Investment Survival." Human likes and dislikes will wreck any investment program. Only logic, reason, information and experience can be listened to if failure is to be avoided.

Holistic Investing will arm you with sound tools against an uncertain market. Always, and I mean always, invest in a stock beating a major market index (S &P 500) before looking for its other virtues. This is the very first step, but more about that later. Holistic Investing will arm you with the tools to fight back, along with other essential common sense attributes I consider important: a balanced emotion, and above all, focus. However, as discussed in part earlier, we will examine important intangibles which may affect your performance. This book will go where no investment book has gone. It will allow you to see yourself in a new light, arming you with additional weapons other than the usual Wall Street buzz of quarterly comparisons, earnings estimates, etc. Most important, you will regain your confidence.

Risk is half the battle. You will learn to buy and sell in a safer way. Most important, you will begin investing with half the risk of the average investor. You will learn WHEN to buy a stock and WHEN not. You will learn WHEN to hold and WHEN to fold (sell). You

## INTRODUCTION

will learn to harness "time" as an ally, not as an enemy of investing. You will learn that mutual funds are important, while fortunes are made in common stocks. And along the way to Holistic Investing, you will build your confidence by making small trades at first, larger ones later, regardless of what the market does.

Peace at the center comes from a sound mind and body, an old Quaker virtue. Being that I was brought up in Trenton, New Jersey, near Philadelphia, some of my early friends were Quaker, no pun intended.

You can beat the market while collecting your dividends. I agree, this is a bold statement, yet yours to gain by reading this book. Before we begin, I want to redefine Holistic Investing.

Holistic Investing will allow you to invest your money with confidence for maximum gain, cutting losses at selected trigger points. It helps you to determine WHEN to sell, the most difficult thing in investing. Some losses may be necessary on the way to riches. Remember, the market is a three-step process: two steps up and one down. Thoughout modern capitalism, especially in the U. S. since 1932, the market rises nearly sixty percent of the time, and down 40 percent. But this doesn't mean that you can't make money in down markets. We'll concentrate on the bullish sixty percent by buying equities and hold bonds and some foreign funds the other forty percent of the time.

A bull market always rages somewhere in the world. All of us know that investing during a bull market is easy, and most of us remain confused when bear markets arrive. It's a pity that most books don't explain much about bear markets. But bear markets are a fact of life.

Holistic Investing will help you navigate market downturns. Most important, it will provide you with the tools to understand and invest globally, where some of the biggest gains will come in the future. This book was written for those with an open mind, beginner or one with more experience. Even if you're new to investing, the techniques included are explained in a personal style. So let's begin our journey.

A recent article in Parade was titled: "Is The American Dream Still Possible?" In this age of terror, high energy prices and political turmoil the wave of the future? We have traveled this road before. Remember the bear market of 2000-2002? The dark days after 9/11? These events had turned buy-and-hold investors into disbelievers, and along the way the "Dot-Com" bubble had swept us into the shadows of Silicon Valley. Today the real estate bust has claimed another generation of disbelievers. History continues to remind us of the dangers of a "sure thing." The changing tide and ticks of time show no mercy.

Now we face an even graver crisis, The Great De-Leveraging of America or super credit contraction from the bust of the real estate bubble. Time ran an article entitled: The End of Prosperity? Does this read like 1929 all over? No.

Credit card debt wasn't a way of life in 1929. Yet the Great Depression became a reality from the passage of the Smoot-Hawley Tariff Act of 1930 when duties were levied on imported goods; trade wars erupted. Fast-forward nearly sixty years later from the neglect of the Securities Acts of 1933-4 and Glass-Steagall, which had worked for seventy-five years (no more 90% margin accounts and insider short selling) in the name of free markets opened the flood gates to another bubble of bubbles, resulting in yet another financial crisis.

Home foreclosures and rising unemployment remain the problems. Along the way, rising auto and credit card defaults followed. At the beginning of 2008, the real estate sub-prime mess bled into the banking system. Investment banks such as Lehman Bros. and Merrill Lynch collapsed. AIG, or American Int'l. Group, an insurance conglomerate waddled into the morass.

Banks were re-capitalized $2 trillion by the government from toxic loan losses. As always, the big guys "spiked" overextended banks and mortgage companies for profits, only to bring the economy down again.

The G-7 nations of the developed world drew to the rescue. Even UBS, a Swiss financial giant, had written down $13.7 billion. So much for Swiss probity. And to make matters worse, hedge and private equity funds lost their magic over a matter of days. ESL Investments bought 24 million shares of Citigroup paying $49-54 per share. The price of Citigroup crashed to the low single digits. Those investors who bought into Blackstone's private equity initial public offering received a bucket of coal for Christmas.

Remember Watergate and the OPEC Oil Embargo of 1973? Have you ever seen the horrors of the Great Depression on the History Channel? It resulted in soup lines and WPA projects in 1933. Workers digging ditches for food. And a half century later we worked our way through another Crash in 1987. History is replete with crashes and recessions, but, as always, America came back. Today is no different.

This book will map out visions, strategies and techniques that will allow you to keep profits in your portfolio, come whatever the demons unleash. Making wealth, to many, had become a fortuitous affair, while keeping your money is way more difficult. We live in a faster paced world, spinning uncertainty daily. A nationalized oil refinery in Venezuela could roll the oil market over. Can a revolution in Egypt or civil war in Libya be any different?

A disapproved drug from the FDA can roll your health stock over. Your portfolio will fall. But this doesn't mean the end.

Sometimes a pullback can become an opportunity. We will point out these fallen angles and when to buy additional shares.

We'll work toward financial empowerment: feeling free from the surprises of the marketplace and sleeping without worry by controlling risk. This also means looking forward to the following morning, so we can better positioned our portfolio for profit, ready to take on the next cycle. I will discuss Holistic Investing In a Risk Averse World in detail, while keeping your risk to a minimum along the way. I truly hope you enjoy the experience.

Why Holistic Investing over "buy-and-hold" or "day trading?" I find the answers obvious.

How many of you have the time to watch the market minute by minute, day by day? I began my investing career trying to find the next IBM. Meanwhile, I had an auditing job during the day. You still hear stories of those buyers of Amazon and Google who bought in at the ground floor. Isn't this more like luck? How many of us really know when a stock strikes the mother load? Even those who work on Wall Street don't really know. I wonder how many thousands of guests on financial talk shows keep searching for these "holy grail" stocks. Most advisors on investment shows rightly recommend a stock for its future growth or its valuation based on company fundamentals. Buy-and-hold can work wonders in a bull market. However, those who fall in love with a company, not its stock, pay the price of tuition in a bear market. In other words, NEVER, I MEAN NEVER, fall in love with a company. And by extension, a stock represents a company. By the way, IBM shareholders found this out in the early 1990s.

Microsoft has gone nowhere for some twenty years.

Day trading is for professional speculators, period. In fact, I attended a Commodity Trading Seminar Chicago in 1986.

Many in our class couldn't wait to try our new found knowledge. We learned all about charts, patterns, moving averages and money management. I wonder how many of us are still in the business. The point is this: day trading commodities may be hazardous to your health. Yes, some traders were and remain good, like Larry Williams and Jake Bernstein, our teachers at the seminar. How many Larry Williams and Jake Bernstein's are out there? Not many. It takes years of acquiring knowledge and developing skills to trade professionally.

Options, especially stock index options (gold, oil and gas, the Philly SOX (semiconductors) present alternatives. These instruments make excellent hedges against losses in your primary portfolio. For example, I speculated in out-of-the money gold options in the summer of 1987 and in one day gained over $1000. I was cruising for a killing. The next day I gave it all back. Such is life. And if your trades turn sour a couple of times, you're wiped out. Jake Bernstein warned us to be fully capitalized before beginning. The principles I learned in Chicago had become invaluable. For one, I became a believer in charts. More about this later.

# INTRODUCTION

My investment tools and strategies revolve around a sound principle. What time (market) is it? It doesn't make much sense for one to plow into the market because the market had a lousy day, or week. Even picking the right stock, at the right time in its company history may prove futile. The worst of bear markets can topple institutions and governments besides your hard earned savings. I read somewhere that when someone made a comment to a question about a stock, he had meant that stock is a no good SOB unless it goes up. Moral:

NEVER FALL IN LOVE WITH A STOCK. It's not only a certificate of ownership but can become a certificate of confiscation—a vehicle into hell; or, under smart management, it can become a vehicle to a richer life: investment management, more about this ater.

Let's look at the four basic asset classes:
Bonds (corporate and treasuries)
Cash and currencies
Commodities and Real estate
Stocks

The above asset classes, including ETF's (Exchange Traded Funds) and mutual funds present a world of diversification, rather than diversification for the sake of diversification. Why aim for applesauce when you can pick the apples?

Thank God Stanley Cohen, my professor at NYU (Financial Planning Program). He explained one evening why he wouldn't buy a stock unless he looked at its chart. Now this made a lot of sense, like seeing a picture of your stock first. Surely, some stocks are all over the chart (the kind you want to avoid). But the Chinese were right: a picture is worth a thousand words.

Today, charting is easy because of the computer. In the old days we had to go to the supply store and get graph paper, spend many hours constructing stock charts. A chart really does give you an edge, another angle to a better feel for a trend. It's true: "the trend is your friend." All you have to do is to look for the nuggets. And you must know what to look for. We'll get into charting. Excellent books on charting can be found at any good library.

By now you must be wondering why I haven't mention anything on earnings, or corporate profits. Earnings are volatile, sometimes unreliable, and even if earnings expectations are met, a stock price can fall for want of rising sales(revenues) or poor prospects. We'll discuss this in chapter one. While I suspect earnings in a sense: I do respect earnings over time, PE ratios (Price- to-earnings). In other words, if a company's stock price growth YTD (year-to-date) percent as measured against its PE is at least two times, then I'm looking at the stock, given its industry group. This filter has saved me from buying a high-flying kamikaze. It will help you too.

Yes, psychology is an important ingredient for successful trading. After all, the market place is a global pool of mass psychology, Wall Street being its hub. Your mission is to beat the market, doing better in a downturn. Not to become a millionaire overnight. Even the programmers who devise these so-called black-box systems fall to the outcries of Tokyo, Chicago or New York. Your enemy may be yourself in which you must overcome. Learn, understand and grow. Unforeseen news sweeping in from the shadows across may not be an enemy after all. At times, seemingly, even a monkey throwing darts at the Wall St. Journal can do a better job. BEWARE OF THE CROWD. Don't follow it. You'll likely buy high and regret it later.

Lastly, I like to talk about the purpose of being focused. The focused investor is a Holistic Investor, the best of investors. This may sound trite but it's really true. This nugget of wisdom has a lot to do with your decisions on executing trades. Being focused is more than meets the eye. Yes, I studied some psychology at college but I was really an accounting major. Being focused is about common sense. Common sense replacing emotions and common sense living has no equal. You can pay dearly the hard way, by being sick or depressed from stress, fatigue or any number of ailments. I'm no doctor and don't pretend to be. In many a race to the finish line, as in a marathon, your battle to overcome yourself must be won before winning the gold. Being focused is Being focused is everything. Common sense, picking the right stock at the right time makes all the difference, not an understanding of stress reduction or nutrition, as good as they are, will save the day.

Why is your particular stock off to the stars? Why has trading been suspended in your favorite stock this morning? Are you too close to the news? Eventually, you'll get caught up in it—and that is bad. Keep a distance from the popular day shows when working. In fact, "I listen to "soft-rock" on the radio." Jake Bernstein, Chicago, 1986.

On weekends I read Barron's, by far the best source for information. But information overload can be dangerous. Don't get worked-up because some journalist wrote a bad report on one of your stocks. Sure, the stock may go down Monday morning, but if the investment has legs, it'll come back. It has happened to me several times.

Take your time, do your homework. Play the devil's advocate and ask yourself: "what can go wrong?" Is the company management honest (MOST IMPORTANT)? Is the company winning market share? Does the company have the right product at the right time? Does the company have a tail wind to its back (right industry group)? Is the company reasonably valued?

These and similar questions and answers will be discussed.

I wish you success at the very beginning of your new investment career. You owe it to yourself. Our world is becoming smaller; things moving faster, but you will see the market in a new light and beat the market on your terms. We will overcome our old self, open to new ideas while discarding the old. We'll learn and reach new levels of skill, confidence and determination.

And if I may, we'll learn to rely more on common sense, replacing the conventional wisdom with tested ideas that I'll discuss. Are you ready for this journey? A journey of novel ideals.

Innovation depends on creative thinking, the foundation for re-invention, new industries or our renewals. Time kicks out the old and welcomes the new: history's most important lesson. You will profit from Holistic Investing. In Omnia Paratus. Bon Voyage.

# PART A:

## THE 5 MYTH BUSTERS:

## PART A: REALITY CHECK

# CHAPTER 1:
# The Earnings Myth

Before we begin, I would like to pay my respects to two pioneers who had enlightened the individual investor, Louis Rukeyser and Mark Haines of CNBC.

Louis Rukeyser passed on May 2, 2006. Lou began his show on public television in 1970, demystifying the risks of common stocks and investments. He brought Wall Street to the living room at a time, the 1970s, when stocks would encounter considerable head winds. I believe his greatest contribution was the empowerment of the individual investor. He passed along credible information, helpful hints, and worthy opinions from his guests. I'll remember Lou for his gems of humor sprinkled with nuggets of wisdom, especially when all around a bear market raged with no end in sight.

Mark Haines began his career on CNBC in 1989. Trained as a lawyer from Penn Law and refined as an iconoclastic journalist, he wasn't afraid of the power and prestige pervading Wall Street. Mark would ask the tough questions most everyone in the business was afraid to even attempt. Once, at a roast in New York, with the likes of Frank Sinatra, Mark encountered Cary Grant in a hallway and Cary stopped, recognized Mark and congratulated him for his show. Mark passed on May 24, 2011. His absence will leave a major void in the morning hours.

# HOLISTIC INVESTING IN A RISK-AVERSE WORLD

Company profits don't necessarily point the way to the promise land of higher stock prices. I will first present a macro view presenting four mega cap(capitalized) companies which everyone will recognize: Bed Bath & Beyond, Microsoft, Pfizer, Inc. and Time Warner. I'll employ a complete business cycle, considered akin to a presidential term of four years, 2001-2005.

Company net earnings(profits) per year will be given along with their respective high and low stock prices for the year.

Another view of this phenomenon will be displayed at the beginning of 2006, the micro view, pointing to the many inconsistencies of earnings and a company's stock price: earnings/share adjusted for stock split.

| STOCK | 2001 | 2002 | 2003 | 2004 | 2005 | NOTE |
|---|---|---|---|---|---|---|
| Microsoft(Software) *E.P.S. | .90 | .94 | .97 | 1.04 | 1.16 | Split(2-1) 2/03 |
| H – L | 38.1- 21.4 | 35.3-20.7 | 30-22.5 | 30.2-24 | 28.3-23.8 | |
| Pfizer, Inc.(Drugs) | 1.31 | 1.53 | 1.75 | 2.20 | 2.02 | |
| H – L | 46.8-34 | 42.5-25.1 | 36.9-27.9 | 38.9-22 | 29.2-20.3 | |
| Time Warner(Media) | (.74) | .24 | .68 | .68 | .62 | |
| H – L | 58.5-27.4 | 32.9-8.7 | 18.3-9.9 | 19.9-15.4 | 19.6-16.1 | |
| Bed Bath & B.(Retail) | .74 | 1.00 | 1.31 | 1.65 | 1.89 | |
| H – L | 35.7-18.7 | 37.9-26.7 | 45-30.2 | 44.4-33.7 | 47-35.5 | |

*Earnings per share

## 2001   2005

| | EARNINGS INCREASE | AVERAGE PRICE | CURRENT PRICE |
|---|---|---|---|
| Microsoft | 28.9% | 29.75 | 26.05 |
| Pfizer, Inc. | 54.2% | 40.4 | 24.75 |
| Time Warner('02 - '05) | 158.3% | 20.8 | 17.85 |
| Bed Bath & Beyond | 155.4% | 27.2 | 41.25 |

{(Average price: (H + L)(High + Low)/2)}
(Excluded negative earnings of Time Warner for '01)
(Earnings data from The Value Line Investment Survey, April 21, 2006)

## THE EARNINGS MYTH

Microsoft approved a stock split in 2003. Stock splits initially depresses price, spreading existing profits over more shares. Share prices tend to recover over time. Three of four of these broadly diversified stocks have experienced flat- to- lower prices over the period(Microsoft, Pfizer, Inc. and Time Warner). Bed Bath & Beyond did not follow this script. Prices did rise in lock step with earnings. The period experienced a recession in 2001 and the 9/11 attacks.

But I believe that investors who invest only in the earnings of a company are missing the big picture, risking capital on an over-popular metric. Surely, other dynamics are in play. And buying on earnings news only, is like investing from the rear view mirror. Yes, a stock price should reflect a company's earnings, but the smart money have already bought the stock before the news. I AGREE EARNINGS ARE IMPORTANT OVER THE LONG PULL—but do we have the time to wait for the numbers to beat Wall Street expectations? Are we supposed to outguess the experts? Do we really know what is going on inside Corporate America? Of course not.

An analysis of earnings isn't complete without eyeballing another perspective of the beast, the micro view. Here we examine earnings in the short-term, in which companies report their "numbers," or earnings data on a day-to-day basis. Some firms report earnings after hours, when trading is over for the day. For example, if the numbers reported at 5 P.M.(the market closes at 4:00 P.M.) are lower than expected as calculated by the analysts(employees who work for the Wall Street firms), then a stock will fall in early trading the following day. On the surface, during the day events may turn a stock around, such as a press release of a greater book-to-bill ratio or the signing of a new contract. Yet an earning minefield remains, as I will describe below.

THE POINT IS COMPLEX VARIABLES (surprises, downgrades, etc.) CAN DERAIL A POPULAR STOCK, ANY TIME, CONTRARY TO EXPECTATIONS.

## THE EARNINGS MINEFIELD

| Date | Company | MISSED STREET ESTIMATES | BROKERAGE DOWNGRADE | DOWNSIDE SURPRISE | INTEREST RATES | OTHER |
|---|---|---|---|---|---|---|
| 1/12/06 | Tradstation | | X | | | |
| " | IBM | | X | | | |
| Date | Company | Estimates | Downgrade | Surprise | Interest | Other |
| 1/13/06 | Lucent | Lower sales | | | | |
| " | Sandisk | | X | | | Probe |
| 1/17/06 | Continental Air | | | | | Higher oil |
| " | Toll Bros. | X | | | | |
| 1/17/06 | IBM | Price higher | | | | |
| 1/18/06 | Intel | Falls 4% | | | | Sales miss too |
| " | U.S. debt | | | | (-)Yield curve | |
| " | Google | | Over valued | | | |
| " | Apple | | | | | Cautious est. |
| 1/19/06 | Motorola | Fell 6% after hours | | | | |
| " | Briggs & Stratton | X | | | | |
| 1/20/06 | Dow Jones | | | | | Drops 213 |
| " | Citigroup | X | | | | Slow sales |
| 1/23/06 | Ford | (-) earning | | | | Restructuring |
| 1/24/06 | 10 Yr. Treas. | two yr. high | | | | |
| 1/26/06 | Microsoft | Lower | | | | |

As shown above, forecasting earnings is no picnic. Because of the nature of the earnings beast, the beagles won't trap the nimble fox in the wild world of earnings, similar to analysts chasing the wrong Cinderella company before an announcement. Many books and studies have argued that earnings are the holy grail of investing. Book values, free cash-flow, enterprise values, price-to-sales ratios, working capital to long-term debt ratios remain alternative constructs, measures of a stock's worth. From my college days in accounting I learned that earnings are like a river which flows over time (you can't step into the same river twice) Heraclitus.

Earnings get updated like a moving target compared to assets which flows over time, unlike a pond or lake, cash, etc., as of a certain day. Going concerns (businesses) experience changing values over time, affecting both income and assets.

However, in January, 2006, our data period, a reporter on the Nightly Business Report commented that earnings guidance, not actual earnings per share hold Wall Street at bay. In other words, an individual investor would have an even harder time predicting earnings streams, competing with the professionals. Don't play the earnings game, don't fall for glib assurances from some analyst next time. With less fuss and bother, spelled out here and in later chapters, you don't have to rack up the hours researching earnings prospects on line or at libraries in Trenton, NJ, Oakland, CA, New York or St. Augustine, FL. Why compete with Wall Street?

# PART A:

## THE 5 MYTH BUSTERS: CONTINUED

# CHAPTER 2:
# Beware the White Noise in our Embroidered Society

News articles, blogs-sphere and financial TV feature many opinions of experts who report on stocks and investments. Most of these stocks may ride this wave of popularity for a short time only to fall down to reality later. Popularity is a great thing, for awhile. Enjoy it while you can. The new guy on the block is always more interesting than the old. And this goes for stocks too. An analyst may sing the praises of the latest biotech craze today. Will investors remember it tomorrow? The buzz of investment correctness may have a thousand fathers cheering for an IT "cloud" company fad, but if its stock doesn't find support, only its mother will love it.

Because of recent events as the new normal: high oil prices, an Asian meltdown, collapse of the EU (Europe Economic Union) or the fall of Apple from the passing of Steve Jobs. Nothing is assured.

"Story stocks" may become sorry stocks when the parade ends. By the time you purchase the next Google or web wunderkind its price will have doubled or more. Underwriters, brokers and wealthy clients buy into the "darlings" at bargain basement prices. At the open of trading, the price of a hot prospect will shoot up because of an order backlog. Usually, the price will spiral out of the box at the open, and continue higher into early afternoon until reality begins to settle in (as in the "internet bubble") of the late nineties.

In the early days of the internet many start-up companies had no earnings. Tons of investors were burned later when the bubble sizzled in early 2000. However, initial public offerings floated in a weak market will disappoint. It's no wonder that new issues are offered in bull markets. The owners and management of these new issues want to profit too. Everybody wins except the individual investor.

An analyst interview: "Looking out to 2007 and beyond, we like defensive stocks with earnings streams that do not reflect the ebbs and flows of the economy."

Interviewer: "Do you own any of these stocks?"

Analyst: "No I don't, but I'll be looking at them."

A recent article in The Philadelphia Inquirer revealed a study compiled by the Federal Reserve in Philadelphia, the Livingston Survey.

Its survey of 44 economists conducted forecasts twice a year of GDP growth, inflation, corporate profit and retail sales. Overall, the forecasters believed the economy would sail into 2007 at three percent growth with weaker retail sales. But they worried about inflation. The forecasters had revised their near-term inflation figures up.

Small wonder, as the price of energy has spiked since Katrina. The real worry was that higher energy costs will continue to work its way into more consumer goods. The survey reported that the numbers on inflation weren't revised up. In March of 2007 the Sub-Prime Mess had begun.

Yes, the market continued to trade into a new high, October, 2007, only to mask trouble ahead.

Years ago a friend and I had responded to an investment seminar advertised in a New York newspaper. We caught the train in Trenton, excited about visiting the Pan Am Building. We looked forward to catching a good deli sandwich afterwards. The seminar was crowded, some standing in the rear of the large brokerage office. The speakers recommended three stocks and a mutual fund. One of the stocks,

Commonwealth United, aroused my curiosity because of the growth of conglomerates. I bought twenty-five shares. I liked the stock because the company was a conglomerate and the sector did well. I figured that at the beginning of the new year the trend would continue.

During the winter and early spring the stock rose a couple of points. I felt vindicated.

However, into the summer Commonwealth United headed south. At times the stock seemed to struggle back a little but the fall was relentless. A bear market was underway after Nixon took office. By late fall the stock was under ten. Originally, I bought at thirteen and a fraction. The stock kept falling, and by January of the following year it fell to around five. I figured Commonwealth would come back, for the businesses seemed to be strong. I bought another twenty-five shares. At the time Nixon being president, a new era at hand. Wall Street went into a swoon and the bear market intensified. The Dow bottomed on May 26th, 1970 at 526.

Commonwealth United was now trading at around one dollar. Of course the company went into Chapter 11 and a few years later I received a check for seven dollars and change. This represented my pro-rata share of the settlement. Little did I know that in that audience the evening my friend an I visited New York were a group of wealthy doctors from Connecticut.

These doctors initiated a class action suit against the company. Later, Commonwealth United was dropped from the New York Exchange after "pink-sheet" status. By the middle seventies, my foray with Wall Street had taken new meaning: take the money and run before it's too late.

But I must say, Ron and I enjoyed the hoagie sandwich at the New York deli. In closing, I would like to pass on some advice from a commentator of PBS "Nightly Business Report," Lou Heckler in December of 2012:

"Listen to your own voice": adapted from Steve Jobs

"Speak your voice with confidence."

# PART A:
## THE 5 MYTH BUSTERS: CONTINUED

# CHAPTER 3:
# Beware the Name Brand Myth: Smaller is Better

Buying large name brand stocks may be hazardous to your pocketbook. For generations we bought telephone or motors and would just stash the shares away into safety deposit boxes.

The strategy worked in the slower paced world of the twentieth century. But it doesn't work anymore because of globalization (competition). Your competitors are no longer across town; they're across the sea.

I remember my uncle Tony telling me about the time he bought more shares of Pennsylvania Railroad. The twilight of the company had arrived, but few knew that Penn Central (a merger of the Pennsylvania and New York Central railroads) had been bleeding because of its falling passenger segment. The freight operations made money, but it wasn't enough to stem its march toward bankruptcy. The end came in 1970. The government operated the old equipment and the PENNSY became Amtrak for passengers and Conrail for freight.

American railroads bled capital beginning in the 1950s. Their heyday including W.W.II attracted Hollywood: troop trains in both world wars, the Broadway Limited and Twentieth Century Limited from New York to Chicago. Elegance on rails tempted businessman to make their appointments in Chicago the following morning, while relaxing in style. But air travel and the interstate highway system eventually replaced the railroads, especially with the introduction of jet airplanes in the late 1950s.

Remember Pan American and Trans World Airlines? Their death rattle had begun with deregulation of the industry and merger mania in the 1980s. Fewer riders occupied tourist class seats as other carriers offered lower fares. Pan Am and TWA depended more on the backbone of its business class passenger. Excess capacity and mega debt loads eventfully grounded the companies. In fact, my first client worked for TWA, founded by an epic and elusive personality,

Howard Hughes, the renowned aviator. My client flew his 747 from New York to Rome and then to Cairo. I advised him to take early retirement so he opted out in 1986. I remember that he and his wife were happy because soon afterwards the company was sold. Of course, TWA was broken up and sold off in pieces. Indeed, a harsh end from a noble beginning.

Brand name stocks have gone to ground not only in the transport sector but in motors.

Let's look at General Motors and Ford. The story of GM can fill a volume and become a best seller. I remember Pat Boone and Hoss Cartwright advertising Chevrolet in the early 1960s.

Hoss would pound on his truck emphasizing its work-horse quality. Pat Boone would drive a '57 Chevy and sing: "see the USA in your Chevrolet." The post war boom brought buyers into showrooms buying Chevys and Fords for their new homes in the suburbs. The Ford Mustang, Pontiac GTO and the Camero became cult cars. The kids, of which I was one, went wild over these machines. But the party was over in the early 1970s: A time when we had to wait almost an hour to buy gas. The big three (GM, Ford and Chrysler) had begun to make those small, ugly boxes which burned less gas. But something else was brewing in the vat.

The Japanese had begun exporting more of those Datsuns and Toyotas. Honda joined the party later. Yet it wasn't so much the relative fuel economy. Quality and performance now mattered. By the mid 1980s Japanese car manufacturers turned to premium brands such as Acura, Infinity and Lexus. Buyers began buying them in place of Mercedes, Oldsmobiles, Lincolns and Cadilacs

GM's historic market share, north of fifty percent, rolled over. In fact, Oldsmobile, which used to sell over a million cars annually, fell to just over six hundred thousand vehicles. A few years later GM discontinued the Olds brand. This sad event ended with the Alero rolling off the line in the early 2000s: an end from a great beginning. GM had lost its standing as the largest auto maker in the world after 2008. Now Toyota has is own problems.

The American "rust belt" around the Great Lakes became known for its iron carcasses of closed steel mills and auto plants. High union wages and benefits costs, foreign competition, outsourcing to Mexico, and that "sucking sound" crippled the auto industry. Ross Perot warned about this in 1992. But GM had reinvested into Saturn and Hughes Electronics by Roger Smith, GM's Chairman, to reposition the company in the 1980s. Meanwhile, Chrysler had reinvented itself under Lee Iococca, thanks to the minivan and some great innovations. Ford had fallen on hard times too, because of its Explorer and Firestone tire fiasco in the 1990s. But the Explorer is back and American trucks continue to rule the road, especially the Ford 150.

Competition and class action suits have checkmated name brand companies like Corning Glass (asbestos), Merck (Viox). Sears and K Mart, now one, remained locked in a turf war with Wall Mart.

Buying the bonds of ailing name brand companies makes sense, a better strategy. In the early 1980s I bought Chrysler bonds when the company was on its knees. Lee Iococca's and his engineers developed the K-Cars, such as the Dodge Aires and Plymouth Reliant. These cars sold.

These small four cylinder vehicles were as reliable as the more expensive cars. Later, Chrysler introduced the first minivan, the Dodge Caravan and Chrysler Town & Country, a resounding success. I had bought a Plymouth Voyager in 1992 and traded it in 2003 for a Town & Country.

I put 146,000 miles on the 3 litre, 6 cylinder with only a replaced fuel pump and compressor for air conditioning. A great car.

Chrysler paid back its government loan and the world took notice. Meanwhile, my Chrysler bonds soared in value while paying about seventeen percent semi-annually. I had bought the bonds at a deep discount in the early 1980s and held on until Chase Manhattan Bank called them in.

In sum, don't buy shares of ailing name brand companies. Better to buy their bonds, because even if there is a liquidation, bondholders are paid before stockholders.

# PART A:
## THE 5 MYTH BUSTERS: CONTINUED:

# CHAPTER 4:
# Beware of Wall Street Bearing Gifts: Yesterday's Darling Can Be Today's Dunce

"Story" stocks are hyped creatures of the Street, the grist which feeds into our over communicative society. The media often focuses on the shares of a new company going public or a company about to introduce the greatest mousetrap. Many new companies don't even have any record of income or sales. Older companies, such as a drug firm about to launch the next miracle cure, due diligence remains crucial. Do your homework. I will discuss later my preferred metrics, data points and sources.

Often, these media marvels come out in a bull market when psychology is riding high along with buckets of positive press coverage. New stock issues accelerate during a bull market, especially its later stages. Don't be caught in the slide after the last "sucker" buys in.

Public offerings, or IPO's, are written and talked about months before their issuance.

Underwriters, brokerage firms, and preferred customers stand in front of the line. Shares are allocated to these customers as payment for services or sold to the privilege few at the issuance price, often at a discount. Usually, the new issue opens at the prescribed market quote, and in a bull market the stock will shoot up soon after the opening bell. During the trading day a popular new issue swells in price. A robust new issue will fade late in trading as profit takers close out positions. However, the stock will close much higher than its opening price.

A darling stock can be an established company acquired by a public figure, such as Bill Gates or Warren Buffett. Microsoft has acquired smaller companies to enhance its business model, a familiar practice. A scenario unfolds: a "buzz" or gossip about Miracle Animations, an assumed name. The company begins making the scene by leaking info to media about a proposed stock offering. The stock begins to rise in value. Respected newspapers and the media report on a conversation with an "unnamed source." Secret meetings take place with the company executives. A higher level of trading volume of "Miracle" stock rides along with a higher price.

Insiders know something but aren't talking–yet. Perhaps late in the day, after the market closes, the buyout by Microsoft or some other company is announced. The following morning Miracle will shoot up in price and settles near the buyout price. Understand the script before buying.

We live in the digital age despite many millions of old, analog TV sets that continue to bring cable and satellite programs into homes. One may ask himself: Why rush and replace my 26" RCA for a flat-panelled DVD screen? We did just that recently. Because the old RCA picture tube broke down. Now we have a 33" flat-panel RCA with built-in DVD and HD (high definition.) Do you remember that flat-panelled commercial in which you would hang the screen on the wall, like a picture? I don't know about you, but I would get a rubber neck after about fifteen minutes.

Many argue that as long as they could clearly feel the disbelief on Cary Grant's face as he races into that Illinois corn field, or Frank Sinatra, eternally flashing the king of hearts in that mid-town

Manhattan bar—why bother with another toy? The new toys are better and also more delicate.

Unfortunately, years can elapse before today's darling stock bears tomorrow's fruit. Wall Street will continue to trump the "China Card" or the next oil play out of the shale deposits of Canada.

The worst offenders are the analysts. General Motors was recently downgraded from an upgrade by the same analyst two weeks earlier.

Myopic visions of grandeur catapulted a book about Dow 36,000 back in the double-digit gains of the late '90s. An earlier book predicted the "Great Depression" of the 1990s. Market mavens and strategists worship the tail winds of the current trend. Most economists have a hard time getting the jobs report right, as they fell shy by 100,000 jobs as job growth came in at only 75,000(May, 2006).

Many see brokerage house analysts ranking near astrologers.

Remember the summer of Snapple, a soft drink beverage. The company plastered the airwaves about its drink. Its cute name and fresh taste did catch Coke, Pepsi and other soft drink companies by surprise. At the time the likes of Ocean Spray and Tropicana hadn't got into bottled fruit drinks in a serious way. It was a wake-up call.

Of course Snapple sales rose because of its novelty and it did represent a good alternative from the colas. The strategy worked. In fact, the strategy worked so well that we have a ton of soft drink-fruit drink-watered-down wannabe companies, Snapple's competition. At last count, I wrote the names of the following drinks: Arizona, Gatorade, Capprisun, Nestle's Juicy Juice, Lipton Ice Tea, Mountain Dew, Dr. Pepper, Fresca, Diet Rite, Sunkist, A&W Root Beer, Fruit 2O Purified Water, Kool-Aid water jammer, Mott's Fruit Punch, Yoohoo Chocolate Drink, Welch's Anytime-Anywhere 6 pack, V8 Fusion & Juices, Cystal Light mixes, Country Time Mix, Tang(remember?), 4C Totally Light Green Tea mixes, Wyler's Light Mixes…and the list goes on and on, circa 2007. Give me a break.

"Story" stocks have a short shelf life. When the story goes stale, the stock goes ail. Many of these 90-day wonders wind up in the Wall Street graveyard when their ability to make monopoly profits end.

The Snapple example beckons competition. As an investor, you want just the opposite.

You want a company occupying a corner of the market, a niche, before the dogs of war (competition) rush in. We'll be discussing this later.

Barriers to entry remain a fact of economic life. Barriers are the difficulty of a firm entering a market segment because the scale of manufacturing or advertising requires tons of capital.

The food and beverage industries require heavy volumes, unit sales, to make up for their razor- thin profit margins. Product lines mature into exotic flavors and varieties, another costly move.

Survival requires brand loyalty, questionable when the next new thing is always coming out. In order to survive, a company must wrap a bear trap around costs. Good luck.

Beware of darling old wolves wearing new clothes. Trojan horses are as old as Homer and remember to question a company's assumptions. Remember the old saw: "if it's too good to be true, it probably is." And once the fizz or genie leaves the bottle, it's too late.

# PART A:
## THE 5 MYTH BUSTERS: CONTINUED:

# CHAPTER 5:
# Why Chase Price?
# Let it Come to You

For ages, our grandfathers and Wall Street preached this method. But nobody bothered to tell us when. An old adage of Wall Street says that they don't ring a bell when it's time to sell.

Wouldn't it be nice if we can read tomorrow's Wall St. Journal today so we can scoop up those cheap stocks and cash in before today's close? Unfortunately, we toil and sail in uncharted waters. The proponents of dollar-cost averaging from automatic payroll deductions may work, at times. Sadly, those poor employees of Enron found out the hard way. Most retirement accounts were tied to stock and they tanked. Even getting out during the crisis was considered unpatriotic.

We live in uncertain times. And uncertainty is poison to stocks. Throughout history, great fortunes have been made from uncertainty. For example, Rothschild's messenger waited at the docks, waiting on news of the battle of Waterloo in June, 1815. A boatman arrived with news of victory to a cheering crowd. Napoleon's army fell after years of war. Rothschild's agent returned immediately to London with the news. Renewed optimism swept throughout England and Europe. Because Nathan Rothschild acted early, he added to his considerable family fortune when his gilts, high quality government bonds, leaped in value. You can say that Rothschild, the ultimate insider, won this battle in his mind before the generals won it in the field.

Often, we ride the waves to fortune only to lose it to the aftermath of turbulent waters. An old saying rings true: any fool can make money, ah...but to keep it. Every bull market in history has corrected, and most bears shoot all prisoners. Most grizzly bears last for at least twelve to eighteen months: 1929-1932, 1937-8, 1939-1941, 1969-1970, 1973-4, 1980-2, 2000-2 and 2007-2009.

Lesser bear markets such as in the 1950s and 1960s were corrections such as 1957-8 and 1966. During these periods macro economic trends or political issues reign in the name of depression, war, inflation, political crisis and terrorism.

Cubby bear markets, my name, last for less than twelve months. These pullbacks correct excesses of an ongoing bull market. Cubby bears run from about three to nine months, and can become great buying opportunities. They usually shake out weak money which drives the stock down to a better value. I'll close this chapter telling you about my Computer Science experience in the early 1970s. Actually, the story began in a helicopter hanger at the Oakland Airport with a world renowned lawyer.

When I began graduate studies at the New School in New York, my parents and I bought Computer Sciences. It was 1977, a decade of inflation and global turmoil. Computer Sciences serviced the burgeoning growth in network systems handling government contracts.

The company held huge service contracts with federal and state governments, school systems, and corporate America. Mainframe systems and mini computers did the crunching on magnetic tape, and companies like IBM, Honeywell, and Electronic Data Systems sold and serviced these systems. Computer Sciences was a relatively new computer services company, doing much of its business in California.

The bear market of 1973-4 came knocking on the door, courtesy of the oil embargo and Watergate. Negative mental attitude arrived like the sea mist, pervading the wharves along the Embarcadero.

## WHY CHASE PRICE? LET IT COME TO YOU

Inflation continued to rise, and new Watergate revelations seem to surfaced daily. By August, 1974, Vice President Ford was sworn in. WIN buttons (Whip Inflation Now) appeared by late summer, a gift from former economic advisor Alan Greenspan. The market continued down along with Computer Sciences.

My stepfather, Cliff, reassured my mother that Computer Sciences would come back. At the time he worked at the Oakland Airport, his company servicing helicopters. One of his customers was F. Lee Bailey, the famous lawyer. On one of Bailey's visits the conversation in the hanger turned to the stock market. Bailey was a "hands-on" guy who would mingle with the crew and mechanics. The talk that afternoon came around to Computer Sciences. Without hesitation, as Cliff told us later, Bailey liked the stock and believed the company was sitting on top of a gold mine. In the Bay Area, talk of a gold mine has more meaning. Bailey reaffirmed what Cliff told us earlier, that computer sciences had been winning many more school district contracts and that the stock was poised to go higher. F. Lee Bailey left the meeting by stating that he would buy more shares.

That evening Cliff told my mother the news and she called me in Trenton, NJ where I was living at the time. They prepared to buy additional shares and suggested that I do likewise. The next day I called my broker, a full service firm (Charles Schwab hadn't introduced discount brokers yet) to buy additional shares. I was too buried into my economic studies to worry about the stock market. I bought additional shares at around seven dollars, my first lot bought at around thirteen dollars per share.

In the summer of 1980 I cashed in on computer sciences at around $25.00. Since my Ford Granada broke down because of a loose lug nut from an oil change, discovered after I returned from New York one evening, I had to buy another car. I bought a '79 Alfa Spider which I enjoyed for the next thirteen years.

We were lucky. We caught Computer Sciences at the beginning of a renewed growth wave.

But many investors who bought tech stocks in the bubble years in the late '90s and held on have lost their money. I have repositioned my monies into other sectors since. And I learned an important lesson: Don't bother looking for the needle in the haystack. Just choose the right haystack.

# PART B:
## THE ANTIDOTE:

# CHAPTER 6:
# The Big Picture: What Time is it?

For ages many advisors have recommended stocks regardless of the business climate. This practice remains because the rationale behind buying a stock is its earnings power. In theory, this may be true, but we know practice and theory seldom meet.

It's better to buy a growth stock wunderkind if the stock is running with the wind. Rather than settle for any growth-driver which may fade. Look for a small company stock inspired from an emerging sector.

Let's look at the energy sector for most of 2005 and early 2006. The independent explorers and drillers have done better than the majors like Exxon-Mobil or Sunoco. Natural gas producers like Southwest Gas, Devon Energy and Chesapeake Energy scored major gains. Even energy service firms like Ensco International and McDermont which service ocean rigs ran with the bulls.

The entire energy complex proved JFK's edict that a rising tide lifts all boats. In short, it's much easier to run with the bulls than being chased by the bears. Buy into a sector running before a true tail wind, rather than buck the headwinds of earnings misses, rising rates and future downgrades. Look at the big picture. Weak companies in a strong sector will move up in a rising sector. But weaklings in a weak sector will crash.

I bought into municipal bonds and financial stocks in July, 2006 during a slowing economy.

Lower interest rates were in the offing, good for financial stocks and bonds. I sold some energy stocks but retained McDermont, a service firm.

Before we leave this chapter, a guide should suffice to clarify my point: "The Big Picture" presented on the following page as an example. Now I'm not expecting you to be an economist, even highly paid Wall Street economists get it wrong at times. Economics is a social science, as I learned at The New School.

In reality, economics can be elusive and humble the best of us. President Truman made a statement about wanting a "one-handed economist." Economics is also an art. It behoves us to understand data and trends. Try to sit in the right seat in the right pew than to take any old seat, if I can use a metaphor. Take stock of the weekly gainers on the New York Stock Exchange.

Stock market sectors rotate with regularity—and their stocks will follow their sector.

Before I leave this chapter I like to make an observation learned the hard way: the school of white knuckles and iron sailors in wicked ports. **BUY A SERVICE COMPANY INSTEAD OF A "GOODS ONLY" COMPANY.** Sure, many goods firms also provide services. But in today's world, especially in high tech and commodities, products or goods tend to decline in price when a new generation is introduced. Years ago my experience with Seagate Technology taught me a lesson. In the early 1990s prices of Seagate's RAM's (random access memory) chips kept falling, so did its stock price. Peter Lynch referred to this as a "never ending Greek Tragedy" in his famous book: "One up on Wall Street." Remember, a lower priced inventory of a goods company means lower profits–and a lower stock price. Why the lower price: Because new products hitting the shelves will replace their elder widgets. Lower demand drives lower price.

A service company has no inventory except its inherent human capital built into its product. My classes with Prof. David Schwartzman explored these concepts three decades ago in micro-economics and industrial organization.

Displayed below is a concept developed by me to illustrate the phases of the economy and its impact on markets: bonds, stocks, commodities and currencies.

### The Big Picture

| Inflationary Expansion: | Non inflationary Expansion: |
|---|---|
| -Commodities | -Stocks |
| 1940s | 1950s |
| 1960s | Mid 1980s/ Mid 1990s mid 2000s |
| | |
| Stagflation: | Deflationary Contraction: |
| -Gold/Currencies | -Cash/Bonds |
| 1970s, 2010s? | 1930s & early 1980s |
| | |

Back in the 1960s when I was just starting to invest I was chasing stocks. Not knowing the big picture.

I considered buying RCA in 1965, because of its color TV. A couple of years later I bought a small freight forwarder called Wings and Wheels in 1967, now defunct. By 1968 metals had risen from obscurity as Anaconda Copper rose from the dead, a mining operation with one its branches in Chile. The stock rose smartly and I made some money, and lucky for me I got out in time.

The mine was nationalized by the government a few months later. My father was with me on this one. Back then he told me to stop throwing money away on those "pink sheet" losers. I finally listened.

# PART B:
## CONTINUED:

# CHAPTER 7:
# A Picture in Time: Personal Revelation of the 1980s

Stock charts are worth more than a 1,000 words. Analysts or reporters can say what they want about a stock, company or the market, but the final arbiter for me remains the stock chart.

Why Personal revelation. Because personal revelations carry a greater truth, on the whole, than the conventional wisdom of the day which have failed the test time. Once I considered charts to be decorative appendages to a stock's financial report in Moody's or The Value Line Investment Survey. Little did I know that charts were to play the major role in my investment education, an ongoing adventure.

In the early 1980s when high interest rates ruled the waves my focus veered away from fundamental analysis. It seemed that the only game in town were corporate bonds and utility stocks. Fundamental analysis didn't provide options that I intuitively wanted, even though I wasn't seeking these additional choices. I studied about PE ratios, earnings yield and discounted- dividend cash flow models in a required finance course at Rider, part of my accounting program. But fair values for stocks or the market derived from above yardsticks would not square with an ongoing bear market. Sure, one can figure a fair price as a snapshot in time, but the real market lays open to other uncertainties from abroad or home: fifty points down because of a spike in interest rates overnight in Europe, or a bad number on consumer sentiment.

This particular bear market of the early '80s made a lasting impression: GM plants closing in the upper mid west, the outsourcing of jobs to Mexico and the downsizing at RCA. The term "rust belt" came into existence and the closing of tool and die shops in Indiana would eventually spread to New Jersey.

One Saturday afternoon while visiting the Trenton Public Library I came across a book by Joe Granville.

His ideas about "on balance volume" piqued my imagination in that a move in volume precedes a move in the price of a stock Volume precedes price. I tested the concept and discovered the premise to be true, especially on big moves. I also discovered that a majority of a market moves is lead by volume, especially at the beginning of an important bull rally.

Soon, I read other books on technical analysis and learned about head-and-shoulder patterns (tops), flags and pennants (continuation moves), and reverse head-and-shoulder (bottoms).

My investment horizons increased by one hundred percent, in other words, my sole reliance on fundamental analysis was over. At the time I was attending graduate school in New York and writing my final thesis for the late Professor Robert Heilbroner at the New School.

In the fall of 1983 I enrolled at New York University into their Financial Planning Diploma Program.

We learned about taxes, estate planning, insurance risk, investments and the details of a financial plan. But it wasn't until the winter of '84 when everything would change. Enter Stanley Cohen, CFP. At the time the market was in a funk because of rising rates.

One evening we plotted the earnings of a company on graph paper and its price on a chart, the two would follow a similar pattern, usually in tandem. But Stanley Cohen added something that I will never forget: "I still wouldn't buy the stock unless I examine its chart." I kept remembering what he said on the train ride back to

Trenton that evening. He was the first person I've known who used both fundamental and technical analysis. Most stock investors were either fundamentalists or technicians, not both. This squared with my thinking.

In November of 1986 I flew to Chicago and attended a Real-Time Trading Seminar by Jake Bernstein and Larry Williams. This was about day trading and I figured that its principles could be applied to stocks. Larry was a proponent of price patterns while Jake spoke more about risk management, trading psychology and a technical method which I use today. In fact Larry Williams went on to win the U. S. Trading Championship in 1987, growing $10,000 into more than $1 million.

Many of us can remember the summer of 1987 when the stock market soared to the moon, paraphrasing Paul Tudor Jones (a moon shot) topping in late August.

At about this time computers had become serious investment tools. At the trading seminar above both Jake and Larry were making real-time trades, most of them winners. I decided to get a PC. For some years I plotted charts of the Value Line Composite on graph paper. Now the leg work can be done on a PC. Soon afterwards in the spring of '87 I bought Metastock II, a very good software package downloaded with about 100 stocks, like IBM and other large companies.

This gave me the ability to download prices and test for profits. This power represented a real turning point in my investment career. Later I've discovered that "black box" indicators are useful but limited. I set out to develop my own proprietary studies and continue to this day.

In early October I packed my bags and flew out to San Francisco to join my parents on their anniversary. We stayed in a high rise above Fisherman's Wharf, enjoying the abalone, sourdough bread and good Nappa house wine. But we didn't enjoy what was about to happen on Wall Street. The market was dying before our eyes.

By Thursday, October 14th I read an interview with Richard Russell in "Investor's Business Daily," keeper of the Dow Theory.

He advised everyone to sell. After falling the preceding four to five days with little rallies in between, I had enough. At the time I remember the conventional wisdom: to hold, to "stay the course." After all, the market always comes back, right? Sure, but when? Of course they don't ring a bell when a multi-year bull market is over. So, after my coffee, I promptly went back to our condo with the sea gulls and sold. Lucky me. For what was to come later was much, much worse. My mother and Cliff agreed. So we got the monkey, read market, off our back and enjoyed our visit to the wine country that weekend.

Yes, Richard Russell announced to the world that the party was over. My clients and computer were 3,000 miles away yet sometimes you must listen to your heart. All hell broke loose Monday morning, October 19th. As it turned out, I was scheduled to fly back to Newark that day. On my return flight I enjoyed a couple of Jack Daniels. The market crashed similar to the calamity in September, 2008. In retrospect, Cliff would always slip me a $20 before boarding.

# PART B:
## CONTINUED:

# CHAPTER 8:
# Follow the Money: The haystack is more important than the needle

In the late 1980's a financial publication featured a star stock picker in its paper. Eventually, he toured the country giving seminars in various cities. On a Friday evening he was to speak at a hotel near Princeton, so we decided to pay our respects and attend. It seemed that this stock picker possessed the Midas touch. Most, if not all of his picks had done well. He chose the kind of companies you see and hear about often: IBM, Sears and familiar names. It was spring, 1987.

Occasionally, FNN, the forerunner to CNBC, interviewed the stock picker. He was asked about his stocks, and he'd talk about his method: earnings of the preceding four years, quarter over quarter, overlaid with earnings of the current quarter. Straight forward stuff.

We attended the seminar to get some new ideas on stocks. As in the stock rating services he gave star quality to stocks he liked because of their rising earnings trend since 1983, the base year.

Even so, I remembered back in the recession of 1981-2 earnings had been driven down because of the recession even if a company with poor management made money since 1983. Perhaps the economy and not the company should get the credit.

During the summer of '87, all stocks rose in a gusher tail wind. At the time, I was fully invested in mutual funds. Everybody was happy. As mentioned, the market peaked in late August. However, a tired bull would begin to lose steam shortly.

Soon, everything would change—The Crash of '87—it seemed to wash away the old guard and I never heard from above stock picker again.

The eighties' stock markets would grind to its unspectacular finish, unravelled by an failed takeover attempt in October of '89. I was driving through the Connecticut countryside that Friday afternoon. The money left the market that day and washed away a decade of thrills and pain, actually, bonds outperformed stocks in the 1980s. All the stock guru personalities of the decade went into permanent house arrest.

I realized, once again, that fame could make or break you. And I knew that if you want to make it, and that goes for anything, then you must pay the price and make your way, not from some previous path. For what may work for someone else in his time may not go for you. Sure, rising year-over-year earnings benefitted all stock pickers from 1983. But even when earnings continued to climb in 1989, many companies wouldn't respond because of memories of the Crash.

People were afraid to buy so Cash was King, the new haystack in town. In fact, the only stocks rising were those poised for takeover.

Another good example of not following the money played out in another hotel on Route 1 near Princeton, this time the mid 1990s. I attended a stockholders meeting on Cytogen, a biotech company I held. The stock was stuck in a narrow range, around $4—5 a share. I held a small position, 100 shares, concerned because the company couldn't get out of its own way. The good news was that they were on the threshold of some major breakthroughs, FDA trials, in alliance with another drug company. The bad news was that they continued to burn money, their "burn rate" (liquid assets expended per week, month without replacement) continued unabated.

## FOLLOW THE MONEY

During the question and answer session following the presentation the chairman began to field some tough questions from the audience. I sat right behind the executive committee. The person behind me asked a question the chairman couldn't answer so he referred this to his treasurer, and she responded. The stockholder wasn't satisfied. He told the treasurer about a story from a business talk show. He explained that optimism expressed by an analyst on Cytogen, despite its "burn rate," and it would be worth the wait.

The Treasurer couldn't answer directly, so she spoke about nonrecurring charges and other accounting adjustments. I was recognized by the chairman and explained to the guy that analysts are sometimes wrong, even on television. Some giggles were heard from the back of the meeting room. After, the meeting, the treasurer turned around. She smiled and thanked me loud and clear, as if to make a statement.

As we got up to leave the guy and his son came over to me and asked: "Is that right, do analysts make mistakes?" I replied: Yeah, they're human too."

In retrospect, I sold the stock about $5 ½ a few weeks later, as it approached its upper range.

Later that year it fell to around the $2-3 area. I guess its "burn rate" had gotten the better of it.

As discussed, if a stock can't move within a reasonable time, then it's time to move into greener pastures. Like a vacuum, money hates idleness, for it yearns to see the sun light of a new day. The above two stories lead us to the point of this chapter—money, like nature itself, seeks power. Therefore, we must think about money in a new way.

Listed below are examples of money deployed over various asset classes. Think in terms of asset classes, not dumping your investment dollars into one stock or mutual fund. Think about categories such as asset classes and industry groups. Don't buy that Gee Whiz technology company making miracle chips or the next pharmaceutical company with the blockbuster drug.

Pick out the asset class where the action is, where the money is flowing, and then pick out that company best suited to ride your new wave into profits. But you must make sure that the asset class: bonds, stocks, commodities or currencies had a prior push, legs or staying power. The asset class, commodities for instance, should continue to profit with the bulls for at least a few months. And when the party is over, you'll have time to reposition. We'll cover ways to analyze these trends. But for now, its important to rethink investments in terms of market sectors, not about that hot stock everyone is talking about, but a class, sector or group attracting money, pulling away from the crowd. Think haystack, not the needle in it.

Allow me to define these terms:

| | |
|---|---|
| Class: | Bonds, stocks, commodities and currencies |
| Sector: | Financial, energy, consumer staples, transportation |
| Group: | Financial (banks, brokers, insurance; mortgage) |
| | Energy (oil exploration, drillers, natural gas, refiners) |
| | Consumer staples (food distributors, beverage, drug retail, health services) |
| | Transportation (airlines, truckers, rail carriers, freight forwarders) |

Remember, common stocks and mutual funds include all four classes, such as corporate bond funds or technology (sector) funds. Likewise, ETF's (exchange traded funds) include all the above and currencies. Some stock funds hold bonds in their portfolio for diversification.

For instance, a $1000 investment can be made in various ETF's at the beginning of April and valued to the end of October, 2006.

Stocks and bonds had outperformed gold, but earlier in the year gold had outperformed.

Of course stocks and bonds cover a very broad area: treasury bonds, municipal bonds, oil stocks, medical equipment stocks, etc. A class will outperform for awhile, and then fail. Another class will rise to take its place. As in a horse race, money seeks the best return.

However, at times it is BEST to remain in cash. Just remain on the sidelines and WAIT FOR THE MARKET COME TO YOU. And believe me, you'll make more and spend less energy. Like the tortoise, you'll beat the hare. Take that holiday, go for a sail, play some golf, go to the mountains for that ski weekend, and live to trade another day.

# CHAPTER 9:
# New Tools of the Trade Technical and Fundamental Tools

Tools amplify your ability to make better decisions: the scope of this book: Holistic Investing in a Risk Averse World. I apply these tools to both Core and Cyclical stocks as a method to LIMIT RISK.

Core Stocks are the true drivers of your portfolio because of capital gains and dividend growth. Mid-cap value stocks with growth potential have a stellar track record over the decades. In addition, these stocks pay their way because their dividend rates should be above market average. Mid-cap companies are smaller, more nimble than their larger brethren. A company's growth curve over time is similar to a 40-50 year cycle of a commodity or a nation's currency. Decades can tell the story of an IBM or a Lorillard.

Of course, some of these thoroughbreds may run a bad race now and then, but they'll be back again. We look further out to those markets our Core Stocks will be dealing with, generation of future sales, the most important thing.

Cyclical or Special Situation Stocks are better addressed from technical studies. The reason for this is the time-value of money concept, addressed in this book. Technical analysis can give you, from chart studies, a **WHEN** criteria, the best time to enter into or out of a position. Core stocks require chart studies too, but from a different perspective: principally, adding additional shares before a rebound to newer highs.

We work with weekly chart data. A lot can happen in a week: reversals, bad news, an upgrade- downgrade, even foreign news. New price highs, lows and the breaking of trend lines six month prior carries more meaning that a one-shot wonder of day trading. A stock near the bottom of its chart trading sideways for weeks is of particular attention. Your stocks or funds may exhibit this pattern, meaning that it may break to the upside on strong volume, a very good sign.

In contrast, daily prices have been known to spike up or down, reverse, running all over the place leaving little clue. This randomness can distort the price data, notwithstanding the margin calls or stop order losses of the trader. In contrast, a weekly reversal is easier to detect before any real damage is done.

In particular, weekly volume data carries more weight that daily volume because more information emerges from the end of the trading week. And if concurrent with high price, a breakout may push price to a new level confirming the current bullish trend. Volume is used to confirm price, on the way up or down—an important concept. It's much easier to look at a weekly chart for "positive volume," associated with a spike in price. Holistic investors ride a trend in sympathy with price and volume, a more complete picture.

The best way to look at price charts is on-line. Also, software companies provide excellent packages of multiple charts: daily, weekly, monthly, etc. along with real-time market data for the active trader.

But Holistic investors aren't active traders. Of course brokers would love traders to be active so they can rack-up commissions. However, the web site: Big Charts (Marketwatch.com) provides this for free. Now this isn't an endorsement. But I use the site

# NEW TOOLS OF THE TRADE

because all the technical and fundamentals tools are out there in the public domain. No need to spend a lot of money for additional equipment or software. Isn't this great! You can join the web site as I have.

Once online, you must create a chart of a company. Look for the stocks of small to mid- size firms. Sure, one can look at Dow stocks and that's OK. However, larger gains and risks are with smaller companies. This is why I choose those small to mid-size companies with price-earnings ratio and year-to-date growth.

Below are the charting tools I use:
- A year-to-date or six-month chart, whichever more convenient
- S & P 500 Index as a comparative tool
- Candlestick weekly price-bars (examples given later)
- Bollinger Bands overlaid on chart data (20 period weighted moving average method)

Technical Indicators:
- Positive Volume with 52 week moving average
- Slow Stochastic Indicator
- Momentum Indicator
- MoneyFlow Indicator

Fundamental Analysis:
YTD (Year-to-date) % growth of stock divided by P/E ratio: higher the value the better
Double-digit % 5 year sales growth.
Double-digit ROE, little long-term debt.
Rising Free Cash Flow % as a percentage of sales*
History of moderate share growth (no dilution)
Lower Institutional holdings, less than 55%.
Better than market dividend exceeding dividend rate of the S & P 500.

* FREE CASH FLOW is earnings +non-cash items depreciation, etc.) (-) CAPITAL OUTLAYS

These aren't hard and fast rules. Work with what works for you. For instance, Apple and Netflix with high institutional holdings can continue higher, but when they fall—watch out! The greater the institutional holdings as a percent of a stock's float (shares held by investors) the weaker the hands of ownership.

# PART B:
## CONTINUED:

# CHAPTER 10:
# Buying Pattern Signals: The Cosmos Moves in Patterns

After we decide what stocks, options or funds to buy, we take the most important step in investing: WHEN to pull the trigger, so to speak. Yes, timing is everything.

Timing can make or break you along your road to financial independence. Deciding on "what" to buy is relatively easy, but deciding "when" to buy or sell is more difficult.

However, I'll address this matter later, taking the "when" out of the buying equation altogether. It's best you learn the technical patterns first.

For now, I'll address the decision to buy a stock in a conventional manner, so as to build a foundation for newcomers. If buying springs from a rational process selling can lead to a more irrational manner, especially in a market downturn. We will address this topic too. Remember, selling is more difficult that buying. Nevertheless, the steps I've listed below will demystify much of the alchemy of buying and selling.

For generations, books have been written on the basics of investing, the search for values, earnings and PE ratios, and this is a first step. Along the way you may discover many other ways to buy a stock. I did. And most of them failed. The steps I've studied after college and on many snowy evenings afterwards had been put to the test, and some of them worked and also broke down at another time. I returned to the drawing board once again. Yet foundations must be laid.

Earnings and cash flows can be deceiving despite of what you hear of their efficacy. Many traders sell on good earnings news, long before the earnings and sales benefit the company. Watch out!

Buying a stock begins with your stock chart on Bigcharts.com., an affiliate of Marketwatch.com. These charts are easy to read and present excellent resources. In the old days I would buy graph paper and work the traditional methods of triangle patterns, double tops and bottoms for example. Now the web saves all the leg work and brings this to the comfort of your home. You may have an idea of what stock you want to buy after tracking it. And the best strategy is to wait for a pullback in price to a predetermined level, e.g., a 33-50% retracement of a prior high, to a level of a stock's 30 week moving average. Many stocks bounce off of this level and rally to its old high.

The following investment zones have simplified my investing experience. The zones provide points of departure and points of no return, setting price boundaries that take the guess work out of investing. This is the beginning of Holistic Investing.

## CYCLICAL STOCKS:
### Buying Zones

Zone 1: Breakout From Base: Bottoming pattern

After a previous high and subsequent price decline to the 30 week average (200 day moving average), buy DOUBLE BOTTOM, of which second bottom is higher than previous bottom and stock has fallen (corrected). BUY if closing price at or near the HIGH for the week with strong volume and price range ABOVE 10 week moving average. This is a safe method for avoiding false breakouts, when a stock breaks higher from a high only to close down for the week. This particular pattern occurs after a 3-8 month consolidation. Buy 25 shares at LIMIT PRICE.

Zone 2: Run Up:
Buy weekly closing high after previous sideways consolidation as price continues to make highs after correction.
Buy 25 additional shares.

Zone 3: Blow Off:
After buying 50 shares from the two previous Zones, the stock, usually, is marching toward an intermediate top. However, you don't want to be caught holding 50 shares while stock falls back into familiar ground (Paraphrasing General Patton: Avoid paying for the same real estate twice). The stock in this phase will march to a new high, or fail, breakdown, and fall into a nasty decline. Buy 25 additional shares in case stock pops into new high territory; however, be prepared to sell ALL SHARES soon. Set sell stop below LOW of week after new high.

The Theory: Final breakout from another 1-3 week topping plateau is possible. But price may spike to another high and reverse the following week. In all likelihood, a good stock should correct 33-50% and fall back into Zone 2 territory, only to march to new highs. But if stock falls back into Zone 1, breaking BELOW its 30 wk. moving average, find another stock.

(1) Buy additional shares of Core Investment (explained later) after a pullback to the 33-50% level from a prior high.

(2) Or buy Core Investment after a pullback to stock's 30 week weighted moving average and stock holds. I prefer weighted moving average. Wait for a bounce off the 30 week on strong volume.

The buying zones described above have built-in risk avoidance because of the reduced shares of repurchases as a stock goes higher.

Remember, we use weekly data. Weekly data eliminates day-to-day volatility, the "static and noise" of a stock's random activity. Stocks do fluctuate from psychological impulses of active traders: Keynes' animal spirits. Weekly data also project trends out over a longer period, thus eliminating excess trading on day to day movement.

Do you want to fill the pockets of your broker? Listed below are graphical illustrations (1)-(5) Appendix.

The following rule (3) is for buying additional shares on the way up, after a stock has rallied from the Buying Zone as described above:

(3) Buy additional shares when following conditions are met: Stochastic-Pop Indicator

(a) When $2^{nd}$ weekly stochastic indicator has crossed above (K >D) from a higher level on chart as indicated by Friday's weekly close* The PV/G (price value growth) concept works with this and will be explained later.

(b) When Money Flow Indicator reaches new high (as indicated by Friday's close)*

(c) And Momentum Indicator confirms above as it moves higher.
*(if Friday's closing price is higher than its weekly opening price with strong volume)

(4) Buy when Japanese Candlestick forms a "T" pattern and its weekly price range is WITHIN previous week's range above Buying Zone. The "T (stock closes at high).

(5) Lastly, buy when stock's price range clears 10 week moving average. Weekly high may rise from another "U" shape pattern (a high, falling into trough and subsequent rally that traces out the letter "U") after a 4-6 week consolidation bottom pattern. I have had much success from this particular pattern.

# BUYING PATTERN SIGNALS: THE COSMOS MOVES IN PATTERNS

Money Flow and Momentum should rise to highs for confirmation. But if these fail to do so, then stock can make a "double (lower) top" (second top lower than first) and fall. If bullish, stock will continue rising most of the day from outset. As stated, the Appendix displays charts which illustrate buying and selling: graphic illustrations, (1)-(5), explained: Appendix.

# CHAPTER 11:
# Selling Pattern Signals

Selling stocks, funds and options become the flip side or opposite of buying. However, this effort is more difficult and really involves more intuition in addition to the art, science of buying explained. Initially, selling can be reduced to a science, but in most cases, you won't get your price on execution excepting sell orders. If you sell at the open, the stock may be thinly traded and price fluctuations more likely. Random psychological factors prior to selling may occur the night before. This will affect price. Lastly, a stop order may be executed below your target price on a stock falling in a tailspin.

Let me leave you with an old saw learned years ago: take your time to buy but run like hell to sell.

Selling Cyclical Stocks:

(1) Sell a stock from a double top, when it fails to make a new weekly high. Volume should fall below its 52 wk. average. The late commodities trader, W. D. Gann believed that most declines originate from a double top, the failure of the second top (usually lower than first) to penetrate an old high. The late great bull market of the late 1990s peaked in March of 2000, and a second but lower high was made in September. The wider the space (time) between the tops the

greater the fall: the 2000-2 bear market went down and remained down until November of 2002.

The Theory: An analog to the last buying example: After making a new high the stock drops 33-50%, from which it advances to another high, lower than previous high: SELL from a level of (Bollinger Bands of +2 standard deviations).

(2) Sell when stock closes below the S & P 500 on a comparative scale. If a stock, year-to-date has moved up 15% but the broad index of the S & P moves to 16 1/2% on a weekly close, its time to move on.

(3) Sell when stock reaches upper level of Bollinger Band (one of my default indicators) on 2nd try and money flow indicator lower than prior week.

(4) Sell when weekly candlestick pattern (Japanese price range) makes Key Reversal, shaded dark, and price closes at or near low when prior week's price range closed at old high, shaded white. In other words: if stock of prior week closes at high compared to current week's price at low and both price ranges equal in size: get ready for a Key Reversal.

(5) Sell Inside Week (entire price range within range of prior week), a dark candle pattern, a Japanese Candlestick pattern. In other words, a higher low than previous week's low and lower high than prior week's high. This signals a reversal of trend—watch out below.

These selling signals work best in upper levels of Bollinger Bands (+2 standard deviations above 20 week moving average of weekly closing prices). A word of caution: If a stock has dropped below it 30 week moving average(or 200 day moving average) then **DO NOT** buy additional shares from a bounce off old lows. This strategy works best with Core Stocks, larger mid-cap companies similar to the S & P 500. **CYCLICAL STOCKS** are typically small to mid cap companies which are more volatile and may fall harder and even further into new lows.

Above sell signals work most of the time, having a greater reliability than their 'buy signal' counterparts. Always remember, in the latter stages of a powerful multi-year bear/bull market, mass hysteria rules the day, and the market is really looking for an excuse to humble investors.

Remember the 416 pt. Dow drop in late February of 2007? And The Mother of all drops of 777 points was in October, 2008. All the yearly gains wiped out and then some.

These rules beat acting on a tip, rushing out to sell after a TV talk show 'expert' bad mouths a stock, or from reading a negative article. Keep your powder dry until you see the white of your enemy's eye, or the actual proof, such as selling pressure on heavy volume.

I like to part with some sage advice from the late W. D. Gann. He stated that the greater the breath, time spent (by a commodity or stock) low to low or from high to high), the greater the rise or fall, respectively, in both price and time.

Listed below are graphic illustrations: Appendix (1)-(5), explained: Appendix: Selling

# PART C:
## HOLISTIC PORTFOLIO THEORY:

# CHAPTER 12:
# The Value 3 Portfolio: Micro View: Positioning Your Money in a Risk/Reward World

We begin by redefining 'risk and reward:' The pocket Merriam Webster Dictionary, Collegiate, 11 ed., 2004.

Webster defines risk as an "exposure to possible loss or injury; the chance that an investment will lose value." In this world of money, we define risk as exposure to an erosion of value, or value tempered by time–a time element. Putting it bluntly, a stock or investment with a time-bomb tied to its belly.

Most of us have heard the story of a person who bought an internet stock at the top of the last market bubble in 2000. Of course the money evaporated into a fraction of its original worth by 2003. In fact, most long term investors had lost faith in long term investing and became short term sellers as their savings flew away into cyberspace.

Another good example of time value is one that some of us have experienced first- hand.

After the war, grandmother decided to put her war savings bonds and stock certificate in a safe deposit box. Years later, she remembered about those AT &T shares and decided to cash in. Her granddaughter was about to begin college.

The stock split many times paying dividends. In 1984 the company split into those Baby Bells,: Bell Atlantic, Bell South, etc. She discovered that she received shares in those other Bells and made even more.(The definition of a classic Core stock, discussed later.) Grandma praised the passage of time.

Time has a way of helping or hurting investments. The AT&T's and IBM's of yesterday's world have become the Google and Netflix of late. Some say that their best days are over.

When talking of time value, compound interest must be considered. The big thing to remember about compound interest is that money will double in time by dividing the current rate into 72, the Rule of 72. In other words, 72 divided by a rate of 6% (72/6=12) or 12 years for money to double.

We are reminded, often, that the "power of earnings growth" will propel a stock higher over time. We view earnings viewed over time, a pattern of earnings proves a more valuable tool. But earnings viewed in a static sense, such as current "earnings target" is worthless except when compared revenues or sale. Are earnings really from revenues or cost cutting? Sure, stocks or companies, like people can be vulnerable and rebound the following quarter. So those who were spooked by the soft numbers of the previously quarter now rush back to buy.

We must view earnings in a new light. The Key is to view earnings as an income stream, like a flowing brook, rather than a pond of water gathering moss. This key works.

Earnings or Free Cash Flow (earnings plus non cash expenses, depreciation, etc. less capital outlays) viewed over time becomes more meaningful, not present earnings, a snapshot in time.

Now we can look at a trend or pattern of earnings flow over time, a one, three or five year period.

Isn't this more meaningful? A good company may miss a couple of quarters of earnings growth, but in the end its numbers will get back on track and it should match the growth of the S&P 500 or better. This is a definition of a Core Investment, a firm outperforming many S&P 500 firms, outperforming, because of its competitive position, unique market position or products.

One of the most important topics of portfolio theory, risk and reward, falls within the realm of behaviour, the mind-set of the investor. I know volumes of books, articles and seminars have addressed this topic. It seems this aspect of investing rivals stock selection and investment timing.

I agree that psychology's impact on trading is magnified because of its time element, market volatility and margin characteristics such as a hog contract for instance. If I can boil it down to one dynamic, it would be this: Know Thyself. The early Greek Philosophers knew human nature, especially its drama. One of my favourites are the words of Heraclitus. His wisdom adroitly reveals our fallacies and propensities toward folly. If there are two books which I would highly recommend they are these:

Expect the Unexpected (Or you won't find it) by Roger Von Oech, THE FREE PRESS, 2001

Extraordinary Popular Delusions and the Madness of Crowds by Charles Mackay, LLD.
Richard Bentley, New Burlington Street, 1841
L. C. Page & Company, 1932: Reprint

We can be our worst enemy, not the shoeshine boy with the "hot tip" of old or the elevator operator at the Waldorf. The movers and shakers of industry are no better or worse than the rest of us in the buying and selling of stocks. They may have better access to inside information, and that's to be expected.

I remember a stockholder's meeting in Boston some years back. A former Attorney General was in attendance which added some spice to the morning. Frankly, he looked pretty good. He was a famous figure fired from Watergate's Saturday Night Massacre. Anyway, we had met at Sybron Tech, a 1996 leader in fibre optics for telecom and advanced electronics the world over.

Things were going rather well with new investments in capacity and products, the usual. After awhile, speakers at the meeting began to touch on the esoteric, moving into hyper drive. The new techniques and products required for new technologies seem another decade away. And even if this wonderful innovation found a market, would it sell? I was spooked. When I arrived home I sold the stock. At the time Sybron traded in the high twenties to early thirties. It had fallen some time later. The moral of the story is this—if you don't feel right, in your gut, for some reason in which you can't put your finger on—then get out. In most cases, you'll be vindicated. I can't find the stock listed in Barron's.

In times of stress, when a market crashes from trouble from the Saudi oil patch or in China, geopolitical turbulence, sell your stock or fund. You have no other option. These problems arrive unannounced. The old saw: Wall Street doesn't ring a bell when it's time to sell.

The question: will the market weather the storm and come back stronger? Will the market return in a reasonable time?

If no coherent answers are forthcoming, then it may be wise to sell. Why wait for another market cycle to bottom and rise again, two-three years later. Meanwhile, your money can find a safe haven in cash.

However, Core Investments, such as IBM in the 1950s and 1960s, GE, Computer Sciences in the 1970s, Microsoft and Cisco Systems in the 1990s would have made ideal candidates for reinvesting, hopefully near the bottom of a multi-year bear market. My parents loaded up on additional shares of Computer Sciences in 1978 near a bear market bottom and made a nice profit later. Emotions are subjective and no one can walk you through the gauntlet. Certainly, I would sell a cyclical stock in a crisis but not a core stock. And speaking of funds, some mutual funds with long term records fit the definition of a Core Stock, like Magellan of Fidelity and Windsor, Windsor II of Vanguard.

I like to end this chapter on the duty for due diligence. When I enrolled in the Financial Planning Program at NYU some years back, this term, due diligence had seemed a novel idea.

# THE VALUE 3 PORTFOLIO: MICRO VIEW: POSITIONING YOUR MONEY

The scope of financial planning: estates and trusts, taxes, budgets, investments and insurance cover five vast disciplines, a world of knowledge. The planner would have to cover these bases in order to formulate a plan for a client. The complexities involved are enormous, and today banks and investment firms offer these services. No one person does all the work and audits the records because of the enormity of the task. And all of this is due diligence. So before you buy a stock or anything, have a good idea of its nature, why you're buying. A corporate bond or a company behind the stock are only as good as the folks running the show. Are these people, the management reliable? A company's management is the MOST IMPORTANT due diligence you can do for yourself. Remember WorldCom and Enron? After due diligence, everything else is so much easier.

Reports and financial statements beg demands on your time. They are tedious, boring and difficult with all that fine print. But they must be examined: the smaller the company the more you must search. But I solve this problem: if a Tech Wunderkind doesn't have any earnings whatsoever, forget it. Remember, your companies must have an earnings stream, talked about earlier.

Positioning your money in a risk/reward world is the heart of portfolio theory. Money management is an integral part of this universe. For you may be the best stock picker in the world and a "cool turkey" in the heat of a bear market. But the battle is not over. A higher principle underwrites all. And it's this: Do you have a system which can be applied: over and over in the pursuit of profit? Are you a sunshine and rainy day investor? Remember, swinging for the fences or just trying to get on base are two different strategies. Home run hitters strike out the most and consistent batters have the highest batting average. Great hitters hold high lifetime averages and have hit many home runs. We remember Willie Mays, Babe Ruth, Lou Gehrig and Joe DiMaggio. All the above had lifetime batting averages over 300 and were considered home run hitters. First, get on base, then steal second.

An investment can be the greatest thing in the universe for months, one or three years.

Sooner or later, it will fade and be forgotten. Those who held Microsoft or Cisco Systems fell with their stocks in the prolonged bear market of 2000-2. It was time to say good-by. Today, March, 2007 these stocks are stuck in the twenties after trading 200-300 % higher seven years ago. A person who bought them in the heady days of late 1999 would still be out of the money.

In earlier decades, IBM, GM, AT & T had claimed the darlings of the day. True, these companies are still good companies and may represent a good buy, but they're heroes of yesteryear.

Do we have the time to wait for your ship to come home? Foundering about in the rough seas of investing may seem like a long time. But we do have time to meet the kid's education, the dream retirement home in Florida, our retirement. Not knowing where you've been doesn't help where you're going. Yet Failure is healthy, if viewed as a stepping stone to better things. We must answer these questions: WHY did I fail? Or WHY did I succeed? A lot of us can't put our finger on it. We may have ideas, but no rhyme or reason, no pattern. Were we too optimistic, too pessimistic? Too timid? If these are questions you have asked, then read on. I believe a better way exists. Read on. Holistic Investing can transcend errors of technique, pressures of time and money management, and most important, self management.

Holistic Investing boils away any arcane art of investing down to a common sense system. Surely, mass psychology can affect investing and it can be harnessed in your favour. Economics and geo-politics trigger such events. For ages we've batten down the hatches and held for the long term, hoping to hit that home run like grand mom did on her tucked away AT&T stock. No more, for we live in a much smaller world that ticks to nanoseconds of information 24/7. Our oceans no longer protect us. But a system that works can protect our portfolio. And one final thought about the long term (investor): "We are all dead," as so deftly put by Keynes.

# CHAPTER 13:
# The Value 3 Portfolio: Macro View: Positioning Your Money in a Risk/Reward World

THE POWER 3 PORTFOLIO: Format:

    (1) Cash/Bond Funds
    (2) Common Stocks/Index Options
    (3) Mutual Fund Sectors

(1) Cash/Bond Funds: a FUSION of 40-60% of monies should be in this category at all times regardless of market condition. Of course, nearly 60% of funds should be parked here in a secular bear market, 40 % for bull markets. Core stocks, your primary drivers comprise category (2) with no positions in special-situation or cyclical stocks. Yes, it's true that back in the days of 5% interest, money market mutual funds would be a good choice, a far cry of .25% money paid now.

Reason: Short-term monies in Treasury bond funds protect the portfolio in down drafts. The bonds will gain value as stocks fall. Also, bonds barely fluctuate in periods of weak interest rates. When rates rise, close out bonds positions and park all monies in cash.

(2) Common Stocks/Index Options

The right common stocks will do wonders for your portfolio—as the reverse with the wrong ones. Core stocks should hail from the mid-cap value group and pay above market-rate dividends. Cyclical or Special Situation stocks should be small -mid cap growth stocks.

Smaller companies aren't mired in organization issues; have greater flexibility; and have good prospects for buy-outs from larger firms with greater growth potential from a smaller base. Index Options are for hedging only. If you determine that the broad market is in for some rough sledding, then buy near the money puts for insurance.

If market heads south, you will profit and if not, all you lose is your option premium which should represent less than two percent of your portfolio. Buy option(s), one-two contracts at beginning of contract.

Reason: Stock market gains should be held in minor corrections. You really don't want to fight the same battle if stocks fall all the way down to original purchase price. By placing a stop order around 7 ½ % below high or at prior week's low, whichever higher, profits of cyclical stocks are locked in. Many stocks retrace 50% of prior gain before resuming higher. If not, a stock may continue down below 50% from high. Close position.

(3) Mutual Fund Sectors:

Market sectors define the market. Rather than hearing about the price of oil driving up gas prices towards $5.00 a gallon, isn't it better to get some of your cash back from

## THE VALUE 3 PORTFOLIO: MACRO VIEW: POSITIONING YOUR MONEY

buying energy or natural resource funds? A few years back Index investing was all the rage because most money managers don't beat the market. Lower cost indexes give them their advantage. But those who kept to their index stock funds in the fall of 2008 saw their hard earned 401k's melt away. Hello bonds. The idea is to determine when the industrials, specialty retailers, energy or the basic materials, etc. are poised for a bounce. Overvaluation/undervaluation, supply shortages, the wealth effect of upscale shoppers, and a host of other fundamental reasons can spook the market. I look at new highs of companies representing a sector. Look at 2-4 companies within sector to verify its bullish scope. If true, then you have the beginning of a move which may prove profitable, even moving contrary to the market.

Mutual funds expanded after the War, The Dreyfus Fund, for instance, comprises most sectors and had given investors an opportunity to participate in all the post-war bull market. **MUTUAL FUNDS CAN ADD VALUE TO YOUR PORTFOLIO.** At this time I have monies in the Dreyfus Select Managers Value Fund and the Invesco Convertible Securities Fund (12-22-13). This year has been stellar as common stocks have risen 20 % plus. I would say that a good 25% of the gains in the Holistic Portfolio are from mutual funds.

Reason: A sector may continue to reap profits for months. You should participate in this gift and supplement gains to your portfolio.

This chapter strikes at the heart of Holistic Investing, especially in this age of globalization and geopolitical uncertainty. If there ever was a time for **TATIACAL NOVELTY** with simplicity, it is now. For ages Wall Street has been preaching for broad diversification in a basket of stocks and bonds, to the tune of sixty percent stocks, forty percent bonds. Yes, this used to work and did provide a measure of stability with market returns. The theory was that if interest rates had risen, then bonds, a hedge against down markets, would keep the investor's ship afloat in stormy waters. But bonds would go down too. Their income along with the better dividend paying stocks would build ballast.

In the 1970s the above approach sank. Rising inflation may have helped some of the stocks to rise, the natural resource and small technology stocks, but the bonds were ravaged. Inflation stripped away the value of the bonds and untold thousands of investors swore that they would never buy bonds again.

In the early 1980s, cash was king and the new Fed Chairman, Paul Volcker was determined to squeeze inflation out of the system. He instituted credit controls early on and later jacked up rates. The severe manufacturing recession resulted in 1981-2, leaving a "rust bowl" of closed plants behind. Now was the time to buy bonds after many years of anguish. In retrospect, bonds out performed stocks in the 1980s, thanks to the Crash of 1987.

The Cold War military build-up of the 1960s-1980s provided a robust fiscal influx into defence contractors and their suppliers. The winds of globalization were barely on the drawing boards.

Money was relatively tight and credit card debt not even a whisper of the monster it is today.

Investment decisions revolved around economic growth—too little or too much—and its cost, interest rates, too high or too low. Global pressures, international money flows and lopsided trade imbalances were yet to make its mark.

Portfolio theory weathered and sometimes had been buffeted by the storms since the Great Depression. Pax Americana had underwritten the rebuilding of Europe and Japan while a manufacturing boom rehired the returning troops. This continued into the 1970s, aided by the "guns and butter" economy except for the oil shocks later. But after the early '80s recession, everything changed.

# THE VALUE 3 PORTFOLIO: MACRO VIEW: POSITIONING YOUR MONEY

General Motors, the auto industry and their suppliers had begun its long descent into hell. Tool and die shops, and even textile and shoe industries began closing plants and cutting jobs in the mid west and New England. At the time, 1981-2, the only game in town was CD's (certificate of deposit). Many folks bought these, and I was one of them. Many households avoided the rollercoaster rides of the Wall Street "casino" and an earlier bond "certificates of confiscation." I bought a CD in a Maryland bank paying over sixteen percent. And despite the economic turbulence we had more fun.

The upshot of the above economic pains, successes, booms and busts had not affected the investment climate and portfolio theory as we knew it. College courses teach us to diversify and hold for the long term, correct. Never bet the ranch, especially in today's real estate market.

However, in our information age with global markets, I-Pads and stock market media, additional information and technological power has not, by itself, make us better investors. Yes, we're better informed. We may get out earlier from a bad trade, but mostly, the market will come back.

The real winners are the brokerage and investment houses. Sadly, holding long term may indeed be long term Greek Tragedy coming from nowhere. And the company may never return.

Thousands of retirement plans fizzled into smoke in 2000 after the "Tech Bubble" of the late '90s. People went to jail.

Why not rethink, reinvent, the way you look at money, your money? After all, it's at stake.

We should visit it often. Holistic Portfolio empowers us. Its simplicity allows you "hands on" management, de-institutionalizing business as usual. The big institutions spend billions selling us the same story. Isn't it time we create our own story? Why settle for sixty percent stocks and forty percent bonds when a sensible alternative exists? You may get market returns with the traditional approach, but with much greater risk.

# CHAPTER 14:
# Core Value Stocks: The Driver

Core stocks drive your portfolio, and if selected with patience, these stocks can power you to riches. The question: what makes a core stock appealing? The short answer: a core stock is an all-weather stock that can survive any market environment: bull and bear markets, in times of roaring inflation or money crunching deflation, international crisis or any other thing the world wants to throw at Wall Street. These stocks are proven survivors, tested in the cauldron of the past.

Core stocks find a home in the S & P 500 and/or a Mid Cap Index. These value stock pay better than market rate dividends, and most important, are capable of growth. By growth industries, I mean familiar companies known by most of us, not some "Buck Rogers" vision of the future which may not prove profitable for years. A firm may build the best mousetrap and ride into an IPO (initial public offering). However, I avoid these stocks because of their vulnerability (high price and unproven track record). Remember, sitting in the right pew means being in the right stock at the right time.

As of mid 2011, my Core stocks were Singapore Fund, ETF, Syngenta and Wynn Resorts.

They may change in the future. I would own no more than five Core Stocks at any time.

Diversification, in some cases, can water-down results and increase transaction costs. This will be explained in following chapter.

The next most important thing in choosing a core stock is its management. Are they taking market share away from its competitors? If they are, all the other good things fall into place: sales growth (the most important), growth in free-cash as a percent of sales, profit margins and ROE (return on equity). Surely, all stock sectors may fall in a bear market but a core stock should fall less because of its stronger industry and better management.

How do you measure management effectiveness? No one knows the day-to-day activities of companies except insiders, directors and those making strategic decisions taken by large companies. Yes, these changes are reported by the media and become stale news by the time most individual investors know. It's too late: good news-price rises and the opposite in bad. I believe the best management yardstick is to measure its proven track record. And I don't mean scanning over those annual reports with reams of fine print to burst ones pupils. Just look at a company's sales growth, free-cash and shares growth (no dilution). End of story.

Getting into the earnings game, as explained earlier, can be a fool's game. Earnings can be manipulated, "padded" as proven way after the fact as numerous companies have restated earnings due to honest or dishonest mistakes. Remember: It's hard to restate sales of a Fortune 500 company.

Historically, stocks with rising dividends had become a popular way to buy a stock. This may work for awhile, and the dividend should cushion the stock in a bear market. But what happens to the company if its industry falls from grace. The stock will fall. Example: financial stocks did well in most of 2006, but now the big guys (the institutions) fear the Fed will not lower rates despite a falling economy in 2007. Why? Inflationary fears keep rearing its ugly head. So financial stocks take gas and natural resource stocks ride the tiger higher. Surely, many financial stocks have excellent managements. But even they cannot fight a tsunami of disbelief as oil prices head higher, food prices follow.

I like to point out another truth about the validity of sales growth in the selection of a core stock. I look at the percentage of sales growth over a typical business cycle, usually four years or the term of a presidential administration. I also measure share growth of the same period. Having these percentages, I divide the sales growth by the share growth (including stock splits) and arrive at number, usually greater than one. If the answer is 1.375, let's say, then I move on the next levels: industry sector and management as discussed. For instance if sales grow by 250% and shares grow by 185% over a four year period (250/185) then sales would outgrow shares by a factor of 1.35135, the higher the number, the better. Also, stock buy-backs reduce share growth.

Before I leave this chapter, I like to include another model in determining core stocks, as the article in The Times-Union of Jacksonville, FL of 4/25/07: "Stocks that tower over competitors," referring to 'Wide Moat Stocks' made famous by Warren Buffett, the Oracle of Omaha. In effect, the companies are castles with towers with moats around them. They exist because of the following advantages: intangibles (patents), low-cost production, customer loyalty, the "network effect," critical mass in the internet (eBay and Google, etc.). In other words, wide moat companies have little competition because of the difficulty for competitors to open shop.

I tracked just four of these stocks for 2007, year-to-date. Bank of America, Fastenal, Medtronic and Walgreen, all listed in the Business section of the paper.

Bank of America was down 5.2%, Fastenal was up 15%, Medtronic was down .2%, and Walgreen was even at 0. I didn't bother to rank the other sixteen companies. And if I did, the results, probably, wouldn't be that much different But here's the real story, the S & P 500 beat the Morningstar Wide Moat 100 Index, over the past three years by 11.1 vs. 5.4 per cents, annualized. Yet the Morningstar Wide Moat Focus Index of 20 stocks returned 14.4% annualized, thus beating the S & P, because this index considered the group underpriced.

Time and leverage are the last element I like to emphasize. This means Core Stock holdings can be held longer than most stocks. Their reinvestment windows allow investors to buy additional shares when their prices are lower, trading near its 30 week or 200 day moving average. I will discuss this later: my version of dollar-cost average will allow investors to buy approximately twice a year(most market corrections occur either in the first two month(Jan.-Feb.) or May-June to the Sept.-to early December time-frame. Most important, many stocks correct within their normal parameters from past corrections during a general market correction.

Core stocks reinvested from the above system will outperform the market over the long haul. Time is on your side.

Core stocks invested and reinvested on the heels of macroeconomic trends, unlike traditional fundamental analysis, pay extra dividends from capital appreciation. For example, I invested in the Singapore Fund because of its bright future in south-east Asia. As China goes so goes southeast Asia, especially Singapore's modern financial hub. Surely, the region will have periodic sell offs as in all global markets, but will return stronger the next time.

I chose Wynn Resorts because this company, especially Steve Wynn, will make the right decision as he demonstrated time and time again. The new game in town is Macau, and yes it's in China. I remember the old days in the 1980s when he and Frank Sinatra made commercials.

Steve was interviewed recently by Michael Eisner. Steve helped turned Las Vegas into a family resort and will do likewise in Macau, spurred by China's rising middle class. The Chinese love gaming. The world loves to wager on the slots. Look at the Power Ball madness.

Lastly I chose Syngenta, a Swiss company traded on the New York Exchange. Syngenta refines and improves commercial seed for agribusiness around the world. In a sense, the company is in the specialty chemical sector which will play a major share in the economy of the future.

## CORE VALUE STOCKS: THE DRIVER

Global warming is a fact of life. Witness the polar icecaps in meltdown. Greenland's glaciers are falling into the Atlantic as this is written, thousands of years of history gone. It's no secret that our weather patterns are changing to extremes, larger floods (Super Storm Sandy) and longer droughts. Tell the NJ Governor that you don't believe in global warming? Commercial seed of the future must be able to withstand drought, the volatile extremes of a warmer climate.

Syngenta remains on the cutting edge of global food supply, and it will become even more important in years to come.

Leverage, the acquisition of debt, for good or bad, makes the world go round. Global booms depend on growth and political stability. An expansion of debt follows. Equities rise from increasing confidence and economic growth, fuelled from an expansion of markets and trade.

Core stocks will behave with the rest of the market. When they fall to a level representing good value you want to buy more shares. Suppose your core stocks falls below its 30 week average along with the market. A sound company will fall with the market but in time, consolidate and move higher. BUY MORE. And if another core company looks more attractive, then track it.

Your core stock should be a well capitalized company. It should be in the right sector: say health care or energy. If your new core candidate continues to outperform the S & P 500, then SWITCH to the new stock.

However, and this is IMPORTANT: do not switch at the market price; switch at predefined LIMIT PRICE, discussed later.

# CHAPTER 15:
# Holistic Portfolio Principles

The Holistic Portfolio will outperform the waves of greed and fear, boom and bust or whatever the market will do. Yes, your Holistic portfolio may be down for a spell, but because of its strategic market position with few competitors and above average dividends reinvested, your stock will continue to advance after the bear market.

Investors are frequently blind-sided by surprises and unanticipated events. These shocks are the meat on the bone which open-up windows of opportunity. If prices zig to extreme overvaluation (funny-money land) then sell those smaller, aggressive cyclical stocks before they zag back to reality. DO NOT SELL CORE STOCK HOLDINGS, as discussed unless a better candidate arises. Yes, they will fluctuate with the market; however, TIME IS YOUR CORE STOCK's BEST FRIEND.

Like the "young-Turk" waiting in the wings, his day will come when the boss retires.

Fundamental Rule for Buying/Selling Core Stocks:

Buying: Buy Core stock after Bull Market Correction:

    Buy PVG (Price Value Growth) STOCKS: stocks with % YTD (year-to-date) price growth expressed in whole number, at least double its PE ratio: ex. Price rise, let's say is 20% and PE is 10, thus Stock YTD: 20 divided by PE of 10, 20/10 =2 or greater. Why: BECAUSE TRENDS HAVE STAYING POWER.

Buy a Core stock after a pullback and then trades sideways, a flat market bumping along bottom of at least 3 months. Buy when stock breaks out on much better than average 52 week volume. Yes, the market may continue sideways, but this stock is considered 'underpriced" and should outperform the market in the next bull market.

Note: Look at stable shares outstanding and long-term debt.

Return on Equity and 5 Yr. Sales Growth%.: Double Digit

Position in its market: Does company have serious competitors?

Ability to generate FCF (free cash flow, as described)

Selling Core Stocks: the rules on page 77 on selling Cyclical Stocks can apply to the sale of Core Stocks. Especially, I would sell if:

(1) Core Stock's YTD Growth % falls below market average (S & P 500). Your stock should OUTPERFORM market averages. Beware of stagnation.

(2) Core Stock's price falls below 30 week (200 day) moving average. (Of course, if stock falls from high, a stop of 7 1/2% below high will protect you.)

(3) Core stock candidate should be gaining market momentum and pop above market averages.

As we build a portfolio we must manage it. Principles and planning for Holistic portfolio management follow. Forget about traditional portfolio managements of fixed per-cents allocation of stocks, bonds and cash. Remember, Holistic Investing maintains at least 40-60% of your money in cash or bond funds. We diversify but in a limited way: market sectors. At any one time I hold about THREE core stocks and no more than THREE cyclical stocks. Remember, core stocks are large mid-cap value companies. Cyclical stocks are smaller companies usually found in the Russell 2000 Index. Cyclical stocks grow faster than Core stocks and are traded on any exchange. I find five-eight stocks and one-three mutual funds easier to manage rather than a basket of let's say 15-20 investments However, an ETF's or exchange traded fund can count as a stock such as my investment in the Singapore Fund a few years ago. I held Singapore and Brazil as cyclical because I consider growth in Singapore's region equal to Brazil with a much better than average dividend. You want to simplify investing.

Some individual investors buy into the diversification thesis by holding twenty to thirty funds (mutual and ETF's). This is too much for the mind to focus on. Active day traders have been known to "burn out" on fewer holdings. Avoid information overload.

The Holistic portfolio favours mutual funds as another investing tool. And speaking of diversification, this is it. But I approach funds as another asset class, not so much a growth vehicle like index investing. Sure, index funds are low cost because of low turnover. These track the S & P or NASDAQ and run on automatic pilot. They're similar to core stocks with low or no turnover, trading expenses kept to a minimum.

I view mutual funds from a sector approach. For instance, I'm holding AIM Global Equity, an international value fund and the AIM Energy Fund. Over in Dreyfus, I hold the International Value and Strategic Value funds because of the weak dollar and better exports of large multinationals. I also hold the Dreyfus Natural Resource Fund because of the current dynamics of rising commodity prices. Of course, this orientation will change as conditions change. Last year I held the AIM Financial Fund with good results. Sector investing works.

You can be in the right church (sector) and wrong pew (stock) and make money; or you can be in the wrong church but right pew AND MAKE less MONEY. Be in the right church and pew.

Interest rates and inflation define the market. At the present time, we have an inverted yield curve (short-term rates higher than long-term rates). Three month treasury securities yield 4.96% while five-year treasury bonds yield 4.59%. This is bad news for banks, especially small banks, because they borrow short (higher rates) and loan long like equity and car loans. Thus, I would avoid bank stocks even if the brokers and insurance companies are reporting good earnings.

Also, a weak dollar doesn't bode well for the financials. The financial sector has underperformed in 2007.

The flip-side of financial stocks are commodity stocks: agriculture, metals including copper, gold, silver and energy including crude oil, natural gas and the oil services sector. At this time my cyclical stocks are Metals Management, a scrap metals dealer out of Chicago, and Gulfmark, a marine services company to the ocean drillers. Demand is outstripping supply because of a global boom for resources. Daily commodity prices fluctuate even if the fundamentals underlying commodities remain in place. Money is to be made.

Lastly, before we get to the actual system, I like to compare some stock funds for possible candidate core fund holdings, a partial list:

Stock Funds that Zigs when market Zags
Courtesy of The Times Union: 4/24/07
Annualized Returns %

Correlation w/S & P 500

| Fund | Type | 1 Yr. | 3 Yr. | % Unlike |
|---|---|---|---|---|
| Vanguard S&P 500 | Lg.Blend | 15.9 | 10.9 | 0 |
| Copley (COPLX) | Lg.Value | 26.3 | 14.6 | 30 |
| John Hancock(TAGRX) | Lg.Blend | 23.5 | 17.7 | 31 |
| Pinnacle Value(FAIRX) | Sm.Value | 18 | 15.2 | 17 |
| Dreyfus Muni Op (DMBZX), Class Z | Muni Bonds | 7.52 | 6.34 | 100 |

Now I like to get to the meat of this chapter: How does the system work?

# HOLISTIC PORTFOLIO PRINCIPLES

The Holistic Portfolio:

Hold bonds with Strong Dollar:

| | | |
|---|---|---|
| Cash/bonds: | 40-60% Ballast: | Buy Bonds up to 10% w falling rates) |
| Core Stocks | 40-30% | Buy and hold/switch |
| Cyclical " | 20-10% | Buy and sell |

Operation: Buy and sell cyclical stocks, small to mid-cap companies on a week-to-week basis.

Winning trades return to Cash. LOSING TRADES RETURN TO THE BEST CORE STOCK INVESTMENT. This principle is important. Proceeds from an earlier loss can buy additional shares of a strong core stock. This not only improves morale but bears fruit later. A good move.

In general, let's say your trading record for cyclical stocks is roughly 50% winning trades and 50% losing trades. Of course I hope your percentages are more like 60-40%. In BULL MARKETS: a mix of 40% cash/mutual fund bonds and 60% stocks. In BEAR MARKETS: 60% cash/bond funds and 40% stocks. Why the high percentage of cash? I'll explain these ratios in another chapter on risk, I call "strategic risk."

Currently, my core positions are Singapore ETF, Wynn Resorts and Monsanto. I study their charts daily by logging into Bigcharts. com. (weekly-prices) by determine performance year-to-date. One can read many things into a chart, and my chapter on charting should help by introducing new tools and ideas.

Forget about a severely undervalued stock which, on first glance, looks good. Rising contracts for new business, book-to-bill ratio, insider trades, etc. Sure, all of these are nice to know but will they really help you make an informed decision? If a stock contains all of these metrics it's deserves it. Beware of a "buy rating" by some analyst, look before you leap. It's down for a reason.

Remember the old saying: "In simplicity there is power." My favourite rating of a strong market is to divide a stock's year-to-date percentage price growth by its PE ratio. The higher the number the better as discussed earlier. Let's say Wynn Resorts has a year to date growth of 15% and its PE is 18. So we divide 15/18 and the answer is .833. Now let's assume Monsanto stock rose 24% year-to-date and its PE ratio is 23. We divide 24/23 and arrive at arrive at 1.04, greater than .833. After this I look at the money flow and momentum numbers Market Watch) and compare it to its slow stochastic indicator. Are they moving in sync? If so, proceed. Make sure the Stochastic Indicator %K rises above %D the second time from a higher level on chart: 2$^{nd}$ Wind Effect. Look for PV/G well above 2.

I also find money flow indicator reliable, a true harbinger of longer term trends, the grist of Core Stocks.

Another way of choosing a core stock is from a combination of fundamental and technical analysis. This involves a new twist from an established stock in the S & P 500, Pfizer, a drug company who said yesterday that it will triple its Phase III portfolio by 2009.

Pfizer had eleven drugs in Phase III clinical trials, the last stage before being sent to the FDA (Food & Drug Administration). Pfizer had 99 total programs in the pipeline of which 20 were for cancer treatments, 17 for pain and inflammation and 17 for neurological disease. They will target four new medicines per year from internal R & D starting in 2011, according to MarketWatch, 8-7-07. However, the stock went nowhere. Money Flow will give you the answer.

The company seems on solid ground:

| | | |
|---|---|---|
| Return on Investment: | 23.6% | annualized |
| Gross Margin: | 87.5% | " |
| Profit " | 40.0% | " |
| Dividend Yield: | 4.75% | " |

As evident, fundamentals can deceive. Moving on, after a short spell in PFE, Pfizer, I bought FMC, the old Food Machinery and Chemical. This stock is into industrial chemicals and the lithium business. Lithium batteries power hybrid autos. Dow Chemical makes most of these batteries. However, FMC will provide residual demand, additional batteries as needed as consumers wean off of

## HOLISTIC PORTFOLIO PRINCIPLES

gasoline. However, it will take years for hybrid vehicles to make critical mass. Higher fuel price will accelerate the conversion.

Another reason why I bought FMC is the development in the field of bio-pharmaceuticals, namely a partnership with Biopharma: the development of a capsule made from a marine compound that will dissolve in the small intestine, not the stomach. This product will revolutionize drug delivery in fighting disease. Medications which dissolve in the stomach may not be effective. **NEVER BET THE RANCH ON AN INITIAL BUY.** Buy into a core stock lightly, and on confirmation, if the stock is the "real deal;" buy additional shares after the stock pulls back from a higher level.

Another core stock I like was Monsanto. As of mid September, 2007, the stock has risen nearly 75% YTD while the Dow rose only 15%. But one would think that this stock is way overvalued. Not so. Monsanto based between June and early September, a good foundation for another move up. On September 20th the company raised its outlook on global growth. The global boom from Asia will spur demand for additional food production. China and India need crop protection, especially in corn. I quote from MarketWatch: "better tax rates, early corn sales, improved herbicide prices add to an upside." I recently bought the stock at 77 and it currently trades at 83-4.

Of course Monsanto may fall back but I believe this company will continue to outperform the major averages. At this time, 9/07, my core positions in the following fields: agribusiness, natural resources, energy, emerging markets, technology and gaming. Why do we buy a Core Stocks after a losing trade? Because your portfolio will grow faster from the Core side of the ledger, the true driver of your wealth. And the sooner this happens the faster your confidence will grow.

Also, by buying more shares of a very good company your wealth will increase. Remember, time rather than market volatility is your friend. Market volatility can be your friend with your smaller growth companies.

Bad streaks in sports as in investing are inevitable. The nature of the beast. Much of market volatility is sheer randomness. Like a ship at sea, the market will eventually right itself and off to the races again. Wait for your second wind. And believe me, it will blow again in your favour.

Remember Frank Sinatra's song: That's Life: "Riding high in April, Shot down in May."

Another reason we buy core stocks after a losing cyclical trade is psychology. Yes, I spoke above about the power of psychology. Now I'm no shrink or priest. But after a loss we need some good news, a victory. And what's better than a victory when a prior losing trade transforms into a money maker. Remember: Core Stocks need time. Cyclical Stocks need volatility.

This concludes the essence of Holistic Portfolio Theory. The ballast of up to 60% cash/bond funds will cushion those certain hard times, protracted bear markets. The bear does growl and claw and slowly walks away to perdition. The good news is that most of your money begins from bear market bottoms, a series of fake moves up, bad new daily, dire predictions. And as sure as people love mom and apple pie, Morning in America arrives at the station. Have a list of strong mid-cap value stocks poised to ride this train higher. Buy them cheap.

Avoid one of the most pressing issues for new investors: experiencing big losses early in a career. THE HOLISTIC PORTFOLIO AVOIDS THIS. Instead, use a down period to grow more in investing: know the traditional ratios—PE, price-to-sales, return on equity, long-term debt, institutional holdings, and most important: Free cash flow. Expand your envelope and be prepared for round two. Investing is about mass psychology at market turns and economics. It's about global politics. Most important, it's about common sense and focus. A strong core stock will ride out these trends.

Go for the small victories at first, hit the singles and doubles. Never bet the ranch, not even on a core stock. You really want to hitch your stocks to a rising star, a sector on the move.

## HOLISTIC PORTFOLIO PRINCIPLES

Stocks rise principally for three reasons:

(1) A company's performance
(2) A sector's movement
(3) The market's trend

Do you know what the management is cooking up before earnings are released? No one does except the insiders. Index funds ride the coattails of a bull market. But bull markets run out of steam. By catching the right sector your stock can catch the wind at it back for weeks, months, sometimes years. And if your company performs from a sincere, smart management the stock market will do the rest.

Remember the Internet bubble of late 1990s? Many got burned because they fell in love with those "profitless wonders." Now the oil companies and China are printing money. This too will end. Be flexible; be nimble and anticipate change. Develop a Plan B: What can go wrong? Think Critically, survive.

# CHAPTER 16:
# A Cubby Bear Correction

Welcome a stock market correction. Stock markets generally pullback from 2-6 weeks and correct from 4-8%. A market decline over ten percent may be the beginning of a bear market, covered in the next chapter. These small corrections are necessary for the bull to catch its breath, and run even higher.

A correction in a bull market allows you to take a deeper look into your positions. And if your stocks fall less than the market averages, the S & P 500 and the NASDAQ 100, then you're doing a good job in stock selection. Contrary to panic at the opening bell or losing sleep, this is the time to sit back and BUY ADDITIONAL SHARES. Set limit orders.

If a core stock falls to your original purchase price or below, why not use some of your cash and buy additional shares, matching the number of shares originally bought. Now you are primed to benefit when the bull returns with double the number of shares. Also, you can switch to another cyclical stock that shows more promise at the same price. Also, set limit orders on buy/sell.

Again, Core stocks are held long term. Your friend is time, not volatility. Your aim is to accumulate as many core shares as possible from successive downturns provided that fundamentals continue stronger. Remember, bull markets need ECONOMIC GROWTH.

Another way to accumulate more core shares is from a losing trade. You can move from cyclical to core stock. For example, I sold the Brazil ETF, a cyclical stock when it had weakened from the "mortgage meltdown" of 2007. I bought additional shares of one of my core stocks, WYNN Resorts. WYNN actually rose during the sub-prime summer of 2007. A good core stock has a low beta, meaning that it will fall less than the market, a stock that zigs when the markets zags.

But I have **ONE MAJOR EXCEPTION** with the holding period for core stocks. If your core stock suffers from a gusher of success, meaning that it rises to extreme overvaluation(a parabolic run-up of 25-50% in a very short period of time), then I would take profits by **SETTING A SELL STOP** down to a reasonable level of 7.5% below the high. **WHY PAY FOR THE SAME REAL ESTATE** (stock) **TWICE?** This is a very good reason why we carry five core stocks in our portfolio of eight stocks (not counting mutual funds). Of the other four core stocks, one of them will be a better buy. Why not buy one of them with the profits of the overvalued core stock sold. And if the other core stocks are overvalued, then park the profits in cash and wait for a pullback.

For instance, Monsanto and Singapore ETF were my other two Core holdings. At any given time WYNN Resorts would go wild and spike much higher in a very short period of time, then I'd place a sell stop at 7 ½ % below its high. When the stock falls back down to this level, then I'd be stopped out. For example, I'd SWITCH to another Core stock provided one is available. If not, place profits in cash and wait for a better opportunity. **DO NOT** buy back the same core stock or new cyclical stock with the profits. The market rarely rewards good luck twice in short order. Cyclical shares are shorter term investments and are treated more like trading vehicles.

A. CYCLICAL STOCKS: Immediate Sell:

Stocks usually make a **SECOND TOP** after making an initial top. Place sell stop near weekly close of second top provided that second top is lower than original and if stock is struggling. Be prepared. If stock is struggling then it has giving you a clue of weakness. But if stock breaks through to a new high look for volume breath, a sigh of relief but retain stop just in case it weakens later. Watch volume.

If volume is strong and stock breaks down, then modify previous stop and place sell stop as near prior high close as possible. If volume is weak and stock continues to climb, this sets up a classic Bearish Divergence: sell using above sell stop techniques.

B. CYCLICAL STOCKS: Buying Additional Shares. Listed below are methods of doing this. The best way to decide if your stock is worth buying is relative strength. Has your stock's group (oil services) let's say, continue to OUTPERFORM the S & P 500? Don't sell. If stock makes a new top but breaks down into a pullback, you have an additional investment set up. In most cases, the stock will bounce back, at least from its 30 week moving average. You can buy additional shares of short-term cyclical stocks at prices at or below original cost in a market pullback. Buy if your stock falls down to its 10 week or 30 week moving average, depending on the severity of its pullback. The additional shares will appreciated with greater value on the next move up. Buy the following:

(1) weekly closing price at or above 10 week moving average. If stock falls below the moving average on a closing basis for the week, **DO NOT BUY.**

(2) stock outperforms market average on the way down by falling less than average on a percent basis.

(3) moneyflow indicator stable over three week period (its powder kept dry for next up.)

When the correction is over, the market should lift your stock higher. If your stock rises, we enter a new dimension. I'll speak about this shortly. If your stock doesn't perform to your wishes, you should be ready to take one of two actions: hold or sell.

By holding a good stock, sometimes the market doesn't catch up to its true worth, after all, the company is making money so the market will discover the stock again. But if the stock doesn't respond to a market rebound, maybe something else is holding the stock back—the wrong industry sector, falling revenues, etc.

As discussed, if the stock is a financial stock and rates begin turning higher on reported higher inflationary expectations, then sell. But let's say the consumer services group reports lower than expected profits. I would hold because the group may encounter a slowdown in consumer spending and your consumer services stock may bounce back when spending picks up.

The debate today is whether the housing slowdown will affect consumer spending. So far it hasn't materially kept the consumer away.

If you're fortunate to see your cyclical stock rise quickly to its old highs but fails to surpass it, then sell. The stock may bounce along the top and retest an old high several times, closing lower. Prepare to sell.

The real test is volume. If volume is higher along the top, then churning is taking place where smart money sells to new takers (institutions) while price remains steady. Volume is near or above its 52 week average. Get out. The stock is waiting for a tipping point and roll over it will. Cash in your profits. Remember, your goal is to hold roughly 40-60% in cash/bond funds. But surely, some of these trades will be losers, the nature of the beast. Don't worry. Sell them and forget them. I repeat: always reinvest losing trades into the best core stock value at any given time.

Something else may be going on here. Your future.

A winning psychology is everything. Remember Mohammed Ali. The way he came back against George Foreman in the "Rumble in the Jungle." Psychology. under difficult personal conditions, Ali kept focused. When training, the natives chanted for him and wrote graffiti in support during his morning run. Ali not only won the fight for himself, but he won for the folks in Africa. Likewise, by turning your losing dollars from cyclical trades into the most promising core stock, you will remain a player, be in the game, and win financially. Most important, you can win the battle over yourself, and wake up one morning with renewed self confidence.

## A CUBBY BEAR CORRECTION

In closing, winning core stocks, like Phillip Morris in the 1950s, IBM in the 1960s, Apple in the 1980s, 2010 and Cisco Systems in the 90s, redefined the time-value of money concept as reinvested capital referred as the new compound interest itself. We also know that money funds outperformed stocks in 1981, 16-17%. It's too bad that the bank called in my Chrysler bonds to roll them into lower rates a few years later.

# CHAPTER 17:
# Navigating Home in a Multi-Year Bear Market: The Basics

This final chapter of Part C deals with the most dreaded experience of any investor, broker and international player in stock market history—the crash. The Crash of 1929 remains the big daddy of multi-year bear markets, lasting from the fall of 1929 to early summer, 1932. The Mississippi Scheme and the South Sea Bubble of 1720 had swept France and England into a wild frenzy of real estate speculation. Tulip-mania brought Holland to penury a century before—the bust and collapse of a mighty bull market felt throughout Europe and the Old World. Millions lost their franks, pounds and guilders in those bears of old. Early speculators, like investors today, were unable to sniff the winds of change. Caught in the snare of inertia, investors refused to sell. And days later all was lost, all except some bankers and ship owners who were able to hear the silent bell ringing: "the party is over."

Denial remains a powerful human emotion, as before. After all, denial can be rationalized away. We heard the distant rumblings of over-valuations yet we bought into the "moon shot" summer of 1987. Our grandfathers ignored the September cracks in the last hurrahs of

1929, yet suffered the nosedive a month later. Interest rates had been benign in that era of the Jazz Age. However, in the summer of 1987 the dollar was crashing. But in 2004-6, easy money had wrought another bubble.

Yet a bubble market, like an aging bull rumbles at full speed cannot pull back in time. A bull at speed with mass and momentum, just can't just stop, it's too late. Our bull has passed his point of no return. He cannot go home again, a point only Hemingway could tell of a Saturday afternoon. Emotions continue to rule this beast in his final days, snorting, charging, taking in less air with each gasp, seeing simple rage, waiting for the Matador to take him home.

What forces or sirens sing the coming of a major bear? We must look back in time to dissect the coming of this major event. On average, it arrives every four to five years. In some decades, it may never occur, such as the 1960s and 1990s.

The roaring 1920s had a major bear market in 1921-2, similar to the 1980s: 1981-2. And in most cases, this grizzly event occurs early in the decade, after a blow-off late from the previous decade.

We celebrated the 1950s as an era of Happy Days. Yet bear markets occurred after the Korean War and in 1957-8. And to add fuel to an unforgiving mood I remember when attending yeoman school at the Coast Guard Training School in Groton, CT, our Atlas rocket blew up off the launch pad, initiating a national pessimism, while the Soviets' Sputnik flew overhead. This just made matters worse, and the market continued down into winter. But of course we came back a few months later with a successful launch.

A. ANATOMY OF CLASSIC BEAR MARKETS IN HISTORY:
(1) Higher interest rates from Fed tightening: 1969 and 1981.
(2) Beginning of a recession, e.g., 1957-8, 1973-4, 1981-2, 1990-2, 2001-2, 2008-9.
(3) Geopolitical meltdown:
    (a) War: Fall of France, The Low Countries, Greece, Pearl Harbour: 1940-2
    (b) Arab oil embargo: 1973-4
    (c) Attack on the World Trade Center, 9/11: 2001-2

# NAVIGATING HOME IN A MULTI-YEAR BEAR MARKET: THE BASICS

(4) Excess Leverage from Debt, Derivatives:
    (a) Real estate bubble, 2004-2006
    (b) Stock market bubbles: 1923-1929, 1983-7
    (c) Asian Contagion(Asian stocks), 1997-8

The above sagas will continue to play out as long as people, now institutions play the market in a gaggle of traders, hedge-fund operators, leverage buyout players, and now private equity dealers. What happened to the little guy of yore?

The individual investor was a big player in the real estate game of late but some say he hid behind his 401k. Unfortunately, the small investor had surface late in the last bull market, chasing higher prices and suffering crippling consequences from falling housing prices. However, the Holistic investor has only half of his or her monies in play, and the remaining half in cash, facing only half the risk when the Big Bear returns.

(B) DEFINITION OF BEAR MARKETS:
(1) S & P falls 5%: A Pullback
(2) " " 10%: A Correction
(3) " " 20% or greater. A Bear Market

Now one can argue that the Dow Industrials should be the standard bearer of the market because people respect it's widespread popularity. True. But the S& P 500 contains greater depth and it more fully reflects the extent of a market decline. In addition, most bear markets last longer than two quarters, at least six months, and continue into multi- year events. A bear market will pull most stocks down into its vortex. A correction, by contrast, won't last as long and carry fewer stocks along for the ride.

The worst bear markets are the prolonged events such as the 2000-2002 Tech Wreck. Like a Chinese water torture, this market fell much greater than fifteen percent yet the time spent falling was punishing for the uninitiated as well as a seasoned professional. Similar to the market meltdown of September 1929 to July of 1932, the market staged a series of false rallies but ultimately met its grave digger at the end. Those who bought tech stocks in the late 90s and held out to the end, like Napoleon's elite guard battered by a superior artillery barrage, groped its last hope, and gave up its ghost. The Emperor and the individual investor were crushed.

Holistic investing isn't about big wins or big losses. We need not participate in a bear market except for our core investments. We'll buy more shares as the opportunity arises later.

We know that market volatility isn't our game. Time is. And time needs no plan except good health. A good Core stock will weather an economic storm, rebuild capital faster and rebound after the Dark Age. So time is on your side; take advantage of it.

On the next move up, a bull market reborn, add additional shares and ride the new wave higher. Remember: Cash is King. Meanwhile, cyclical stocks become cyclical bonds. Yet we hold on to our core stocks. FMC, Monsanto, Singapore and Wynn Resorts remained Core investments after the storm subsided. That small Asian nation and the gaming industry in Macau will continue to win new markets and attract a new generation of players, especially a China reborn.

A popular gauge of market condition is the earnings yield (1 divided by market's P.E. ratio greater than current 30 year bond yield. If PE ratio during a bear market is 13, then 1 divided by 13='s .077 or 7.7% and if treasury bonds yield LESS then stocks present better value: a BUYING OPPORTUNITY.

Also, the Rule of 6 presents another tool, or six percent benchmark. Some professionals use this. If the earnings yield is greater than 6% and bond yields lower, than stocks remains a better alternative over high-grade bonds. Most professionals use the S & P 500 as a bench mark. I plot the S & P on my charts.

The earnings yield is an old but true friend in times of turmoil, yet it has saved investors by keeping them in bonds when they yielded 6% or greater exceeded the earnings yield. And speaking of bonds, in the very early 'crash phase' of a new bear market, treasury notes, in the middle of the yield curve, present a safer haven than T-Bonds.

# NAVIGATING HOME IN A MULTI-YEAR BEAR MARKET: THE BASICS

A. EARLY STAGE BEAR MARKET: S & P 500, weekly, closes below 30 week average.

Management:

Sell Cyclical stocks since they had failed to cross above their 10 week average. Timing the sale may be difficult. Of course LIMIT sells should have been trigger prior to S & P crossing BELOW its 30 week moving average. Don't sell into a panic. Many investors do and regret it years later. Sell in a cool, collected manner. This means that a rally or "dead-cat" bounce occurs after the panic. Remember, no market, whether a rocket bull move or a panic sell-down moves in a straight line. Sooner or later, the market will catch its breath and reverse direction. If you're holding a cyclical stock down in price from your purchase, the stock will attempt to move back up after the panic and retrace at least 25% of its previous fall. When your stock bounces back, don't fall in love with it. Sell your stock, cut your losses and move on. Also, don't follow the usual rule of buying additional stock shares.

You buy additional shares in a flat to positive market.

The market, at this point will trade below its 30 week moving average. All monies from sales of cyclical stock sales are returned to cash. Later, when the panic portion of the bear market is over, you may want to look at bonds: intermediate grade treasuries. The best place to find government and high-grade bonds are in mutual funds. Even if the market continues to fall, quality bonds will return their income and a little capital appreciation. But "Fed Tapering" may raise rates.

Most bear markets bottom the second year in a multi- year event: 1957-8 (bottom in early 1958), 1969-70 (bottom in May, 1970), 1973-4 (bottom in late 1974), 1981-2 (bottom in August, 1982), 1990-1991(bottom in early 1991, 2000-2002 (bottom in October, 2002): the second year.

I recommend strong currency bonds because early in a protracted bear market, bonds are a safe harbour, appreciate in value and return income.

Bonds become the alternative from stocks in a bear market. Yet this doesn't mean that you should sell your core stocks, because down on the farm (the company) businesses become leaner and improve products ready to launch into the next bull market.

I like the Dreyfus Intermediate Term Income Fund. As of 6/30/07, its performance compares well against Lehman Bros. U. S. Aggregate Index:

Total Return (Yield + Capital Appreciation): % Cumulative

Dreyfus Intmd. Income:1-Yr. 6.5, 3-Yr. 14.92, 5-Yr. 27.1, 10-Yr. 91.39

Lehman Bros. Index 1-Yr. 6.12, 3-Yr. 12.43, 5-Yr. 24.5 10-Yr. 79.37.

MIDDLE-LATE STAGE BEAR MARKET: S & P 500 fails to cross above its 30 week avg.

Large cap consumer staples: beverages, food, drug, utility stocks, the necessities of life are the only game in town. This area, historically, has done the best and will pays dividends. Buy cyclical stocks which pay RISING dividends. Buy staples, no big purchases.

Good sources for above stock selections are your local library reference section, either on line or on the shelf: Moody's, Standard and Poor's and The Value Line Survey. These sources have helped me considerably before the web and I continue to research some stocks whenever I'm near a good library. You can buy some of these companies as conditions allow but remember, for now consider them cyclical stocks. Meanwhile, your cash position should remain at about 50% or greater in cash and bond mutual funds.

Corporate bonds can supplement your portfolio. Usually, about mid way through a bear market some corporate bonds offer attractive yields. The important thing to remember when buying corporate bonds is the solvency of the underlying company. However, I would buy these bonds in a mutual fund. For instance, if a bond is paying a 15% yield, is this company on the verge of insolvency? DON'T BUY. There's a reason for this. If the company's bond yield is priced that high, then something is wrong. The company may be on the brink of Chapter 11. Better to buy a bond of a "going concern" at let's say 8-10% (get your entire principal back rather than losing it after a bankruptcy filing.

## NAVIGATING HOME IN A MULTI-YEAR BEAR MARKET: THE BASICS

Near the end of a multi-year bear market, and Wall St. doesn't ring a bell to announce this, the asset class of choice is financial stocks. However, in this time of financial crisis financials may be a bad idea because of the uncertainty from Dodd and Frank, financial regulations. However, these stocks usually rise when the outlook for their underlying investments resume while interest rates remain weak. Initially, money-center banks are my favourite at this stage of the cycle. Later, as the bull reawakens and takes a life of its own, consider the broker dealers like Merrill Lynch or Charles Schwab. These stocks are traditionally the sector which triggers the first stage of the next bull market. Keep your eye on these financials, especially the broker-dealers.

Once the bear market is over, you can go back to a normal mode of investing, buying some small caps or "cyclical stocks"(stocks which rise with the economy). Consider retail stocks. These stocks, along with the financials ride the initial wave of a bull market because of a pickup in consumer spending.

Most manufacturing and technology firms follow the financials and retail as the market confirms its bull status. Boeing and other aircraft manufacturers, the autos or chemical companies also fit this mold. In this stage of the business cycle the economy rises along with durable good orders. The torch is handed to manufacturing companies as the bull catches its second breath.

The best money is made after the first correction of a new multi-year bull market. After the financials, retail and health companies have had their run, the manufacturers kick into Phase 2, ACCUMULATION STAGE, following the LIFT OFF or Phase 1. Stocks included in Phase 2 group are technology and industrials. It makes sense: first you finance it, then you make it, then you buy it. I see no reason for this to change. The Three Bull Market Groups:

1: Lift Off Phase: financials, retail, transports, health care and consumer stocks

2: Accumulation Phase: manufacturing, chemicals, technology, defence

3: Consolidation Phase: metals, mining, natural resources, energy, commodities, real estate.

As for globalization and bear markets, it may be smart to buy some foreign funds. I have bought the Singapore ETF with great success for its growth and dividends. But be sure that the dollar is weak. American multinationals benefit from greater exports. Globalization means that markets are more in sync with each other. Yes, maybe nations like Turkey or Japan may do better than the United States and Europe in a multi-year bear market.

AVOID FOREIGN STOCKS. Better to buy those funds representing foreign investments.

Be sure to eagle-eye these foreign investments because you can wake up the following morning and find your investment had evaporated. Be careful, these have baggage like accounting issues and trade in illiquid markets. .

In sum, outlined below are the stages of investment in a multi-year bear market:

STAGE 1: Crash: Treasury Notes as the new cyclical investment. No additional investment in core stocks. All trades returned to CASH. Position: 50%+ CASH/BOND FUNDS.

STAGE 2: Meltdown: After rally from Crash. Large cap dividend paying stocks and high-grade corporate bonds become second wave of cyclical investments. Sell prior to next stage. Return all trades to CASH: Position 60% CASH.

STAGE 3: Exhaustion and Bottom: After market makes prolonged bottom (from 3 to 6 months), and no one knows the exact bottom of a bear market, begin to use some of the surplus CASH to buy additional shares of your strongest Core stock (Core stock outperforming the S & P 500). Has Core stock outperformed the broad market average on the way down?

## NAVIGATING HOME IN A MULTI-YEAR BEAR MARKET: THE BASICS

Meanwhile, prepare to take cyclical positions in the financial sector as mentioned above. Note: the dollar should strengthen as new bull market begins. CASH remains at 60%+ but will move toward level of 50% after new bull market gets underway. Happy hunting.

# PART D:
## HOLISTIC INVESTMENT R & D:

# CHAPTER 18:
# Researching Common Stocks

This section is not about finding the next techno thriller out of Silicon Valley. This is about the methodical journey we must take in cyberspace or at a good library to find a solid, reliable stock, an all-weather soldier for our portfolio.

Marty Whitman was recently interview on CNBC. He explained: "Don't worry about market risk. You ought to put an adjective before the word risk." Marty manages the 3rd Avenue Investment Fund, about $30 billion in assets. He focused on investment risk only, buying a stock at a discount to net asset value, Power Lunch, CNBC, 9/6/07.

Money management is one-half of the battle for investment survival, and by buying at a discount you will power your returns into the stratosphere, beating the market. THE NAME OF THE GAME IS TO BEAT THE MARKET, especially by falling less on the downside. To park money in a mutual fund and go on a cruise can be dangerous, especially at the beginning of a bear market. And even the experts don't know when a bear market had begun, even after the market falls. One must be vigilant, always, and cut losses of those cyclical stocks which may not come back. Remember, a SELL STOP is your best defence. You can determine your exit point easily. In any event, HOLD your core stocks because they'll be back.

For example: WYNN Resorts rose some 70 points from my purchase price of 93, to a high of around 168 in early October, 2007. The stock was trashed by analysts because it rose too much and from lower than expected revenues from Macau. The other casino on Macau, The Sands, also sold off. WYNN dropped some 15-20 points from its high, down to the 140s. I didn't blink because its management is in strong hands. Steve Wynn continues to groom his race horse, like Seabiscuit, to run and win another day. Yesterday, the stock returned to the 150s, and the global boom will continue to bring visitors to Macau and Las Vegas. As an afterthought, I sold WYNN at 151 from a limit sell order. I felt the stock struggling, weaker volume at the top–not a good sign. Yes, good core stocks can be sold. DON'T COVER THE SAME GROUND TWICE. In March, 2008, WYNN fell to the low 90s.

Now we begin to address the meat of this chapter, common stock research. I believe four sources remain the best for tapping into those common stocks you need for your holistic portfolio. Whether you go on-line or visit your local library, these companies are the best:

> Barron's: The Wall Street Journal
> Investor's Business Daily
> Standard & Poors
> Value Line Investment Survey

I like to talk about each one and expand on their merits. Yes, this is subjective and other advisors will differ, and they should because of different investment styles. Surely, the above sources can fit most investor styles. Most important, the holistic portfolio can benefit from all the above. But before we begin, I like to draw your attention to the **PVG Momentum Rank** in the Appendix. This of course does not replace in any manner the principles laid out in this chapter. Good fundamental analysis has no substitute.

# RESEARCHING COMMON STOCKS

Barron's is an excellent source of information with tons of data for the individual investor.

Also, for years I've read the "Up and Down Wall Street" column by a most talented, humorous, satirist, the late Alan Ableson. Also, The "Market Lab" section has a ton of information.

In September, 2007, Barron's published the Barron's 400, an index based on a "disciplined stock-selection process." The Index has beaten popular stock indexes over the past 10 years, some by a wide margin. It is based on research by Market Grader (www.MarketGrader.com), a Miami firm which tracks a company's growth, profitability, cash flow and valuation. The period includes both bull and bear markets. For example, the B400 racked up a gain of 54% while the S & P 500 rose about 33%. Investors can use this resource for finding good core and cyclical stocks for your Holistic portfolio.

2007 YTD as of 9/27/07

| | | | |
|---|---|---|---|
| Barron's 400 | 13.56% | Barron's 400 | 11.58% |
| Dow Jones Ind. | 12.71 | Dow Jones Ind. | 16.29 |
| S & P 500 | 9.05 | S & P 500 | 13.62 |

Source: Barron's

However, no one index will win the performance race every year. It's just the nature of markets. Much depends on market allocation, sectors, capitalization, growth vs. value, multi- national benefits from trade, etc. Rather, a multi-year trend is the best measure. For example, the B400 beat both the Dow Jones Ind. and the S & P 500. The B400 had fallen 1.77% in 2001 and 10.76% in 2002. Dow Jones and S & P fell 7.1% and 16.76%, 13.04% and 23.37% respectively in 2001 and 2002.

Investor's Business Daily becomes our nest source. This daily has covered the investment and economic environment since the 1980s. Its specialty is common stocks and the various tables and charts for the more serious investor. The newspaper's "key tools" screen stocks and educate investors in the subtleties and nature of the stock market.

For example, Investor's Business Daily educates the investor in the following:

(1) On becoming a better investor
(2) Stocks Do's and Don'ts
(3) A column on investor concerns, "Investor's Corner"
(4) An educational column with insights on smart investing

Investor's Business Daily zeros in on those stocks in the news, i.e., a stock update. The newspaper publishes a daily screen of those stocks favoured by institutional investors. Charts on when to buy and sell are available.

For the new investor, this seems a good way to begin, or get into the game so to speak. A new investor may have numerous ideas, some conflicting, and perhaps suffer from inertia. IBD sort of coaches you along the way, and I may add: take a very small position on your favourite stock—you can always buy more later.

Perhaps the most important tool of IBD is the IBD 100. This index is a computer generated list of leading U. S. companies and their various stages of the current market cycle. The IBD Top Ten Market Monitor clarifies the best performing companies. A holistic investor may want to pay attention to this particular index because momentum plays a very important part. Surely, a top ten company will tend to be overvalued, but the company deserves to be overvalued in most cases. Yes, overvalued companies aren't cheap, yet many continue to ride higher and higher.

Good examples are IBM of old and Apple; moreover, Google and Netflix had won this distinction today. However, I would go about this differently.

Top Ten companies tend to repeat daily, but soon enough a new company will break into this group. Watch to see if this new company continues to remain in the top ten. If so, then this stock may be a good buy before it gets any more expensive. Eliminate those companies which are about to be bought out. Their volatility may land

## RESEARCHING COMMON STOCKS

them in the IBD Top Ten, and these stocks only trade up to its "buy out" price before running out of steam. Further, a top ten company, if a leader of a particular industry group tends to drag its smaller competitors higher, for instance the fertilizer group. The group leader tends to run with the wind before winding down. Meanwhile, you may want to profit before momentum winds down.

The next resource every serious investor should consult is Standard & Poor's. The S & P 500 remains the professional money-manager's nirvana. Beating the S & P 500 ensures job security. In fact, well over half of institutional money managers fail to beat this benchmark over and entire market cycle of bull and bear markets. In fact, the S & P, like Barron's posts those companies included in their indexes on their web sites. This search can be accomplished by clicking Standard & Poor's—indices–products & services–index changes. For instance, on 9/5/07 additions included Life Cell Corp (LIFE) and deletions were Komag, Inc. (KOMG).

The S & P 500 covers some 75% of U. S. stocks, weighted by market capitalization. The public-float (outstanding shares) of the S & P is at least 50% of the index. Its asset value was recently some $10.7 trillion of leading U. S. Companies of all exchanges, NYSE, NASDAQ and the American. This index is considered the grand daddy of all benchmarks dating back to 1923. In 1957 the S & P expanded to 500 companies, where it stands today.

From a research point of view, S & P relies on a star rating system, 5 stars being the highest.

The index also rates income stocks for those investors who wish to forego capital gains. Written stock reports and analysis make it easier for an investor to understand why a stock should be accumulated or sold. These reviews should help the beginning investor. I've spent untold hours leafing through S & P reports in libraries since the 1970s. If anything, S & P's opinion on your stock should be another clincher, or second opinion so to speak.

After a thorough analysis, trust your gut, a "gut feeling" isn't rational, but often rationality cannot answer all the pros and cons which make up buy or sell decisions. Yes, seek validation from investment sources before you act. It may save you money—and sleepless nights.

The last investment resource I'll discuss is Value Line Investment Survey, my favourite.

Value Line and I remain old friends, discovered in my early days of stock research just out of college. I remember driving downtown to the Trenton Public Library, and even today I visit the Ewing Library, Mercer Branch, to see what's new in Value Line. Old habits die hard. But some old habits are good, even fortuitous when it comes to Value Line. Many a winner, some losers came from the annuals of Value Line because of its cornucopia of quarterly statistical data such as per share sales, cash flow, capital spending and % returns on capital, equity plus a concise narrative on recent company developments. I wholeheartedly support their research and even in this day of on-line statistics, reviews and opinions, the Value Line Investment Survey wins my vote of confidence. However, I don't rely on any particular source for stock selections because the market demands a multitude of tacks and sources to complete your research.

Be open-minded, eclectic and ALWAYS be suspicious of ads on TV or direct mail touting the next big gold mine in South America or wunderkind high tech start up.

Technical analysis can give you a better feel of WHEN to pull the trigger, or when to buy.

Study chart price patterns, look at volume; seek a low entry point. But for now, we'll do our fundamental research, where all good investments research begins.

I like to illustrate one of my stocks, Monsanto, pulled from the Value Line Investment Survey, page 1970, dated 8/17/07. The company bottomed twice, in mid-late 2002 and again in early 2003. From the bottoms, the stock had risen ever since. Monsanto (MON) split two-for-one in mid 2006. Clearly, Value Line's chart shows this, a real plus. The shaded area in 2001 means recession. Price projections to 2010-2012 are 105-70, high and low.

## RESEARCHING COMMON STOCKS

Monsanto is in agricultural seeds and genomics (biotech) and herbicides. However, I'm against any insecticide or genetically modified food. However, a greater global adoption of its corn seed into feed and ethanol for fuel will enhance both growth and scale in draught stricken nations. For example, in Monsanto, I looked at Cash Flow growth and Capital Spending growth, projected. Deduct capital spending from cash flow to arrive at Free Cash Flow, out to a 3-5 year benchmark. I also looked at common shares outstanding to assess its projected % growth, as compared with Free Cash Flow. If Free Cash Flow grows at a faster rate than Common Shares, then I'm interested. For instance, from 2008 to the 2012 period:

|  | 2008 | 2012 | % Growth |
|---|---|---|---|
| Per Share Cash Flow | $3.30/sh. | $4.70/sh. | |
| Capital Spending | .85/sh. | 1.00/sh. | |
| Free Cash Flow | 2.45/sh. | 3.70/sh. | 51 |
| | | | |
| Common Sh. Growth | 545m | 545m | 0 |

In other words, Monsanto's Free Cash is projected to grow 51% with no additional dilution.

Ever since the industrial revolution the combine or later the corporation has had to borrow money or issue stock, leverage, in order to expand and grow. Monsanto acquired Delta and Pine Land Company earlier on a short-term loan and refinanced from commercial paper, yet the company is projected to issue no additional shares. Good. Remember, the greater the number of shares, the more potential dilution. Dilution is an Achilles Heel since cash flow/share is spread out over a greater number of shares. Wall Street considers earnings per share as the prevailing benchmark.

However, Value Line has issued a caveat. Because the price-to-earnings PE) multiple is historically high, Value Line cautions that capital gains into 2010-2012 may be limited. Good advice. Value Line is worth your time.

# PART D:
## CONTINUED:

# CHAPTER 19:
# Researching Trends: Again: Follow the Money

Follow the money means to follow the big boys: institutional large block(volume) speculators. Foreign monies may be included in this category. George Soros and/or a Japanese or European Group will bet "big bucks" on a market leader. Our global market never sleeps, even on week-ends. Deals are forged into heavy trading the following week. This action is best reflected in the final hour of trading, from 3-4 PM, New York, Monday, indicating market direction. Often, on Tuesday, a reversal would take place, turn around Tuesday. But the key is volume. If the market turns on the final hour of Tuesday in light volume, less volume than the previous day, then the trend for the week remains in place. Again, this had worked only if Monday is a big volume day, volume above its 52-week moving average. This example represents heavy block volume, institutional buying, as reported in Barron's.

The large commercial speculators are a good proxy for institutional monies, and its movement is what really matters. WHERE is the money's final destination?

This information is available for the individual investor. Barron's publishes a list of industry groups, really sub-groups, of stocks: Dow Jones U. S. Market Industry Groups in their Market

Market Lab section of their weekly edition. Extracts below were reported to my readers:

Asian Surpluses Move Markets

The Top Five Industry Groups follow the money into those market sectors: commodities, industrials, consumer staples, etc. which tend to lead the market. The greater the money flowing into any one industry, the more volume required, the greater the price gains. Look at volume as oxygen for a stock. For instance, an excess of funds into any one sector would cause the price of a market leader to rise within the group. Also, an excess of monies out of any group would cause a falling price, but we're not concerned with this for now. We're interested in money inflows and the possibility for a new trend to begin.

Listed below, is Bi-Weekly activity beginning at the 2nd Quarter, 2007.

| 4/2 | 4/16 | 4/30 | 5/14 | 5/28 | 6/11 | 6/25 |
|---|---|---|---|---|---|---|
| Tires | Tires | Tires | Tires | Tires | Tires | Tires |
| Steel | Steel | Steel | Steel | Coal | Steel H. | Constr. |
| Mining | Mining | Trucking | Metals | Alum. | H. Constr. | C. Vehicles |
| Trucking | Metals | Gold, etc. | H. Constr. | Steel | Mining | Steel |
| Metals | Trucking | Metals | Mining | H.Constr. | Alum. | Alum. |
| | | | | | | |
| 7/16 | 7/30 | 8/13 | 8/27 | 9/3 | 9/17 | 10/1 |
| Tires H. H. Constr. Alum. C. Vehicles Metals | Constr. H. Metals Tires Oil Equip. Cons. Elec. | Constr. Cons. Elec Tires Metals Oil Equip. | No Data — — — | H. Constr. Cons. Elec Tires Oil Equip C. Veh. | H. Constr. Cons. Elec. Metals Oil Equip. C. Veh.. | H. Constr. Metals Cons. Elec. Tires Oil Eq. |

The Top Five Industry Groups remain steady. The above rankings are year-to-date information. Of course, on a weekly basis, the rankings flip-flop because of volatility and little continuity would ensue. Our aim is to catch a trend, not to jump around and trade every other day. Bi-weekly data are given to save space. My records reflect weekly data from Barron's.

For the most recent week, 10/8(week ended 10/5/07), the Travel group broke into 5th place.

This sort of resembles a major league baseball standing: National League East, etc. The population of all groups is 150, so 5th place means that Travel is doing better, YTD, than the other 145 groups. Tires ranked first into late spring because of a shortage. The theme for the Top Five remains steady: metals, gold & other precious metals, heavy equipment, mining, trucking and oil equipment & services. Consumer Electronics had a good run in late summer, probably because of Apple's I-Phone.

This is where the money is. Most of this represents buying in a bull market and some selling.

Of course in a bear market most will represent selling and some buying. **THE MOST IMPORTANT THING: BE ON THE RIGHT SIDE OF THE MARKET.** Consider the positions above an important tool, like a direction finder or GPS if you will.

It's well known that the winners of this global boom reside to the east and south of the United States, China, India and Brazil. These emerging nations have a rising middle class, catching up after decades of little or no growth. Manufacturing and infrastructure spending sit at the top of their shopping bag, with a thirst for assets to continue growth. An astute investor can take stock of these trends.

However, at this time emerging market nations including Ireland and Eastern Europe aren't doing too well. The Global Economy remains mired in a downtrend as the rest of the world.

Beware. China has raised interest rates a number of times to tame inflation. And when the world gets moving again, you can bet that the above emerging economies will lead the parade.

# CHAPTER 20:
# Leave the Market to the Media: The Glory of Cash/Bonds

Remember the quote earlier from Marty Whitman, a long-time investor and manager of the $30 billion 3rd Ave Investment Fund: "Don't worry about market risk. You ought to put an adjective before risk." I can't emphasize his point enough. Marty simply buys stocks at deep discounts to net asset value. He recently bought the Radium Group, now struggling because its industry fell victim to the housing crisis in the second half of 2007. The stock has fallen, but Marty went on to say that he holds a good stock for five years. This is another definition of a CORE STOCK: a stock that recovers in value AFTER A CRISIS and positions itself stronger after the storm. I'm confident Marty will prove right once again.

Selling a stock is the most difficult thing in investing. A stock "fully valued" is and remains the criteria for most professionals. A PE ratio well above the market of most indices is perhaps the most popular. But the trouble is that PE expansion can continue late into a bull market, typical of fast growing companies like Google or Apple.

A holistic investor will set limit sells or trailing stops at predefine levels. I've found that a reasonable limit of 7 and ½ percent below a recent high works. HOWEVER, I WOULD SELL ONE HALF of my position if I really believe that this baby will bounce back making new highs later. By selling one-half, you protect your profits by returning funds to cash/bonds. If you're right and the stock continues falling to its 30 week average, HOLD. If so, buy the same number of shares sold at a LOWER price and considered the difference as added capital to your portfolio.

Your cash/bond account should be around the 50% level in uncertain markets. Core stocks should make up the remainder of your investments. These stocks weather market volatility.

A severe market decline will affect all portfolios, from Harvard's Endowment Fund to Warren Buffet's Berkshire Hathaway. When the stress, the headlines clear, the market usually settles into a trading bottom, maybe lasting for many months. DID YOUR INVESTMENTS FALL LESS THAN THE MARKET? The Holistic investor's portfolio will beat the market on the way down by falling less because of its larger cash/bond position. Why? (1)Cash and bond funds will hold value and return even more income if rates rise again (after a boom the Fed will raise rates to lower inflationary fears). Treasuries rise in panic selling.

(2) Many Core Stocks will fall less than the market because of their larger capitalizations and overseas exposure. Witness the "nifty 50" during the market decline of 1973-4, stocks favoured by the big institutions (IBM, Colgate, Johnson & Johnson, etc.). These were the years of stagflation, oil shocks and Watergate: a flight to safety. Large-cap stocks fall less than their smaller brethren.

(3) Cyclical or Special Situation stocks such as gold and silver mining stock do well provided that rates aren't rising faster than inflation(nominal inflation greater that rates). If natural resource or material stocks belong to an outperforming sector when the correction began, then chances are that they will fall less than the market on the way down. Rarely will a Top Five Sector stock fall more than the market in a normal pullback. If rates rise, financial and utility stocks underperform. If the economy rolls over, consumer discretionary stocks take gas.

For example, in the beginning of the Great Depression, deflation gripped the nation but food and coal stocks were in demand. People

## LEAVE THE MARKET TO THE MEDIA: THE GLORY OF CASH/BONDS

must eat and keep warm in winter. Coal did well because it was the primary source of energy. In other words, if your stock is in the right church, right pew, so to speak it will weather the gale better–another good reason to keep a log of the weekly Barron's Top Five Stocks,

Work your portfolio, and your portfolio will work for you. SELL an overvalued cyclical stock by means of a stop-loss order. Keep a TRAILING STOP in a run-away bull market, rather than panic when it spikes down later. Sell the stock and return the monies to Cash. Relax.

Before I leave this section, portfolio research, I like to further clarify the value of CASH or Strong Currency Bond funds. A traditional brokerage or professional money manager will scoff at the idea of such a large cash/bond position of 40% in bull markets and 60% in bear markets. Well, for openers, most money managers fail to outperform the market over the full market cycle of roughly four years.

Many managers will beat the market on the way up, but their performance sort of melts away on the way down. I maintain that one CAN beat the market with only 40-60% in a large cash or bond position. You don't need all that wind to your back to move the boat forward. Running a sailboat before the wind is the slowest point of sailing. Sailing close hauled or a beam reach gets you moving as wind is hitting the bow at an angle of 45-90 degrees. It's apparent wind which drives the vessel forward, the wind created by the sails. Just think, if you can beat the market with less risk, isn't this the best of all worlds?

CASH used to earn 5%. Today some mid-cap value stocks pay greater than 5% dividends.

Holistic Investing takes on Wall Street's conventional wisdom by reducing risk and at least matching performance. You can smell the roses in the winner's circle. It's sweet getting the better of The Street. It's also smart to love dogs for their one year of which they'll trade seven additional years to your life.

In Esquire, April, 2003, the magazine presented "The Secret Cash Stash," "Man at his Best."

The magazine, in their typical tongue-in-cheek style, referred to the benefits of stashing cash away, in an attic, in vents, ducks, floorboards, the "Cold Roll of ten Ben Franklins" hidden away.

That was an allusion to panics, disasters, small pox, "electromagnetic pulse," and other fears associated with the economy.

Fear remains a primitive, permanent black hole in our psyche as Psychology 101 taught.

Unfortunately, some of us learned this time and time again. Cash (wealth), health and family remain at the top. Or is it Family, health or cash. Cash may be the root of all evil, or again, its excess may be the root of all evil. The social sciences have been kicking this around forever. I studied these issues when I've attended the New School.

The course in Keynesian economics, now post Keynesian economics opened my eyes. Does supply create its own demand or does demand create its own supply? Keynes criticized the classical economists of the late 19th century. In 1935, Keynes spoke of this while soup kitchens dotted the cities of Britain and America, nearly 25% of the workforce out of work. Is it better to build the Hoover Dam and TVA in a depression or work on a job site out of state? I would have gone to work and hope that something better would come along later. My grandfather was the foreman of a crew that surveyed some of this work during the Depression.

So CASH or Bond funds aren't an orphan in the Holistic portfolio. The clock of time will swing back and forth between prosperity and hardship. And when hardship rolls around once more, cash is not a bad thing to own. Come to think of it, CASH isn't a bad thing to own anytime.

Lastly, another way to look at the value of Cash/Bonds in a portfolio is illustrated below.

Let's compare a Holistic Portfolio with a Popular Portfolio espoused by many brokers.

## LEAVE THE MARKET TO THE MEDIA: THE GLORY OF CASH/BONDS

|  | Holistic Portfolio | Popular Bear | Popular Bull |
|---|---|---|---|
| Stocks | 50% | Bear 40% | Stocks: 60% |
|  |  |  | Bonds 40% |
| Cash/Bonds | 50% | 60% | Cash 0 |
| Totals | 100% | 100% | 100% |

Generally, the long-term rate of return for the stock market is in the neighborhood of 7.5%, give or take a few points. But from 1995-99 the rate of return was in excess of 10%. The bear market of 2000-2 brought it down to single digit levels. Money funds were around 4.5% (today it's less than .25%). In the late 1970s and 1980s cash paid double digit rates. I remember the Dreyfus World Wide Dollar fund was paying over 10% during the period, and some CD's paying around 17%. We have $20,000 as beginning capital:

|  | Holistic Portfolio Risk | Standard Portfolio Risk |
|---|---|---|
|  | 40-60% | 100% |
| Capital: | $10,000 | $20,000 |
| Return @ 4.5% | 450 | 900 |
| Return @ 10.5% | 1050 | $2100 |
| Totals | 1500 | $3000 |

In other words, a Holistic Investor would have to earn an additional 10.5% to meet the Standard Portfolio's Performance. However, only 50% of capital is at risk. This is a good trade-off because a severe correction can wipe out 50% of value and this would require a 100% gain to make up the loss, in this example. We are assuming a bull market with $10,000 of capital compared to $20,000 at risk (standard portfolio) of most investors. But now it gets interesting. Not all portfolios are created equal. As of 8/31/07, the Dreyfus Premier Strategic Value, Class A shares had a 10 year average total return of 8.42% without sales charge. For the six-months ended 2/28/07, the Dreyfus Premier International Value Fund produced a total return of 9.4%, Class A shares. And for the six-month period ended 3/31/07, the Dreyfus Premier Natural Resources Fund had a total return of 16.58%, Class A shares. We see divergences of 8.42 to 16.58 per cents, almost double, in the test period.

Meanwhile, a Holistic Portfolio can invest in hard asset (strong currency) bond funds, internationally, especially during a weak domestic economy. As discussed, we diversify first by asset class, stocks vs. bonds, then by sector, industrials vs. financial for instance. We also diversify by region, Singapore vs. Europe and by type, growth vs. value. Since our core stocks represent durable long-term holdings, they should be able to weather financial storms better than most stocks. As for cash, there is no more to be said: CASH NEEDS NO DIVERSIFICATION.

I'm comfortable forfeiting 5 and 1/2% additional gains in a bull market for sleeping more soundly at night. Are you? And horrors, sooner or later a big, bad ugly bear will be lopping along. And you will know what to do: raise more cash, short-to-intermediate term bonds, consider foreign currency bond funds if the dollar continues to fall and look at high grade corporate bonds in a falling rate environment.

Stock funds denominated in strong currencies are a good bet. Also, American food and beverage stocks and casinos rarely go out of style. Wynn Resorts, Coca-Cola and McDonalds screamed back in 2009.

# PART E:
## WHY MACROECONOMIC TRENDS MATTER

# CHAPTER 21:
# The Big Picture: And Why it makes all the difference

Have you ever walked into a movie half way groping to find out its gist or entered a meeting near its end clueless? I have. It's challenging to catch hidden meanings shaping decisions especially in your absence. In a sense, this similar walk into the darkness awaits an unprepared investor. Market reality sails a new Zeitgeist underwritten by an emerging global tide, and no longer dances to the same old tune of corporate America. Especially in the post 9/11 world, macro-economic trends drive market sectors which power returns. Emerging economies need American know how, commodities, materials, equipment to build out infrastructure.

Being in the right economic (market) sector, at the right time will make all the difference.

Agribusiness, energy and chemicals, for instance, rise and fall in cycles like any other stock. In time the financials, retail and consumer staples rally when the dollar rallies. A strong dollar is deflationary in the United States. This means consumers pay less for food and at the gas pump.

Consumer spending benefits America. Emerging markets need the opposite, a weak dollar to export.

A weaker dollar in the first half of 2008 powered commodities higher. The commodity sector rose while the financials, i.e. banks, brokers, insurance companies had fallen. Retail items such as consumer staples, i.e., drug stores, food and beverages did better. Market sectors are viewed in a broad sense, because agriculture, energy and material stocks are really sub-sectors of the commodity complex.

Witness our oil crisis and raw materials shortages from globalization. Robust demand from emerging economies drive oil prices higher, marginal demand, in- addition to demand from western economies and other smaller nations. Since crude oil is based in dollars, foreign currency swings have rocked some speculators (being on the wrong side of a trade) during an energy crisis. Asian and Latin American players now wag the tail of the dog from their unsatiating thirst for energy and raw materials. And diversification for the sake of diversification no longer wins the day. We need another strategy.

This new strategy is to diversify among economic sectors such as commodities, currencies, equities, bonds and cash. Real estate, of course is another matter. Real estate, considered a one- way street by investors for decades, fell hard during the Great Recession and continues falling, (7/28/11).

Real estate isn't liquid, not easily traded and requires expense to maintain. Even though an investor's home may be his castle, his largest asset, he no longer views his house as an investment.

Retirement accounts remain the principle source of income in later years. Yet millions have walked away from upside-down mortgages, i.e., equity worth less that outstanding loan.

Real estate makes up at least twenty percent of the economy and with its absence, economic growth will remain stagnant.

Slower economic growth means a weaker dollar. Sure, it's good for American trade, good for multinational and mid-cap stocks while adding to inflationary pressures at home. Gold, a safe haven in times of stress has done well along with resource stocks and agribusiness.

# THE BIG PICTURE: AND WHY IT MAKES ALL THE DIFFERENCE

However, commodity inflation puts pressure on financials and bonds. Pity the poor seniors whose only source of income is social security and CD's paying squat.

The strong dollar of the 1980s had boosted bonds which had outperformed equities.

Globalization has changed the game as outsourcing had accelerated during the 1980s and trade had become a one-way street: China exports from cheap labor, Americas buy cheap goods, China and India surpluses parked into American industry and U. S. bonds. What happened to free trade: value for value? The result, the destruction of American jobs, weaker consumer spending, and a dwindling middle class with mountains of debt. Along the way a massive transfer of wealth from middle America found its way to the trading desks of Wall Street and to the emerging economies.

A few years ago Venezuela had discontinued shipping oil to Exxon-Mobil. At the time the country had nationalized a cyclical stock of mine, Ternium, a Latin American steel producer. The price of oil rose and Ternium eventually recovered. I held on to Ternium because I felt the government of Venezuela just wanted to make a statement. In short order, the embargo was lifted. I sold the stock after a rally, keeping in mind this escapade can happen again.

We experienced issues of global politics back in the 1970s. Remember OPEC? But the nationalization of Exxon-Mobil refineries, serious as they are, pale in comparison to the wholesale buying up of American assets from Chinese and Middle Eastern interests. My dad told me back in 1987 that the Japanese "can't put Rockefeller Center in their hip pocket and take it back to Tokyo." Sure enough, the recession that hit Japan in 1990 slaughtered their stock market, falling for the next ten years. I believe the Japanese sold Rockefeller Center back to America interests at a deep discount in 1992. The wheel keeps turning.

Foreigners don't have to buy hard assets like real estate. All they have to do is take a huge equity stake in an American bank or business. This may change everything: who sits on the Board of Directors, what they make or sell, and who steers future investment including the outsourcing of jobs. It gets worse. If a foreign group of investors own a going concern, like a software firm or a popular leisure company, casino/hotel resort, what is to prevent them from selling the company to another foreign consortium only to break up the American company and its pieces: a spin off.

Capitalism: the gale of creative destruction.

Recently, the service sector trended down for its first negative reading ever. Aren't we supposed to be a service economy? In January, 2008, the real estate market was its worst in twenty years. Defaults kept rising and now we have an economic stimulus to a nation of debtors, owing around a trillion dollars. I don't think consumers are going to run out to the nearest auto showroom. And if they pay off some of their debt it won't help the economy much. Consumer spending makes up seventy percent of GDP. Even Starbucks has scaled back, I guess those McDonalds' coffees aren't that bad after all. Actually, I tried one of their coffees and it's good, but I like my homemade breakfast brew better.

Asians own an abundance of American wealth expressed from trade surplus dollars: more than a trillion and counting. American made foreign autos make up almost half of the domestic market, with Japan Inc., Germany and Korea with the rest of pie. China is about to introduce its automobile but for now, it will be too small for Americans. Remember those little Toyota boxes forty years ago?

China will catch up, and fast. However, GM alone sells over a million vehicles in China and Latin America, not counting Europe. So it's a two-way street. Poor GM had to write down some $30 bl. of assets from restructuring: early retirements, plant closings and health care.

Where will it all end? The only monopoly we hold is aircraft and defence.

Our military is second to none. Companies in this sector are off limits to foreign interests for obvious reasons. But if we have a nation of unemployed or under- employed people, where is the nation's tax revenue going to come from to pay for the wars on terror?

# THE BIG PICTURE: AND WHY IT MAKES ALL THE DIFFERENCE

Years ago American conglomerates ruled the world. China and the Soviet Union struggled under communism. The communists still control power, forsaking their Marxist fathers to make more Yankee dollars. We won the Cold War only to lose the peace.

Globalization, love it or hate it, is here to stay. Perhaps free trade may morph into fair trade.

Just today the WTO (World Trade Organization) handed the U.S. a victory over China in a trade dispute. I believe China will heed this, especially in their coming of age on hosting the Olympic Games this summer (2008).

My point is that an investor must guide his strategy in sync with globalization and its ramifications. Emerging markets have a rising middle class. Just ten percent of China's middle class is 120 million consumers who want the good life. Can you blame them? Surely, the Asian Bubble will burst some day. In the meantime buy only funds of emerging markets. And the best way to invest is to buy mutual funds. **NEVER BUY EMERGING FOREIGN STOCKS.**

Buy bonds of stronger currency nations like Switzerland, Germany or even U.S. Bonds. Also, natural resources do well in an inflationary environment. Canada and the western United States represent a treasure of gold, silver, uranium, natural gas, soybeans, corn, wheat and other opportunities. A great stock is always the Union Pacific Railroad. In the future, good fresh water, as in bottled water will be as rare as a silver dollar. The best way to invest in clean water is through an ETF fund. Later, I'll explain ways to analyze, invest, reinvest and understand this big picture.

One final word on the importance of natural resource stocks. A famous book on investing came out in 1935 which survived fifteen printings until the 1965 edition which I purchased in June of that year. At the time I was one year out of college and had begun to get interested in common stocks. This classic was called The Battle for Investment Survival by Gerald M. Loeb.

I remember a chapter on mining stocks among the many topics including convertible bonds, dollar-cost averaging, women and the market (a revolutionary concept at the time), dividends, taxes, market news, price, among others.

Mining shares, according to Loeb, contained an extra dimension: the perceived value of the metal, gold or copper for instance. These metals rise as the economy expands. At times natural resources carry greater value than other periods. In addition, shortages of the metal will drive price higher which in turn will drive its underlying stock higher. Clearly, the forces of supply and demand dictate.

Time works in favour of resource companies because of global trade and population growth.

Meanwhile, a depleting quantity of mineral wealth remains the variable. Supply remains stable from new production techniques, yet demand expands annually. But can we double our supply of crude oil in seven years? I doubt it. An if we can match demand with supply by 2015, barring a global depression, getting this oil out of the ground or sea will be more expensive than today. In other words, the global forces of demand will win over supply unless technology becomes greener. This equation applies for other industrial metals: copper, lithium, platinum, palladium, silver, uranium and zinc.

Loeb goes on to advise the investor about a mine or company's cost of production. Some mines are very efficient as their ore veins are easier to extract than others. He warns investors that prices will fluctuate since the mining group moves in cycles as other industries—a feature that I have stressed throughout.

Loeb wrote about "preserving purchasing power for current use." In a period of inflation, or dollar "devaluation," mining shares shine. I quote from the book: "gold shares are devaluation hedges. The desire for gold is the most universal and deeply rooted commercial instinct of the human race." Lastly, another important passage for owing mining shares in a portfolio: "...the income return tends to be high and the fact that a return of capital is included is an advantage that is sometimes overlooked at first sight." Gerald Loeb concludes on the topic of a "perpetual investment." This is about the automatic amortization

# THE BIG PICTURE: AND WHY IT MAKES ALL THE DIFFERENCE

of mining. Mines are depleted from operation over time, therefore; a return of capital included in the income tends to be higher than most income dividends, releasing more purchasing to the investor over the life of the investment.

I recommend that investors get a copy of this book from a good library.

# CHAPTER 22:
# A Time to Sow, A Time to Reap: Why Economic Cycles Matter

You may recall earlier I spoke about The Big Picture, or economic sectors. I diversify by sectors, not by some arbitrary diversification of asset classes of stocks and bonds. For instance, why burden your core stock portfolio with financial stocks when the financial world collapsed from the Bear Stearns and Lehman Brothers' failures? Lehman fell from an oversupply of worthless paper of sub-prime mortgages and its securitization. Citigroup struggled after the crash forcing the stock to do a reverse stock split, a very bad sign. The Wall Street banks had perceived a never ending real estate boom, riding the tiger from 2003 to the summer of 2006.

I remember investing in the AIM Real Estate Fund. Yes, the pickings were easy for awhile.

Home equity loans had become the rage as some folks considered their home an ATM machine. I owned BB&T, a cyclical stock. The regional bank is a robust, up and coming bank based in Charlotte, NC, now one the largest in the U. S. BB& T arrived on the radar screen from out of nowhere. The stock specialized in business-to-business relations and software innovations able to cut transaction costs, really important in this climate of mega-transactions. At the time my core stock holdings were FMC, McDermont and Monsanto–commodity, industrial and agribusiness, (winter-spring, 2008). I reacquired the Singapore Fund, a ETF. and held BB&T and Ternium, discussed above. The market topped the previous October.

Adam Smith, the father of classical economics wrote The Wealth of Nations. By 1776 economics had come a long way from biblical times, when scholars wrote of a time for sowing and reaping. Economic cycles, in other words, begin in a time of sowing and end at a time of reaping. Included in these are social forces, political corruption, and golden eras. The Roman Empire fell from a loss of social and economic cohesion: corruption, an overextended military and soaring inflation from lost provinces.

After the Revolutionary and Civil Wars, the United States had debased its currency from the huge debt paying for the wars. A whiskey rebellion in western Pennsylvania resulted from the higher tax on spirits in the 1780s. In the latter 1860s inflation peaked from the ravages of Civil War. The nation went into decline over the following two decades. We fast forward to the 1920s.

A Russian economist named Nickolai Kondratief wrote about the long economic waves, 50-60 year economic cycles, called the Kondratief Wave of the West: Britain, France, Germany and the U. S. Later, he was persecuted by Stalin and shipped to Siberia because of his leanings toward capitalism. He died in a "Gulag" prison.

In the 19th century, Austrian economists argued about business gluts that occurred every ten years or so. The problem was a surplus of unsold inventory resulting from stagnation. Modern economic cycles became known to the world around this time. The harsh Treaty of Versailles, after W.W. I, brought Germany to its knees. By 1924 Germany experienced hyperinflation, the result of reparation payments in kind (coal, iron ore, etc., to the victors. The immediate aftermath of World War 1 resulted in an inflationary blow off resulting in a sharp deflation in the early 1920s. Business cycles are the result of wars, global shortages, famine, drought (weather) and over-speculation in markets creating manic bubbles: tulips, commodities, stocks, and now real estate.

# A TIME TO SOW, A TIME TO REAP: WHY ECONOMIC CYCLES MATTER

The Random Walk theory of the 1970s (stocks don't move in any predictable fashion, like a drunken sailor walking down an alley) breaks down in times of speculative fever or business downturns. Most stocks move in unison from the ebb and flows of global tides. Even in socialism, societies such as Sweden and the old Soviet Union, these nations suffered from the ravages of western capitalism as the rest of the world. From the smallest African village to the manic trading rooms of Hong Kong, we dance to the tune of the business cycle. Long live the business cycle.

In the spring issue of Cycles magazine, May-June 1991, a prediction of real estate prices graced the front cover. At the time, little heed was taken from the chart printed on the front cover: "The Ideal 18-Year Real Estate Cycle." The real estate market had peaked in the summer of 1987. Eighteen years later, the summer of 2005 into 2006, the real estate market peaked again as predicted. The Bubble triggered those wonderful credit default swaps which investment banks bundled and sold to the world, resulting in the greatest recession since 1929.

Mickey Mantle slammed a record 565 foot blast in 1956 in a game with the old Washington Senators at the nation's capital. His home run was epic. Yet just as epic, and unnoticed, was Cycles road map of America's greatest source of wealth, the home. Its future predicted value was forecasted years before the actual event. The author, Richard Mogey noted that real estate peaked around 1890, 1905, 1925, etc. Also, corporate AAA bond yields would swing to a 54 year cycle, peaking in 1867, early 1920s, 1979, etc.

He went on to explain that real estate "begins (peaking) just prior to a major interest rate low (as in the late 1870s and 1930s)." In the example cited, the prior peak in 1987 yielded to a decline to a low in 1996, about eight years. The latest advance had begun in 1996 to a peak in 2005-6, a period of ten years. I know from market theory that declines fall harder and takes less time than an advance, which rises more slowly (rising against gravity?). In reality, this current cycle did peak in mid 2005 at the height of the sub-prime frenzy. The Foundation for the Study of Cycles was established in 1941 by Edward R. Dewey.

# CHAPTER 23: Suspending the Law of Probability - At least for awhile

If a slot player knew that he could beat the house because of a new software secretly downloaded into a slot machine the casino would take a hit, for awhile. Of course spotters would determine the commotion and they would shutdown the machine. Software codes would be tested. Fewer players would visit Gambler's Anonymous, and most of the casinos would call in their geeks to root out the disabling software. Casinos have become little Disney Lands to keep families coming to their Land of Oz. This "pipe dream" or something similar remains a reverie to the millions who visit Vegas and Atlantic City.

However, in the world of Holistic Investing, smart investors can beat the street, or the house. No need to read about "random walk theory" when people like Peter Lynch, Warren Buffett, George Soros and Bill Gross have made a career of beating the system. What do they know that most of us don't? Well, for one, a keen sense of value and a market that needs respect.

Taking a position on an "unloved company," the British Pound or municipal bonds, a Peter Lynch or George Soros know something that most of us don't: THE MARKET OVERSHOOTS IN BULL AND BEAR MARKETS. Prices are often exaggerated up or down.

They often buy at the right price, the right time and at the point of maximum pain as the late Sir John Templeton had done.

John Templeton's long career had begun back in early World War II, when the Axis Powers had the upper hand, 1942. He bought all of the Dow Jones stocks selling for under $1.00 per share. Soon after the battles of Stalingrad and Midway, the tide of war had turned in favour of the Allies. The market rose and John Templeton went on to fortunes. I believed he borrowed the money from a relative to make his purchases.

Any system will work some of the time but can it work all the time? No. A system will work most of the time until it's compromised by market disruptions. The "time" element, time in market of stock or investment is crucial. No number of trades can beat time invested from a good stock, up or down. For example, a 20% gain from a good core stock in a bull market, sector not- withstanding, would beat many profitable trades because of commission costs and lack of dividends. The answer: time in investment. Furthermore, additional gains from share repurchases during pullbacks will add to the capital gains from above example: the winning key for the Holistic investor.

Ben Franklin said that "time is the stuff of life." The time element remains central, not only in timing cyclical stocks but for holding core stocks through "thick or thin." Ignore time at your peril.

How do we account for a time-invested portfolio over the long haul? My favourite term addressing this is the following: YOU MUST ENTER THE INVESTMENT ON THE RIGHT SIDE OF THE MARKET. Buy a stock or fund about to move higher, not lower. Yes, this isn't an easy thing to do. That's why we set LIMIT buy or sell orders, above or below the 10 week moving average respectively. Limit orders take the mystery out of the equation: the entry point or WHEN do we pull the trigger. Answer: there's no trigger to pull.

When do we know that a new wave, if buying, the beginning of an advance or, if selling, the end of an old wave? And speaking of waves is really speaking about cycles, the subject of the previous chapter. In most cases, a market will decline from a DOUBLE TOP

# SUSPENDING THE LAW OF PROBABILITY - AT LEAST FOR AWHILE

where second top is LOWER. And on buying, a market will advance from a DOUBLE BOTTOM where second bottom is higher than previous, as discussed.

I don't advocate shorting, betting that a stock will go down. Professionals over the years have had their heads handed to them because of an inability of reading market cycles or from extreme volatility. In addition, I'm against margin trading, another dead end. Yet it's possible to buy sell-side or bearish ETF funds. But I haven't found this necessary because of the nature of Holistic investing: holding core stocks in down periods and trading cyclical stocks, setting sell stops after new highs.

A necessary ingredient in buying into a new wave or selling from an old wave is to recognize BREAKOUTS and BREAKDOWNS, before buying and selling respectively.

A breakout occurs after a stock trades SIDEWAYS from three to eight weeks after a short term fall. Most stocks do not breakout from "V" formation bottoms. Don't even bother to look at stocks which have fallen over 50%. There is a reason for this: the company is in long-term trouble. Avoid.

If, after a company performing well in the prior cycle, BEATING THE S & P 500 on the way up and down, look into the company as a candidate. Most likely, a short dip by this stock will be short lived. When your candidate stock trades around 25-38% lower, more than likely it will bottom and trade sideways. Eventually, a time will come when the stock will move up. The breakout to the upside should be on volume equal to or greater than its 52-week average. Also, weekly closing price should close (closing price) near the high. Buy after the breakout and set a sell stop at upper end of the channel (price high of the previous 3-8 week base).

A breakdown occurs after a topping period of a stock which had outperformed the S & P 500. This stock has gotten ahead of itself, like my core stocks: WYNN Resorts and Monsanto.

Sure, these are great stocks, but a great stock won't soar to the moon without limits.

Eventually, it will fall and fall hard. Set a sell stop to prevent disaster, as discussed. But let's say that the stock had previously topped, and is now going through a topping phase ( a pattern or channel of indecision week after week). Sooner or later, it will fall. Look for a pattern of lower highs. A stock may rally back to an old high from short covering, or a short squeeze, another reason why I DON'T RECOMMEND SHORTING. I recommend SELLING CORE STOCKS only when their fundamentals have change from your rationale when first bought.

Better to buy a stock's opposite number: if oil stock fall–look at the airlines, financials or bonds. If commodity stocks rise, sell financials and consider buying gold shares in a mutual fund.

Invesco and U.S. Global have strong gold funds. Likewise, if semiconductor shares rise, an economic up-tick is signalled. Look at technology such as the Dreyfus Tech Growth tracking good relative performance and at least matching the S & P 500. NEVER BUY A STOCK/FUND THAT HAS UNDERPERFORMED THE S & P 500. Amen.

I like to end this chapter on explaining ways to determine when your candidate stock is beating the S & P 500, on the way up in a rally and falling LESS in a market decline. Below are methods: explained.

How do we determine how our stock candidate matches up against the S & P 500?

Look in a financial weekly which has YTD (year-to-date) comparisons: performance, PE, etc.

For instance, if your target stock is up 3% and the S & P is down -5% YTD: that's good. You found a good starting point. But in your search, many stocks may merit your attention. Your selection may be among many stocks which have outperformed but remember, you also want to buy your candidate stock after a pullback. In most cases, both the S & P and your candidate are down from short-term volatility. However, I like to discuss another way to arrive at this: the Chart Approach.

# SUSPENDING THE LAW OF PROBABILITY - AT LEAST FOR AWHILE

Charts are the best tools to determine timing. Stocks and markets move in rhythms. Don't let anyone tell you that the market is random. It's not, provided you know what to look for. Yes, to the untrained eye, everything is random. Stocks and market move in sync, like the tides and seasons of the year. A chart will give you an instant picture of a stock's health. Sure all stocks go down in a bear market, but the good ones always come back. A big clue is that good stocks will fall less in a bear market. Meaning: a good stock will be one of the first to rise in the next uptrend.

I'm not discounting fundamentals. The problem with fundamentals is that they follow the market. Their impact felt after the fact. Remember, the market is a discounting mechanism.

Meaning: the market ANTICIPATES news be it earnings, dilution, a stronger dollar, recession, rate increases, etc and move before the fact, as I discussed in an earlier chapter. Visit Marketwatch. Com. to look up related news on a stock or the market.

Yahoo Finance is another good web site where I get historical prices. Also, I visit my broker's web site to get another perspective. Even so, I like Marketwatch the best, a Dow Jones news subsidiary. Once you're logged on, go to Tools and Analysis (research) section. Type in a stock symbol where indicated and click "chart" to bring up a picture of your stock. Remember to use weekly prices to get a longer term vision. Daily activity contains many events that cancel.

Noise.

At the chart menu, I go to advance charts. In the top (header) section click 6 months or YTD if after July 1st, weekly (price ranges) as mentioned. For comparison sake, choose S & P 500 (stock indexes) 30 week average and click. I like weighted average better than simple or exponential averages Hopefully, your candidate stock will be ABOVE the S & P 500 30 week average.

Good. You have a worthy candidate.

Now we need a confirmation to vindicate our analysis: a SECOND OPINION so to speak.

In a mini bear market or pullback, most stocks will fall to a level ABOVE its 30 week or 200 day moving average in tandem with the S & P 500. This test defines a stock's relative strength presenting the best promise in the following bull market. I use Price/Value Growth YTD, mentioned earlier.

For instance, if a stock has risen 15% YTD and its PE ratio is 15, then its P/VG is 1. Now let's say that a stock has risen 25% YTD and its PE is 35, then its P/VG is 25/35 or .714.

Meaning: overpriced and more volatile. Let's say another stock has increase 10% YTD and its PE ratio is 8, or a P/VG (price to growth ratio) of 10/8 = 1.25. This stock would seem a safer bet but I wouldn't buy it. Why, because first, your Core stocks have safety factored in, otherwise they wouldn't meet their definition. Core stocks weather the long haul. Remember? By definition, cyclical stocks are more volatile, shorter term investments. In many cases your cyclical stock will behave like a core stock, beating the S & P with relative safety. Happy day. Hold on to it longer but remember to place a sell stop after a new high.

I would choose the stock with a P/VG of 2 or greater. And the best place to look for this is the Russell 2000, (CNN.com/data/markets/Russell 2000.) Yes, these stocks may be more volatile but its chances of rallying back up to former highs are greater. Very Important: the more volatile the stock the more you must depend on sell stops after a wild rise to the stars. And you may get a dream stock with a price increase of 30% with a PE of 12, or a P/G of 30/12=2.5. Wow, I would really look into this provided pre-existing fundamentals check out.

Risk management means vigilance. Risk management is just as important as stock selection.

Never walk or jet away from a volatile stock to the surf, sun and fun. Set a reasonable price stop before you leave and enjoy the evening balmy breezes at your tropical paradise.

One final note: stocks with high P/E ratios deserve high P/E ratios. And stocks with low P/E ratios have problems, usually. Value

# SUSPENDING THE LAW OF PROBABILITY - AT LEAST FOR AWHILE

investors may disagree. After they'll wait five years for their train to arrive, the market will have turned a complete cycle. And value investors have no guarantee that their wunderkind will return the favour. Don't get stuck in a "value trap" stock. Anyway, most of us don't have the time. I'm talking about emotions, worry, uncertainty and mind games.

IS IT REALLY WORTH THE WAIT? I've seen stocks like IBM and Microsoft in the 1990s and 2000s wallow in the dregs of hell for years, missing the bull markets of 1991 and 2003. NEVER FALL IN LOVE WITH A STOCK. When the situation turns favourable, tilt the odds in your favour. In stocks, as in life, the odds are stacked against you. BEAT THE SYSTEM FOR ONCE, and may the force be with you.

# CHAPTER 24:
# The Power of Precious Metals -Heaven's Answer to a Weak Dollar

Gold and precious metals have intrigued the world for centuries. Precious metals are the true alternative to common stocks. ETF's (exchange traded funds) allow the investor to buy an interest in bullion. At this time (10-12-11), I own the Central Fund of Canada, a stock based in gold bullion traded on the NYSE.

But gold and silver are really half the story. Platinum and palladium, used in catalytic converters by the automotive industry, are considered precious metals, once considered industrial metals. Actually, silver is more of an industrial metal used in electrical components and the film industry, once a mainstay of silver. Silver dollars continue to attract collectors.

Gold is the first metal when one mentions "precious metals," because of its antiquity as a store of value. Asia and the Middle East remains the epic-center of gold in terms of interest and mystique. Western banks hoard the bright yellow metal for its reserve value. As for jewellery, gold and silver reside with diamonds and gemstones enchanting emperors and maharajas of old. In times of war or scarcity gold had remained the currency of choice because of its durability and portability.

The new world, America, had beckoned Columbus to sail west under the flag of Spain–in search of gold. The resulting pillage of Latin America emboldened pirates to rob Spanish gallons for their precious cargo. The seventeenth century was the century of colonization for the European powers in no small part for the riches of the new world.

Later, the gold rushes of California kicked off global bull markets prior to the Civil War and Alaska prior to the First World War. Devastation and inflation resulted, especially the hyperinflation of 1924 in Weimar Germany, the perfect setting for the rise of fascism in Italy, Spain and Germany. Yes, gold and precious metals have and will continue to intrigue the world.

In 1971 President Nixon shut the gold window so that the United States would no longer redeem foreign debt in gold bullion. Before that, President Roosevelt had decreed gold illegal in March, 1933, the famous Banker's Holiday, to revalue the metal to $35 dollars an ounce. The nation's money supply increased yet the nation continued to wallow in the Great Depression.

Before we speak of the investment possibilities for gold and precious metals–what makes them tick? Let's begin with gold's behaviour in the investment world. We mention that gold was a store of value and currency in the ancient world. Yes, gold continues to function along these lines. However, Goldfinger of James Bond fame would've become a very wealthy man if his plan had worked to nuke Fort Knox. His gold supply in Switzerland would have soared to the stratosphere if it wasn't from the change of heart from Pussy Galore.

Gold has the following attributes and behaves accordingly:
(1) Gold is an inflation hedge by protecting purchasing power
(2) Gold is an investment hedge when the dollar weakens

(3) Gold as an alternative investment can outperform stocks, especially in a recessionary economy, especially stagflation.
(4) Gold is indestructible, meaning that if found in a mine buried over millennia or at the bottom of the sea, the metal remains intact.
(5) In July, 2011, precious metals rose on the back of a U. S. sovereign debt crisis: the more sovereign debt, the greater gold's potential value.

I will elaborate on the above. Gold continues to cheer for inflation, because its price rises as inflation rises. No new gold is being created. All the mined gold in the world remains but as the world population increases, more and more people will demand more gold, not only for rings and necklaces but for economic reasons. Gold must fill the needs from rising incomes and a growing middle class, especially in the Middle East and Asia. Stocks and bonds are viewed with suspicion in these nations because they carry great risk in down cycles. Gold is considered more stable.

I prepared the following study on gold's tendency to outperform over the second half of the year: entitled: "Gold's 2nd Half Year Rally" in my market letter of 7/11/08. The precious metals have outperformed its first half (Jan 1 to June 30) over a 20 year period. In years that the economy experienced a strong dollar or even balanced the budget (a very rare event), **GOLD WOULD UNDERPERFORM**. The facts speak for themselves. In years of a weak or unstable dollar, especially in times of geopolitical uncertainty, **GOLD HAS OUTPERFORMED**.

Listed below is the table.
Gold: 2nd Half Effect
1988 to 2007
Closing Price, rounded

| 1988 | 7/25-12/12 | 447-423 | Following January | 1989: 1/9 | 406 | Minus |
| 1989 | 6/26-12/8 | 378-427 | " " | 1990: 1/5 | 418 | Plus |
| 1990 | 6/22-12/10 | 353-372 | " " | 1991: 1/7 | 387 | Plus + |
| 1991 | 6/24-12/9 | 368-372 | " " | 1992: 1/3 | 351 | 0 - |
| 1992 | 6/19-12/31 | 342-333 | " " | 1993: 1/29 | 331 | Minus |
| 1993 | 6/18-12/31 | 372-392 | " " | 1994: 1/28 | 379 | Plus |
| 1994 | 6/17-12/30 | 394-384 | " " | 1995: 1/27 | 379 | Minus |
| 1995 | 6/16-12/29 | 393-388 | " " | 1996: 1/26 | 409 | 0 + |
| 1996 | 7/12-12/27 | 384-371 | " " | 1997: 1/24 | 353 | Minus |
| 1997 | 7/11-12/26 | 322-296 | " " | 1998: 1/23 | 300 | 0+ |
| 1998 | 7/17-12/31 | 295-289 | " " | 1999: 1/29 | 288 | 0 - |
| 1999 | 7/16-12/31 | 254-290 | " " | 2000: 1/28 | 286 | Plus |
| 2000 | 7/14-12/29 | 282-274 | " " | 2001: 1/26 | 265 | Minus |
| 2001 | 7/13-12/28 | 267-277 | " " | 2002: 1/25 | 279 | Plus |
| 2002 | 7/12-12/27 | 316-350 | " " | 2003: 1/24 | 368 | Plus + |
| 2003 | 7/4 -12/19 | 351-409 | " " | 2004: 1/16 | 407 | Plus |
| 2004 | 7/2 -12/17 | 399-443 | " " | 2005: 1/14 | 423 | Plus |
| 2005 | 7/1 -12/16 | 428-506 | " " | 2006: 1/13 | 557 | Plus + |
| 2006 | 6/29 -12/15 | 616-619 | " " | 2007: 1/12 | 627 | 0 + |
| 2007 | 6/29 -12/14 | 651-798 | " " | 2008: 1/11 | 898 | Plus + |

The above table isn't an absolute certainty, but gold's tendency to move higher in the second half of the year remains better than even. As mentioned, this is because the dollar and inflation move in opposite directions (weaker dollar–higher inflation). For instance, the Plaza Accord of the G-7 developed nations brought the dollar down by a concerted effort from central banks by selling dollars in 1985. In 1984 the strong dollar was a thorn in the side of multinational firms as weaker foreign sales pinched earnings. Money flowed into money funds as yields had risen over the course of the year.

## THE POWER OF PRECIOUS METALS - HEAVEN'S ANSWER

Now back to an analysis on gold's Second Half Effect.:

| Number of Years | Number of Years |
| Higher Prices | Higher Prices Incl. January |
| | |
| 10/16(events) | 12.5/16(events) |
| | |
| 62.5% | 78.125% |

Clearly, these stats beat a random flip of the coin over an infinite number of tosses.

The recession years of 2001-2 were positive for gold's second half, especially in 2001-2. But in 1992 gold closed down from deflationary pressures. The years between 1996-8 the Clinton administration repaid the national debt thus running budget surpluses. Gold didn't do well. In years of a stable-to-weaker dollar, coupled with 9/11 and geopolitical uncertainty gold outperformed. In the years with no geopolitics, 1989 and 1999, gold outperformed again. I like these odds. However, during the time of this writing, September, 2008, the dollar had rebounded and one should not be in gold, foreign stocks or other inflation hedges. Coupled with a very poor equity market, i.e., a multi-year bear market and a nasty election year, one should be in cash or a mutual bond fund such as intermediate treasuries and some core stocks. The Holistic Portfolio had nearly 60% in cash/bonds for such events.

# CHAPTER 25: Managing Your Money in a Financial Crisis -Don't Buy: Wait

I consider this chapter one of the most important in this book. It's great to buy and sell on the right side of the market but "smart" buying and selling will add to your returns. Yes, be cool and wait for things to settle. Emotion is a killer. Events and news drive the market. Your mission is to beat the market and preserve your capital because holistic investing directs your assets into CASH or BONDS up to 60% in a market downturn. Let others lament the ruin of their 401 k's

Your money is protected by Uncle Sam from intermediate term Treasury Bonds or GNMA bonds, (Government National Mortgage Association) despite the fiscal woes of Washington. The dollar's reserve currency status makes it one of the strongest currencies in a downturn.

Wall Street tells you that the next bull market is around the corner. Sure. As stocks continue falling into new lows and analysts remain in the woodwork. Keep your cool.

Doesn't it feel better to hold your discipline when most of your assets sit in cash or government bonds? Yet the time will come to get ready for the next bull market.

With your large cash position you will be ready to buy into some great bargains. Let others squander their remaining assets as the market continues lower. CASH IS KING in any bear market. Even so, another good substitute for cash in a lousy market is HIGH GRADE CORPORATE BONDS.

Currently, August, 2011, I hold roughly 50 percent in corporate and government bonds.

However, this won't always be true, especially in times of rising interest rates. I'll return to this subject in more detail later in this chapter.

In mid September, 2008, the market began to crack. However, a crash won't happen unless a tragic global or systemic economic collapse happens first: The Housing Bubble. In 2007 the housing crisis and mortgage meltdown morphed into a global financial crisis. Rumblings of this were telegraphed in advance. In July the news turned sour as more housing foreclosures continued. But the financial system remained strong throughout most of 2007. The market topped in October, as foreclosures continued. However, the market, though weak wasn't crashing. In January, 2008, the market opened weak but rallied in March and April. In May and June another sell-off continued. After a respite in July, the market cracked in August. The situation deteriorated even though the market rallied for a couple weeks. A gut feeling told me to reappraise my situation.

At the time my core stocks, FMC, McDermont and Monsanto were commodity based and commodity prices were falling. These depressed core stocks, though fundamentally sound, had no chance in this deflationary environment. However, I didn't panic, knowing that I would wait and sell at a rebound. I prepared for a bounce, since many stocks rise before resuming their decline (a "dead cat bounce."). Of course no one knows WHEN such bounce would occur but I prepared anyway. I place limit sells on FMC at 65, McDermont at 45 and Monsanto at 107.

Limit sells were placed online at a price higher than current market value. I had bought these stocks in 2007: FMC in the mid thirties, McDermont in mid forties and Monsanto in the early nineties. They were trading below my buy prices. I waited a few days and the market rallied.

And my limit prices were met, selling out of an untenable situation.

I want you to remember the mathematics of market loss—very important. If you have a $100 stock and it drops to $50, you lost 50%, but, in this example, YOU MUST GAIN 100% to get back to $100.

Most of us don't have the time to wait for wayward stocks to return to a better value. And, as mentioned earlier, EMOTION is a factor. Sure, Wall St. wisdom preaches Buy and Hold, and we all know what happened in panics: 1987, 2001. In panics, most investors fear the worst. Emotion rules the day. This drives prices even lower, forcing other more prudent investors to sell later at LOWER PRICES. Why: Market psychology. A little like musical chairs. If you're the last person standing, you must leave the game. Wall Street won't tell you when the market will come back. And to be honest, even Wall Street doesn't know—witness the conflicting opinions in the media. No one rings a bell at Trinity Cathedral, bless this historic church. So here we're watching the financial news, surfing Marketwatch.com or reading about the aftermath the following morning: Answer, take action before the ugly panic: SET SELL LIMITS BEFORE THE EVENT.

Prepare for the rainy day. And if and when it does arrive, you'll be able to sleep at night and your threshold of pain never reached.

I've taken action in August, 2008. The market crashed the following month. Always remember, your large CASH or BOND funds position of 60% in a bear market will protect MOST OF YOUR PORTFOLIO (the market had topped in October, 2007 at 14,164 and had been trading lower since—a bear market).

SECTOR INVESTING DOESN'T WORK IN A FINANCIAL PANIC. ALL STOCKS FALL including gold stocks. Remember, panic is the name of the game. The only safety is cash and Treasury bonds, traditional harbours. Even so, sometimes longer-term treasuries can fall because monies leaving notes and bonds are fleeing into treasury bills. Even municipal bonds can fall because scarred investors feel that local issuing authorities may crack under the financial strain. The only safe "green zone" so to speak is cash or treasury bonds. CASH IS KING.

Later, as the panic settles down, an economic contraction takes hold—a recession. Bonds are preferred and monies should be moved out of cash, buying bonds. Buy them as you would buy cyclical stocks in normal times. Buy high quality corporate bonds and the best way to do this is through a mutual fund. Usually, a protracted bear market will make a second but higher bottom, after bouncing along the bottom for awhile. An example is the bottom in late 2002, a higher bottom than the panic bottom in 2001. The market drop of 2000-2002 lasted for 851 days and fell 47.78%, the longest in fifty years.

# CHAPTER 26:
# Navigating Home in a Multi-year Bear Market and Surviving Deflation: Part 2
# It's all about Demand

Remember in chapter 17 we discussed selling in a multi-year bear market? Now we take another step in a more difficult topic and add financial crisis and deflation to the brew. In my life they're been two bears trapped in the claws of deflation: 1981-2 and 2008-9. Normally, bear markets begin from rising rates or the beginning of a recession, or a period of stagflation. Banks have collapsed from weak demand. Now, as in the 1930s, many banks have collapsed and received "bail-out" monies. Since then the big banks have paid back the bailouts. The negative "wealth effect" arose from stock market losses and credit contraction. Households were especially hit with mortgages under water (mortgage worth more than house). In both instances deflation sprang from weak market demand. The economy shrinks when consumers and businesses take cover; as supply considerations, such as oil reserves or copper inventories count for little. Deflation triggers credit contraction and demand falls even further. Buy treasury bonds.

Remember the happy days of credit expansion, the economic booms when credit card applications flooded mail boxes? Cheap money made this possible, creating the dot-com and real estate bubbles floating on a sea of low interest rates. Teaser loans for home refinancing and balance transfers created the "shop till you drop" ethos. Well, the party is over.

Inflation needs gobs and gobs of money hitting an economy running at full tilt, like in the late 1960s of the Viet Nam War and the late 1970s of runaway energy inflation and gasoline lines.

Now in October, 2008, forty years later we have the opposite dynamic: credit contraction from the fall of "trickle down" economics. I wrote a market letter to my clients entitled: The Fall of Trickle Down, dated 10/13/08.

The above dynamics resulted in the crash of Wall Street's investment houses: Bear Stearns and Lehman Brothers. The very institutions who created the mess received major bailouts, not "rescue" as government officials preferred. Admittedly, some of the banks didn't need the bailout. Yet, this time around gobs and gobs of money went into the market, not the small shops on Main Street.

Small businesses found themselves strapped with little potential, declining profits, lousy returns on capital—events not experienced since the 1930s Great Depression—a Fyodor Dostoevsky event. And speaking of the Great Depression, many programs morphed into alphabet soup: CCC, TVA, FDIC. Hoovervilles, in a lame effort to jump start demand (too little-too late, exacerbated by declining global trade), a frantic President Herbert Hoover trying to turn the tide of falling demand. Note:

President Hoover was really a great man. President Truman tapped him to rebuild Europe after World War II.

Infusions of monies to prop up demand didn't work. The market, crashing in October, 1929 fell every year, eventually hitting bottom in the summer of 1932. An unemployment rate of 25% faced the new president, Franklin Roosevelt, better known as FDR. British economist John Maynard Keynes had argued for massive government spending. Does this sound familiar? He referred to the deflationary debacle of 1929-1932 as "pushing on a string," the liquidity trap.

If Supply-side or "trickledown economics" have tipped us into this mess, arguably, then demand side or demand-pull, as I call it, can pull us out—the flip side of supply-side. But the answer isn't wanton spending–the answer is capital spending and made in America. (Capital spending on infrastructure and creating jobs for instance, with a prolonged life reaping benefits for society lasting years).

Even as things in the early 1930s were grim, spending our way out of the mess didn't work. Europe was rearming by the mid '30s and everyone knew that war would arrive, sooner or later. Chamberlain's appeasement in 1938 wouldn't stop Hitler. The defence industries rev-up on both sides of the Atlantic, Hitler's Germany and British and American factories: jeeps, tanks, aircraft. Japan was buying our scrap steel. Unemployment fell and the War, especially after Pearl Harbor helped retooled America. Demand was back, once again, and unemployment ended.

The recent "flip this house" scheme gave birth to the real estate bubble and commodity boom, high prices for McMansions and energy shortages. Supply or costs would push crude prices to $147 oil per barrel and gold back above $1000 per ounce. China and India were running at full capacity exporting their produce while we paid the Arabs $700 billion a year for imported oil with recycle Chinese dollars. Tons of Chinese goods hit the shelves at WallMart. And folks with low incomes scrambled to scoop them up.

High finance is confusing but all you have to know is that trickledown (economics) came crashing down in September, 2008–ushering in a new era. I call this Demand Pull or Wealth created from the Bottom Up: more durable. Anyway, I believe true, lasting wealth, as in the post war boom of the mid 1940s to mid 1960s gave birth to the middle class. "I like Ike," the Levittowns and the 1957 Chevy. This wealth had a "shelf life," lasting and being capable of being passed down to the "boomers" in a massive transfer from the Greatest Generation.

## HOLISTIC INVESTING IN A RISK-AVERSE WORLD

Holistic investing tracks money and where it's going. Money moves stocks and bonds, not hope. Demand pull economics, as JFK referred: as a rising tide lifting all boats. In periods of low demand, Value stocks are in, growth stocks are out. By definition, value stocks trade at a low price-earnings ratio, PE.

Now for some fundamental basics. I measure working capital in excess of long-term debt.

Working capital is current assets less current liabilities and long-term debt are those liabilities maturing over one year. Others may look at value stocks as inherent (potential) value. But here you get into some problems such as methods of inventory valuation (LIFO) or Last in, First out. This means that inventory may be priced differently. Book value per share can be murky because of methods of accounting, really another matter and beyond the scope of this book. The simple Working Capital/Long-term debt ratio works. Keep it simple.

Usually, the class of companies which do well in recessions are health care, food and beverages or consumer staples. Consumer staples (drug stores), the gaming industry, defence contractors and entertainment industries have also done well. It doesn't matter whether the company is a large or small because if sales are rising and costs are contained, all the better. Another reason why I like mid- cap stocks. One can spend hours flipping through S & P and Value Line gathering statistics, only to chance upon another company more exciting. I've looked for stocks with rising backlog orders and rising sales. This would certainly warrant a look.

Dividends are important in a deflationary environment. However, In a growth climate I rather buy a stock that ploughs its money back into the company. For instance, if a stock with a 5% dividend remains flat, that 5% dividend remains a morale booster. All the better if its dividend rate rises with its sales growth.

The principles laid out in earlier chapters on buying and selling apply. When buying, wait for a market bottom in an IMPROVING economic environment. If a stock bottoms, seemingly, only to rollover, it will simply fall to a new bottom. A good candidate stock is one that moves sideways for at least 6-8 weeks, waiting for a trigger to lift it higher. If this stock moves higher on significant volume, important, then it has a much better chance of continuing higher. DON'T BUY breakouts on weak volume—this is a trap. AVOID.

Buying principles are great, but its only ONE/HALF of the battle. What price do you pay?

Other books have spent chapters upon chapters on this very subject. As mentioned, set a limit buy; avoid market buys. Set your price on a higher weekly close, after trending sideways 6-8 weeks on significant volume. BUY WEEKLY CLOSE above 6-8 week channel confirmed by money flow.

If you buy at a strong market open, chances are that you will overpay. If you buy at a weak open, you may save some money but your stock may fall in sympathy with the market or its group. SET your LIMIT BUY below market price and SET LIMIT SELL above market price.

On management of your portfolio: buy few shares at the outset. I mean less than a hundred.

If your selection is good, the stock will rise into a new higher plateau, again consolidate, before moving up. This may take another 6-8 weeks or so. So what. Wait for that SECOND WIND, or second move higher. I consider this the big kahuna. Most stocks move more in this second phase of its market cycle before reaching an intermediate term top. If you bought 25-50 shares on the initial move up, then I would buy another 25-50 shares on this second move higher using the same principles as before. And if your stock doesn't work out, then 25-50 shares are a relatively small risk profile.

In case of a failed order, place a STOP ORDER 7 at 1/2% below your original purchase price or a TRAILING STOP after a new high. Why seven and a half? This arbitrary number seems to encapsulate an amount deep enough to provide room for a new rally but not deep enough to cause severe pain. Don't fall in love with your stock. And most important, your stock may not move in sync with the market, rising as the market goes down.

In the early 2000s Invesco/AIM Funds compared the performance of Growth vs. Value stocks (Russell 3000 Growth-Value Index. Value has underperformed in good times and has outperformed in bad times-recession.

Money management in a bear market is more important than money management in other market environments. The time-value of money is crucial, especially at a time when interest rates are very low.

In the current bear market which began in October, 2007 interest rates, meaning money market mutual funds were paying around three percent. This is low by recent historical standards being that rates were running 500 basis points higher, or around eight percent a couple of decades earlier. In the early 1980s, rates were above double digit levels as inflation was cooling down during the recession of 1981-2. At the time, the dollar was strengthening and European currencies were weakening. The Dreyfus Family of Funds developed the Worldwide Dollar Fund, a money market fund denominated in foreign short-term commercial paper which reflected higher rates, later in the decade. I remember investing in this fund at a double-digit rate, since the stock market was going nowhere anyway. Sadly, today in the midst of a deflationary debt crisis, the opposite is the case—low rates paying 0.25 %.

Obviously, low rates repudiate the efficacy of the "cash is king" argument. But cash doesn't fall in hard times. Normally, trades are redeemed into cash for lack of alternatives. I mentioned that losing stock trades should go into your best core stock paying ABOVE MARKET RATES from a LIMIT BUY.

Should you place monies paying 0.25 into cash when municipal bonds are paying 4.5-5%? Yes.

Municipal bonds are historically sound; however, one must be sure that the muni is safe. For instance, Puerto Rican bonds, for example are considered unsafe municipals because of their enormous debt. Even if uninsured, these investments from mutual funds provide another barrier of safety.

In the Great Depression, very few municipalities failed, well under one percent of all municipalities and authorities (highway or water) in the continental 48 states. In fact, Joe Kennedy, father of JFK, put all of his profits from the 1920s into municipal bonds, avoiding the anguish of 1929. Even back then, good advice paid dividends.

IMPORTANT: Even though muni-bonds pay well above current money market rates, the capital value of the bond may fall along with the rest of the stock market, but not as much.

For example, I recently invested some of my cash, less than 5%, into the Dreyfus General Municipal Bond Fund at the price of $10.49 per share. Now the price stands at $10.40 per share.

However, the funds pays in the vicinity of 4.75% for a drop of .00858 %, less than one percent in about three weeks. A drop of one percent would be 10 and ½ cents. Thus, my total return would be around 3.75% plus (.0475 minus .01 or .00858), let's say .0375 or 3.75%, **WELL ABOVE** the 0.25% rate of current mutual fund yields. Municipal bonds are safe places to park money, especially when a bear market has nearly hit bottom and trades sideways for an extended period. In addition, after a crash the economy enters a disinflationary period, good for bonds.

The last important point: During a protracted bear market, when new bottoms are being made, almost weekly; remember: CASH IS KING. After the crisis phase put some of your monies in a bond fund paying a higher yield or a strong currency bond fund. And always, in an **INFLATIONARY** crisis, **AVOID** any bonds, even international bonds because chances are that inflation is pervasive in a global economy. Capital values are eaten up with little solace from dividends.

We focus on the bear market period of 2000-2002. In 2000, the market topped in March and again in September, yet the year ended down. Value outperformed in the "Tech Bubble" while Growth was negative. Yet both Value and Growth finished negative in this prolonged bear market.

# CHAPTER 27:
# The Rebirth of Economic Recovery -The Longer the Bottom, the Bigger the Rise

Sooner or later the economy will recover. Many voices on Wall Street beat the drums of recovery months before the fact. Late in a recession optimism wells up like dairy cream. Yet, the recession lumbers long into the cold night. Who do you believe when a famous economist of the 1960s, Paul Samuelson, said that the "stock market has predicted 9 of last 5 recessions." Can the market do any better predicting economic recovery? Maybe. Does the serious investor have time for the tea leaves? No. Barron's and the Wall St. Journal, esteemed publications, feature analysts and market seers telescoping this very event: boom around the corner.

To make my point, an analyst published a book in 1999 with an off-the-wall prediction that the Dow Jones would hit 36,000. This was published a year before the Dot-Com bust of 2000.

Now, to be kind, what publisher is so naive to publish this misinformation? As we speak, the DJI is around 8500. Blowing bubbles into the wind may excite a kindergarten, but gross hyperbole keeps company with fools.

This morning, Alan Greenspan, former Fed Chairmen, testified before Congress. He laid the blame in the "once in a hundred year" collapse of the financial system on the "miss-pricing" of derivatives of sub-prime loans. Investment banks sold these to maximize profits on a sea of higher real estate prices. The world ran like cattle to the slaughter in buying "credit default swaps," now worthless. He added that it would be months before real estate and the economy return to normal. Greenspan said that America will come back, but who will tell the millions who have foreclosed.

Economics, sometimes referred to as the "dismal science" drives the news. When things go right, who cares about economics except economists. Now we'd learned that we must keep an eye on our retirement accounts. And just think, the previous administration wanted to privatize Social Security as a sop to Wall Street. Good for business? Making up losses are difficult, as I explained in my math example. I repeat a quote from Patton: "I don't want to fight for the same real estate twice." Now let's get to work.

The current bear market has given up 41% as of 10/23/08. A bear market drops 20% or more. Since The Great Depression the average loss in a bear market, most multi-year in duration is around 37%. The worst bear market was the granddaddy of bears, 1929-1932. The Dot-Com Bust of 2000-2002 aided by the 9/11 attack fell 57%. This Chinese water torture lasted from March of 2000 to October of 2002, nearly a three year event. This bear was global, fraught with the war on terror.

The fulcrum of the current bear market is the banking collapse. Soon, this bear will refuel from economic recovery, less on the financial condition of banks. This indicates the bear will extend into 2009, possibly 2010(in reality the Bear lasted into early March, 2009). The last bull market began in November, 2003 and ended in October, 2007, a period of four years. Bear markets run shorter that bull markets. Over a four year or presidential cycle bull markets last some 60% of the time and bear markets make up the difference or some

# THE REBIRTH OF ECONOMIC RECOVERY

40%. If presidents are re-elected bull markets last longer as in the Reagan, Clinton administrations.

Since your Holistic portfolio is holding 60% of your monies in CASH or Bond Funds, the remaining 40% of your investments, core stocks, can become vehicles for dollar-cost averaging.

**DOLLAR COST AVERAGING** is buying more shares for less than your original purchase. Of course your current stock MUST BE fundamentally sound, and the firm's working capital and free cash remains positive, growing as a percentage of sales with little long-term debt. Be sure your stock is NOT issuing more shares to finance operations.

Markets have seasonal rallies: basically UP from November to April and DOWN from May to October. Other data seems to confirm: bullish from March -April, August- early September and November to late December and bearish the rest of the time as compiled from futures data (KCBT, Value Line Report, Moore Research Center, Inc. 8/11/01). Another consideration is this: is your company gaining market share on its competitors? A good indicator of this is the company's backlog. Is it growing? Good company fundamentals can counter the above, but it is easier making money with the wind to your back.

For instance, one of my earlier stocks: Airgas, ARG, is a distributor of industrial gases, propane. It distributes this gas to manufacturing and to health care facilities. The stock, currently around 29 was purchased at 44, but I wasn't worried. I bought additional shares at a lower price before because I felt the stock hadn't reached its full potential.

THREE STEPS AND A RISE:

1. In the current recession, the first real step to economic recovery is the end of foreclosures. As I write this there are nearly 3,000 foreclosures daily. This has to stop. Foreclosures drive a stake into the construction industry, a large part of the economy.

2. The second step is jobs, jobs. Unemployment will rise as the recession deepens. The current debt-driven recession is not like recessions of the past. Back in the 1950s and 1980s interest rate increases or surplus inventory sparked the beginning of a recession. The current recession feeds off the write-offs of debt and the poor debt condition of the public. Consumer spending will be weak as we continue into 2009.

The government has spent trillions bailing financial institutions from their mistakes.

Some states may run out of unemployment money as the recession deepens.

3. The final step will be the stock market itself. The market is a discounting mechanism and adds wealth to the economy. The important fact is this: financial stocks must outperform the market once again. If a sustainable rally holds on heavy volume, a new bull market is born as in 1983 and 2003.

## THE ROAD TO RECOVERY:

The market will eventually settle, make a few false starts (a euphoric rise, lasting a few days only to fall back down). No one really knows WHEN the bell rings on Wall Street: A new bull is born. Everyone cheers. The gravy train returns and the rising tide will lift most stocks. But your concern isn't to catch the new bull by the horns. Your concern is to be prepared, by being in the right market sector—the sector which OUTPERFORMS the S & P 500. This is best achieved by mutual funds. Your core stocks will ride the tide anyway.

Listed below are those market sectors, tested over the years that have outperformed the market at the beginning of a new bull market:

Rotation of Stocks in New Bull Market:

1. Banks and Brokers
2. Insurance/Mortgage Finance

# THE REBIRTH OF ECONOMIC RECOVERY

3. Retail (discretionary) especially upscale stores.
4. Consumer Electronics
5. Furnishings/Household Products

The above groups aren't an exact science. For instance, Basic Retail, such as Target or Sears may do better than investment services or insurance companies, and consumer electronics may do better than household products, i.e., Bed, Bath and Beyond. This guide intends to call your attention to these groups before committing investment dollars. Just go online and run a relative strength test of your stock vs. the S & P 500. An easy way to do this is to see if your stock is trading above its 30 week (200 day) moving average.

At the genesis of a new bull market a few stocks will be trading above their 30 week average. And as the market heads higher your stock ought to do likewise. Another important yardstick is the 10 week or 50 day moving average. Many traders key into this metric when price crosses above or below this average. However, Holistic Investing isn't trading. We consider stocks and funds as vehicles of rising value over time. Most important: CONTENT DRIVES VALUE (Good Core Stocks).

Conversely, look out below if a stock closes below its weekly 30 week average. But on many occasions a 30 week moving average presents formidable resistance for a stock, rallying, above this important yardstick. A weekly close on heavy volume above the 30 week weighted moving average presents a buying opportunity. Set Limit Buy following Monday provided that its close is greater than 30 week average.

# PART F:

## FINAL THOUGHTS: THE FUTURE OF HOLISTIC INVESTING

# CHAPTER 28: Time Value of Money The Great Grimm Reaper

Time is everything—the only thing which matters. We all know this truth, but in finance time takes an even more important perception: value. A thing of treasure today may be headed for the scrapheap tomorrow. Have you ever walked through an old house, all of the furniture intact of a time when people had cherished those large stuffy sofas, had eaten those wholesome meals at the bulky kitchen table and had slept in those high mattress beds with curtains overhead, wearing caps at night to keep warm. Just the sheer size of these items would take up the entire room of most modern homes.

Collectors would jump at the opportunity to buy some of these treasures of yore, and I would like to get hold of a mid nineteenth century oil lamp which would light an upper floor landing of a New England home. But to furnish my home with nineteenth century beds, sofas and tables—no, because we already have two bulky sofas which require covers. The original covers probably wore out in the early twentieth century.

The point is that inflation is not your only enemy. Time itself is. We intuitively know this.

We want to stay in shape from good food, exercising, to buy time, quality time. But this isn't a book on health or positive thinking, inasmuch as I subscribe wholeheartedly to these.

Will your portfolio weather the ravages of time, the investment cycle millions have faced through their lifetimes? Holistic investing addresses this head on: core stocks which add value over time from dividends and capital appreciation.

Illustrated below are two ways to interpret the time value of money from an investment viewpoint. Suppose I make $2500 a year over a four year period. Percentage return will be measured 'since inception' in the first table and 'year-to-date,' YTD (year-to-date) in the second table.

Beginning capital is $5,000.

### Time Value of Money Since Inception

| Year 1: | $2500 profit divided by $5000 | ='s | 50% return | | | |
|---|---|---|---|---|---|---|
| " 2 | $5000(years 1+2) | " | " | = | 100% divided by | 2 ='s 50% |
| " 3 | $7500(years1 +2+3) | " | " | = | 150% " | 3 ='s 50% |
| " 4 | $10,000(years 1+2+3+4) | " | " | = | 200% " | 4 ='s 50% |

### Time Value of Money Year-to Date

| Year 1: | $2500 profit divided by $5000 | | | | ='s 50% return |
|---|---|---|---|---|---|
| " 2 | $2500 profit divided by $7500(profit + beg.capital) | | | | ='s 33% " |
| " 3 | $2500 | " | " | "$10,000(profit+prior profit + beg.cap. | ='s 25% " |
| " 4 | $2500 | " | " | "$12,500(profit=prior profits+ beg.cap. | ='s 20% " |

A graph entitled "The Time Value of Money" can illustrate the above more clearly.

In reality, an annual profit of $2,500 starting with capital of $5,000, or 50% isn't realistic.

Making a return of 50% or more implies significant risk, and the greater the risk, the greater the reward, or loss. Hedge fund managers like their backs to the wind, dreaming of commodity or tech booms to make easy money in options and futures of 50% or more. However, secular bull markets like these multi decade events:

tech stocks in the late '90s and commodities in '2010-11 aren't sustainable. Swinging for home runs mean more strikeouts. Hitting singles and doubles means lower but SAFER returns. In times of uncertainty, holistic investing is all about hitting singles and doubles. Later, when a major bottom is in place, you can swing for the longer ball.

A Time-Value of Money illustration can show an ideal path of invested money over time.

Imagine a Y or vertical axis that shows value in $2,500 increments from $5,000 of beginning capital. The X or horizontal axis shows time in yearly increments of 1-5 years. Rarely is the ideal path met because of business cycles (the four year presidential cycle). The market is up 60-65% of the time and down 40-35%. Let's say it's up 62 1/2% and down 37 ½%. A typical bull market will fail and top, usually in a general election year: '56, '60, '64-5, '68, '72, '80, '84, '87-8, ,'92, '2000, '2008, turning the ideal $2,500 gain into a loss. A Hyper market won't last, and will fall hard. A Normal market will rise for months, but eventually top out and fall at a slower pace. A final word on the Time-Value of Money: Inflation. Everyone knows that inflation remains a fact of life. All that money swirling around the world had been parked in U. S. Treasuries: petrol dollars, Asian surpluses and now bailouts of major banks. In times of crisis, Euros and Yen fly to the dollar. The commodities and real estate bubbles of 2007-8 were the recipe for a disaster. The energy induced inflation of the 1970s triggered a severe 'Rust Belt' recession of the early 1980s.

All those trillions of dollars out there will return to haunt us and the next President: (witness the debt battles between President Obama and the Republicans.) The recent boom was generated from a revitalized Asia and Brazil demanding more natural resources for infrastructure. This meant more manufacturing and exporting to the developing world. However, oil at $147 a barrel had become unsustainable. In effect, oil and the housing bubble crashed at about the same time.

Now global economies are in decline, and will continue into most of 2009-2011.

Inflation will become disinflation with home values dropping, and auto dealerships begging for sales. Autos need massive promotions to sell and weak consumer spending doesn't help. Meanwhile, all that money remains out there waiting for a new energy and housing boom. And I believe the next BOOM will arrive sometime around the middle of this decade, into the late teens (2017-2019). By then, most home foreclosures will have been settled and most of the jobs returned. I believe inflation will accelerate slowly, like most booms of the past.

In the last few years of a presidential cycle, in this case 2018 and 2019, we'll see the economy revving up from the Great Global Recession of 2008-2011. The economy should enter the "real" recovery phase of 2013-2017. I believe we're in a 30 year cycle, similar to the stagnation of the 1940s, 1970s, early 2000s. A new boom is waiting to blossom in mid decade.

The early 1970s bear market began in January, 1969 and bottomed in late May, 1970. A new bull market began in the spring of 1971 and lasted into December, 1972. An Arab oil embargo ended the great Post War Boom in 1973. The Watergate hearings did not t help. President Nixon resigned in August, 1974 adding uncertainty to the bear market which had begun in early 1973. By late 1975 a new bull market had begun which lasted into the election of Ronald Reagan in 1980. The market traded down into the fall of 1981 as the Rust Belt Recession had begun.

In 1980, inflation had been gathering steam rising to 14%. The Fed Chairman restricted the growth of money, placing limits on loans and the economy fell into recession, lasting through early 1982. The era of 1970s stagflation morphed into a great buying opportunity in spring, 1985.

The second half of the 1980s had its genesis from a weaker dollar, the 'Plaza Accord. All went well into the early fall of 1987 and then October 19th: The Crash, the worst collapse of the market since

October, 1929. Being more precise, economic stagnation or recession had, in the 20th century, taken place in early decade, years 1 & 2; recovery takes place in mid-decade(years ending in 3- 6; and a economic boom takes place in late decade, years ending 7—9, the usual pattern. I believe the above point is important and worth keeping in mind.

The spectre of another oil crunch waits, lurching for a new day. It will take years to get electric cars in mass off assembly lines. Natural gas and bio fuels can bridge the gap alleviating the crisis. Meanwhile, windmills, solar, and clean coal are available technologies. But alternative critical mass isn't anywhere near what it should be.

Consider this: at the beginning of 2008, an oil specialist on **CNBC**, said that we would have to replace 20 million barrels of oil a day to offset depletion of world reserves He went on to say that we would have to run faster to stay in place. Saudi Arabia doesn't report oil reserves, and some think that Saudi and Russian oil reserves have peaked. Nothing lasts forever. And surely, global growth will return spiking demand for oil--prices will rise once again. Sadly, Democrats and Republicans will be fighting over last year's energy policy.

The good news. The United States is now the world's largest producer of energy including its vast resources of natural gas. Maybe we can run a little bit slower.

# CHAPTER 29:
# The Fall of Trickle Down Economics: Return of the Purple Decade

In 1982 a Tom Wolfe reader was published: The Purple Decades by Farrar Straus and McGraw-Hill Ryerson Ltd., Toronto. I advise you to read the chapter on "The Me Decade and the Third Great Awakening." Wolfe, true to form vividly described generational changes gripping American society at the time. The 1960s and the early 1970s were cataclysmic indeed, beginning with the battle for civil rights and ending with the drug culture and Viet Nam War. Bigger than life personalities roamed the landscape: the Kennedys, Martin Luther King, Nixon and the Beatles.

The culture was about free expression, a repudiation of the establishment. Meanwhile, conservatism and the New South arose after the battle for civil rights, 1964, and had become a Republican stronghold since. Jimmy Carter was the last Democrat to carry the south as Georgia governor in 1976.

By the 2000s, digitally savvy generations had begun to exert their values: generation Y, sons and daughters of the beat generation and the Boomers. I focus on the millennial generation for their sheer size of numbers, sons and daughters of the Boomers, the grandchildren of the Greatest Generation, the World War II generation.

The millennial generation, born in the 1980s are the most educated, technological and pragmatic generation since the flowering of the industrial revolution in the 1890s. They demand answers, and answers they will get. I believe this generation, with good cooperative working skills will help bring America back. A note: As of this writing they occupy Wall Street as a '99% Percenter,' a lost middle class ravaged by out-source jobs and drowning in student loans.

My generation, the "beat generation," born in the Depression era of course were fewer in numbers. Generation Y are our children, born in the late 1960s and 1970s. This generation, more individualistic and rebellious like the "beats" work better alone, creating and seeing the world in a rather satiric way. Satire is a powerful weapon, just watch Saturday Night Live and the early performances of Chevy Chase influencing the election of 1976.

Likewise, Sarah Palin, portrayed as a bumbling iconoclast who couldn't answer Katie Couric's question on a CBS interview: "what do you read?" Is this cruel or unfair? Of course not. The essence of a person's character has always been captured in satire. In other words, every generation reverses itself which, I believe, is a good thing. It's no secret that most parents and their children, have always viewed the world differently.

The children of boomers may have more in common with their grandparents, the "greatest generation." They bond easier than Gen Y because of their early group bonding.

Remember, Gen Y, grandchildren of the "beat generation," keep cool and go it alone. Now this isn't a bad thing; but I believe social change seems to come easier from group participation. Remember their parents, who fought and protested the Viet Nam war? More importantly, Millennials are the most computer savvy-social media 'facebook' generation. Text messages, wireless downloads and sharing, not only of music but important documents and video- conferencing define a more productive information society. As we know,

# THE FALL OF TRICKLE DOWN ECONOMICS

information is the salt and pepper of our economy, no longer the raw materials of iron and copper wire. Alan Greenspan, former Fed chief said that "GDP is weighing less and less these days."

The fall of trickle-down economics had occurred in 2007 which triggered The Great Recession. This happened at a time when the millennials were relatively young. Their fathers, the Boomers, had never experienced a financial crisis, global in scope, a 1930s style catastrophe.

Aside from the real estate bubble, a grave disparity of wealth fermented while millions of jobs were lost to China and Indian outsourcing. Actually wealth disparity had begun in the 1980s as the financial economy grew: the acceleration of credit. Today one percent of the population own some 20% of wealth and 3 percent own around 40%. The concentration of wealth also had occurred in the Gilded Age of the 1890s. Trust busting followed from President Teddy Roosevelt.

This called into question a fundamental rethinking of the culture and the economy. Are we headed in the right path? The contradictions gave way to a rise of trickle-up economics: the rebirth of wealth created from the ground up, the middle class. This favoured small business and cottage-industries. True, the large corporation shall remain a power in today's economy, but more jobs are created from the ranks of small business. Small business means more U. S made goods and services and more jobs.

However, foreign trade, a bastion of the multinational corporation depends on foreign sales.

A weak dollar is friendlier to larger companies who ship overseas. Of course this isn't to say that small businesses don't ship overseas. They do and continue in increasing numbers because of the internet. In other words, small innovative companies will grab an ever increasing share of the pie or rise in wealth. This is desired.

Products you see advertised on late night TV, especially Saturday evening have been and continue to generate global sales. These products are the bastion of small business, not the multinational firm. The problem for the big firm is production costs because of global competition. Smaller firms have an advantage because of lower fixed costs.

All of the above bodes well for small stocks (the Russell 2000) in the newer economy: beyond The Great Recession. But you must be careful. Products you see on Saturday night TV aren't listed on any exchange. Pass over them. Instead, thousands of small firms out there in most sectors prosper from healthy growth: manufacturing, specialty retail, energy, medical equipment and biotechnology for instance.

I believe another sector stands out, alternate energy. Progress on alternate fuel sources begets even more progress down the road. Sooner or later, a LNG (liquidized natural gas) vehicle with solar panels may put a huge dent in gasoline engines at the right price. Regretfully, another energy crisis will have to drive this home because of the power of the oil lobby and the "bunker mentality" in Congress.

An example of a small company is the following: Marteck Biotech makes infant formulas which include plant-source DHA, an ingredient for child brain development. The company has signed into agreements with the Chinese and Japanese governments as major buyers. Even pet foods have DHA as an ingredient, in puppy and senior formulas. It's recognized that the compound promotes better communication in brain function, a no brainer–pardon this pun.

I bought MATK at twenty, waiting for nearly a month when the stock dropped down to my limit buy. The stock traded in low forties at its high and recently closed at 17.84 (4/21/09). I bought only 20 shares and plan to buy more if price falls below 15. If MATK falls to 15 or below on strong volume ABOVE its 52 week average I wouldn't buy, just hold. However, I would buy an additional 20 shares on its next breakout above 20.

Another small company I would consider is Energy Conversion Systems. However, I don't expect energy prices to rise anytime soon because of the recession. But...a day will come when oil and gas prices will shoot up. The symbol is ENER, and they make flexible solar panels. These panels, now used in the commercial market, etc.

# THE FALL OF TRICKLE DOWN ECONOMICS

office buildings will eventually migrate to the residential market. Most solar panels are fixed, meaning that they can't be bent around corners, peaks or valleys of roofs. Energy Conversion has solved this problem. The panels are thinner than the standard older generation panels. Federal and state governments have invested in this product and business will get a boost post-recession.

Later this year energy stocks will spike higher because of the beginning of economic recovery.

Energy prices are a function of global demand and geopolitical developments. Some pundits are calling for $300. oil which I consider ridiculous. Natural gas, hampered by oversupply will break out over time as more usage builds.

A sub-title of this chapter is "Return of the Purple Decade," the 1970s. The 1970s was a time of pulling in from the turbulent 1960s of political turmoil and social change. The seventies were a cooling off period. Early in the decade the "nifty fifty" companies of large multinational companies like Coca-Cola, Proctor & Gamble, etc., commanded attention. The deep recession of 1973-4 called for conservative investing. But later in the decade things began to loosen up, and small stocks came back from the dead. Mining shares rose as gold and precious metals rose from rising inflation.

Disinflation is good for larger firms because of lower rates. But as inflation spiked from 1977-1980, the "nifty-fifty" fell away from the investors radar screen. Small firms replaced them and popped into popularity as more nimble. Small companies can cope better with rising inflation.

Computer companies like Computer Sciences became part of this shift which my parents and I profited from. After falling to 7, Cliff wanted to buy more shares of Computer Sciences. My mom wasn't sure but Cliff was right on. Later, I sold the stock at 24 and my parents did even better.

Another small company, at the time, Apple Computer, was a little start up making computers, primarily for the school market. Today Apple has billions in cash. The PC wasn't out yet so Apple had this market all to itself. The stock rose, up, up and away. I didn't catch this but my boss at work, Don C. told me about it and I thought the price was too high. Apple continued higher. At the time I was attending the New School commuting to New York., yearning to chill for the weekend. Disco was in and Cherry Hill was it.

I should've listened to Don, my boss at the NJ Dept. of Transportation. He told me about Apple's prospects while on special assignment in 1980.

# CHAPTER 30:
# The Rebirth of Bonds: - A Recession's Best Friend

Recently, I wrote a market letter entitled: The Yogi Bear Market. This espoused the great achievements of Yogi Berra, both as player and pundit. I enjoyed reading the book by David Kaplan: 'Take It!: When you come to a Fork in the Road." Aside from striking out 414 times out of 7,555 times at bat, the inimitable Yogi made a presence as an indefatigable catcher. His famous clutch hitting, especially in the world series is a story of legends. Even in his playing days we admired him for his tongue and cheek expressions. One of my favourites was the time he was with Milton Friedman, the late economist.

Yogi said: "You know, a nickel isn't worth a dime anymore." Milton Friedman just laughed, no reply needed.

The recession is deepening as I speak (2009), yet the market somehow feels as if all is well.

We're on the verge of making the seventh straight week of stock market gains. Yet a false sense of hope abounds despite rising unemployment and foreclosures. Yes, the market, a discounting machine anticipates a recovery on the horizon. I just don't see this happening.

First of all, credit, the lifeblood of the economy has barely budged out of the gate. Mortgage refinancing and fleet auto loans are up but the rest of the credit economy is down. Consumer spending remains anemic as consumers cut back on discretionary items. In fact, they're paying down their debt. Retail auto sales are down fifty percent, and business spending remains in the basement.

This morning Microsoft reported its sales down for the first time since 1986. Its profits have met expectations, but all they'll do is buy in more shares to please Wall Street. Remember Chapter 1: The Earnings Myth?

We need more small business jobs. But that won't happen until demand returns and profits pick up in a serious way: hopefully, in late 2009 and 2010. Meanwhile, the economy won't be going anywhere. Yogi was right after all. So this sea change calls for a new investment strategy: bonds, a gentleman's second best friend besides Rover.

Bonds work well in a recession because they pay consistent returns and avoid volatility. However, bond yield are very low.

Recessions are fraught with subpar percentage stock rallies and bad percentage stock declines.

After all, percent gains are great from a low base, decline to decline, back and forth like a squirrel unable to hide his acorn. These fake market moves become meaningless and soak up wasted energy. Why not hold on to something real: bonds with a decent yield and opportunity for capital gains? This doesn't mean I'll sell stocks to buy bonds. Far from it. Keep your cool and hold good core stocks intact. Cash raised earlier from the sale of cyclical stocks can fund bond purchases. In fact, recessions present a chance to double down (re-leverage) core stock positions after bonds are sold. Meanwhile, maintain your cash position of 50-60%.

My cash position is 52.4%, early Spring, 2009. My cash position will buy additional bonds at this time, switching from treasuries to Ginnie Maes to municipals when conditions allow. I also look out for those mid-large cap value stocks to pick up at a lower price. Just after a recession buy larger companies with large cash positions. At the time, (4/24/09), I was eight percent in bonds 6.2% global-intermediate treasury, corporate bonds and 1.8% municipal bonds). These

# THE REBIRTH OF BONDS: - A RECESSION'S BEST FRIEND

bonds are the Dreyfus Intermediate Income and General Municipal Bond Funds. Avoid buying individual bonds from brokers because these are expensive and lack diversification. Credits risks could be a problem. Mutual funds are diversified by nature and offer a better buy.

Below are some statistics on how bonds behaved in the last recession: 2000-2:

Dreyfus Intermediate Income Fund (Class A)

YTD (year-to-date) Total Return: interest + capital gains:
2000 " " 12.34%
2001 " " 6.20 "
2002 " " 6.81 "

Another interesting facet of bonds offer diversity of instruments, such as Ginnie Mae Bonds or Government National Mortgage Association: (GNMA) bonds. These bonds are backed by the government fund the mortgage market. Banks work with GNMA to write mortgages and loan to buyers. As everyone knows, the mortgage market is huge and very liquid. Interest rates move opposite treasury bond prices up or down. Listed below is a table of year-to-date returns (YTD)

Dreyfus GNMA Fund: Dreyfus GNMA Fund (Class Z)

| 2001: YTD | 7.69% | 2006: YTD | 3.41 |
| --- | --- | --- | --- |
| 2002 " | 9.02 | 2007 " | 5.83 |
| 2003 | 2.30 | 2008 | 5.47 |
| 2004 | 3.10 | 2009 | 6.03 |
| 2005 | 2.56 | 2010 | 6.48 |

The Federal Reserve buys treasury bonds to fund bank and financial institution bailouts.

This action will set a floor under bond prices over the course of the recession. Interest rates won't rise since the Fed will not want to harm struggling businesses and consumers. In addition, foreign capital will continue to pour into the United States, especially from Europe's weaker economies. Consumers will continue to pay down credit cards depressing consumer spending.

Credit contraction is a deflationary move. This climate bodes well for bonds, the best time in a decade.

In times of crisis, during a crash, buy Treasuries. Later buy U. S. Government obligations and AA corporate bonds: domestic and foreign take over from treasuries. I especially like strong currency European bonds, German, because of their stronger economy. I would also buy Local Currency Foreign bonds for diversification and their safer position, backed by a stronger currency.

In conclusion, I like to emphasize stocks and bonds can coexist in a recessionary portfolio.

## The Holistic Portfolio as of April 24, 2009:

| Position | Percent | Sector |
|---|---|---|
| Cash | 52.4 | Money Market |
| Airgas) | 7.5 | Commodity Chemicals |
| Chesapeake Energy) | 5.5 | Natural gas |
| Energy Conv. Sys.) | 5.6 | Solar panels(flexible) |
| Fuel Sys. Solutions) | 5.0 | Natural gas vehicles, equip. |
| Knight Capital) | 3.0 | Global brokerage |
| Martek Biotech) | 2.5 | DHA/ARA infant nutrition |
| Teva Pharma) | 10.5 | Generic drugs, global |
| Dreyfus Interm. Inc. | 6.2 | Treasury, corporate bonds |
| " Muni Bonds | 1.8 | U.S. municipal short-intm. |

# CHAPTER 31:
# The Tangible Common Stock - A sober friend or an imposter?

Common stocks reflect the sum of all hopes and fears. In many ways their personalities resemble people, the best and worst of investors and traders on a given day, affected by things known and unknown. It's true that news makes the market at given segments over the trading day, and news affect stocks in any number of ways.

Political and macroeconomic events affect most stocks, such as interest rates or recession fears. At least eighty-five percent of stocks rise or fall in step with the winds of change. But what about the other fifteen percent? Are they winners? The answer: those stocks which hold to the character of their group (sector) are winners, and those which fall out of character are losers.

A tangible common stock outperforms its sector. Think Apple or Perrigo because of its creative management providing products that people actually want or need. These stocks lead their group and when the wheel of fortune turns they become better buys. They act according to script and present no ugly surprises when the wheel of fortune turns. Wall Street has a nasty habit of throwing rocks at your darling, a 'truth to tell' moment, so be ready for a surprise. We will explore ways to prevent these nasty surprises and keep those analysts at bay.

Fund managers will tell you to hang it up: why be bothered with Wall Street's wildly ways, existential moments when your fortune may implode. After all, your fund is safely tucked away in a well diversified fund. This is good advice. A good company, its stock, a tangible common stock will bounce back with the market, provided its group or sector remains intact.

A good example of market risk was my investment in Fuel System Solutions, FSYS, a company which converted internal combustion engines into natural gas users. The stock moved with the market, both up and down. An analyst added that the strong dollar would hurt foreign sales and the weak economy would hurt the company. Wall Street analysts put down the stock.

In a few months the market recovered. Fuel Systems came back about fifty percent. Was I worried? No. The economy may be down but it will return. Accumulate more shares of FSYS or your best Core stock when the market recovers. However, keep those bonds. Welcome those downturns, for they allow you to buy additional shares of a tangible common stock, stocks with a predictable character paying a good dividend.

The President means to change our dependence on foreign oil, a spark ignited by President Carter thirty years before. YOU CAN'T DRILL YOUR WAY OUT OF A DOWNTURN. The lack of demand won't allow you. In the middle 1980s gas prices went down and alternate energy projects crawled into hibernation. Remember those ads by T. Boone Pickens during the election of 2008? And Boone is the consummate 'oil man.' Boone believed natural gas and solar heat have a future despite coal and "big oil." As many have said: Do you really want to ship your money to OPEC?

The age of electric hybrid cars have arrived. We're just at the beginning. The idea of "carbon footprints" is being taught in grade school. Do the math. When these kids grow to adulthood they will represent an even louder voice for alternate energy sources. And not only autos but homes will become more energy efficient. Today, office buildings are converting to solar by installing panels on roofs. But enough of this soap box, let's get back to common stocks with character.

What are the attributes of the tangible common stock? Before we begin, let's begin with people. People with strong character hold similar attributes to tangible (durable) common stocks competing in the marketplace. A person who invests emotional sweat into a trade or skill is more reliable than a pretender. Hear from a person I'm sure all of you know, who lives and breathes character from the content of his personality, his movies: Robert De Niro:

"I didn't have a problem with rejection, because when you go into an audition, you're rejected already. There are hundreds of other actors. You're behind the eight ball when you go in there."

"Money makes your life easier. If you're lucky to have it, you're lucky."

> Esquire, "What I've learned"
> January 2003

Earlier I said that stocks which mirror their group have character and those which don't lack character. Sometimes your oil stock won't ride with its oil group, or retail stocks for instance. This stale performance may be company specific. However, most energy stocks will rise with the energy sector as most stores will rise with the retail sector—the most important measure of a stock's character.

Holistic Investing reflects the power of sector investing. Look at small to mid-cap companies in a rising sector. I classify these as cyclical or special situation stocks. In recent recessions, investors who thought that they were "buy and hold" panicked and had dumped stocks out of fear. Mutual funds will tell you to "stay the course." Better yet, stay the course in bond funds and hitch your star to high dividend consumer staple stocks.

The Crash of 2008 destroyed 40% of shareholder value by November. And some investors had fared much worse, i.e., hedge funds, where losses fell into a black hole. In theory, buy and hold works wonderful—in a bull market. But how many individual investors know when the lights go out at the party with the proverbial punch bowl.

Those who dollar-cost averaged in a bear market had their head handed to them. A bad idea. Do this after the recession when the market remains low. Talk of a recovery begins to dominate the news. Anyway, most bottoms trend sideways for awhile. Look for a breakout of your stock to new recovery highs on strong volume. Staying the course may have worked for an old time whaler, steering his schooner into a particular tack before making a run on the whales. And indeed staying the course with your stock portfolio may work for awhile. Yet Bears are tricky animals and they'll return again and again. All markets, from copper to coffee to Yen to pork bellies move in zig-zag fashion, up or down. Likewise, your stock or fund will trend in similar wave patterns.

In the 1980s I determined that bear markets consume around 39.6% of the market cycle (the typical four year presidential cycle). In other words, the market is down or weak some 40% of the time. Of course, the good news is that bull markets run about sixty percent of the time. At the time the study went back over a couple of decades. This means, during these periods, markets will trend sideways at the top or bottom. In the mid to late 1990s an anomaly occurred. The market had risen for five consecutive years with double-digit returns, a once in a century event. Every fund or advisor looked good. Volumes of magazines and fund literature hammered down the virtue of buy and hold. Everyone accepted the mantra until the "Tech Bubble" bust of 2000. The market didn't bottom until October, 2002: a bear market which began in March of 2000. In 2000 the market made an attempt to ride higher but fell short in September, a lower high and forerunner to an ugly February, 2001 when the market cratered. Of course head fakes and false starts continued until 9/11, and afterwards all was lost well into 2002.

There's other worthy attributes to a tangible common stock. Let's spell these out.

A tangible common stock has inherent value, meaning that the company is a going concern, booking sales growth and free cash flow

## THE TANGIBLE COMMON STOCK - A SOBER FRIEND

over time, with little dilution. For example, a speculative biotech start-up may have little or no sales, zero cash flow and tons of start-up costs. This is not a going concern and the FDA may not approve its next "wunderkind" blockbuster. It's better for this company to partner with a drug company, a going concern with deeper pockets of cash.

Pass over the high-flyers.

Another good example of a going concern wannabe are small companies in the mining industry. The company may books sales even if their mining costs are running away at twice its sales, not including overhead, fixed costs. Its stock may be in the bargain basement selling for under a dollar. The problem is that most banks won't touch this company with a ten foot pole.

So what does the company do? It Issues more shares—dilution. Stock dilution is one of the cardinal sins—avoid like the plague. Look out for those companies with shaky balance sheets: debts greater than assets, the result, a dollar stock which can morph into a penny stock.

What is a quick way to spot a durable operating firm. One can log into Marketwatch.com or Yahoo Finance. However, I like to consult Value Line Investment Survey. First determine working capital: current assets less current liabilities. Second, look at a company's long-term debt, debts over one year in duration. Third, subtract a company's long-term debt from its working capital and arrive at a positive number. Good. Working capital should be at least TWICE a company's long-term debt. Value Line displays company's working capital per share and long-term debt over time, as well as its cash flow. Also, and this is important, this service will project a firm's common shares outstanding out into the next three years. You want to see expanding net working capital (working capital less long-term debt) with steady shares outstanding into the next few years.

The above analysis is a "static" picture (an economic concept) as opposed to a dynamic construct. Static numbers represent a given day, usually the end of year or quarter. Dynamic constructs look at stock's value over time, the market, or a chart of the company.

As mentioned earlier in the book, I like to look at a stock's percent growth divided by its PE ratio, looking for a value of 2 or greater. This dynamic only works better in a bull market. Of course, in bear markets most stocks are negative anyway. Luckily, bear markets last forty percent of the time.

But will the net working capital method work in a down market? Maybe. Even if your stock has a large surplus of net working capital, don't jump into it yet. One must ALWAYS look at a chart before buying, or selling. Is your target company flush with net working capital? Good. Is it unloved and trading down at least thirty-eight percent from its prior high? Good. If so, set a target (limit) buy price and wait for the stock to come to you. Why rush and buy at today's price? LET THE MARKET COME TO YOU.

You will appreciate the day when the stock turns higher.

One last point about the Money Flow indicator: a measure of buying pressure from institutions. Money Flow should be trending up confirming upswings in a stock's price. If not, reconsider an alternate candidate. I've seen many stocks on the up-tick with little or no money flow increases. Other indicators may rise, a case of sufficient but not necessary. Money flow must confirm your stock on the way up.

Another essential for a tangible common stock is its ability to run with the dollar. A rising dollar means a stronger economy and a stronger economy is good for stocks. Dollar elasticity will pull cyclical stocks higher.

But natural resource stocks run against the dollar. Energy and mining stocks do better with a weaker dollar. Like gold, these stocks have the built-in elasticity to move against the dollar with ease. Resource stocks have a higher PE ratio, thus more volatile then safe stocks like consumer staples or healthcare for example.

In the old days, before globalization, most stocks were safe because the dollar was strong.

No more. Yes, the dollar remains the world's reserve currency, and crude oil is priced in dollars. And our output of oil and natural gas will only grow over time.

But the perfect storm of dollar de-stabilization remains. For years, the Asians (Japan and China) have run trade surpluses with the United States. We buy their goods and they recycle their surplus dollars back into U.S. Treasuries. Recently, the Chinese have been buying U. S. stocks. No doubt Chinese fund managers are conservative, buying the large caps of U. S. brand-names and European stocks. Lately, the U. S. government has issued over two trillion in economic stimulus monies, unfunded. This means that these new monies, potentially inflationary, can spike prices higher when the economy picks up. Picture an economy floating on a rising tide of devalued currency. The dollar may slide deeper unless we pay down debt. Meanwhile our growing economy attracts more investment from overseas. If not, the Fed may be forced to raises rates quickly, defending the dollar. This 'exit strategy' has been 'sliced and diced' in Congressional hearings and the press. As a result, commodity and gold ETF's have traded higher. An expanding economy can withstand Fed Tapering (Fed buying less treasuries as quantitative easing lessens.)

An astute investor can profit from dollar swings. I look at the dollar/yen relationship. A rising dollar versus the yen implies a rising U. S. Stock market.

(1) When the dollar is strong and rising, raise or buy U.S. stocks and bonds. A stronger dollar is a vote for America. Yes, rates on cash are comatose, near 0 at present (Oct., 2009), but the immediate effect of a stronger dollar erases gains when the dollar was weaker. After the dollar settles down, think about going into stocks unaffected by rate increases, such as the Leisure Sector. For example, I like Marvel Technology or Wynn Resorts. If a weaker dollar is bad for Americans traveling abroad then a stronger dollar would boost travel. Services such as medical or security or data storage firms maintain value longer in a deflationary environment even if their profit margins are squeezed. Wait for the dollar to become more stable before going back into traditional stocks, like industrial and technology companies.

(2) When the dollar turns down, unload bonds and financial stocks. Buy natural resource or commodity companies.

How will you know WHEN the dollar weakens in a meaningful way: When gold outperforms treasuries. Look for new highs on a comparative chart. For instance, I track gold futures vs. T-Notes over 34 weeks. This is a standard relative strength chart. Compare T-Notes to Gold. Look for new lows and highs. Buy gold when Gold hits new highs relative to treasuries or Notes when they hit new highs. Bonds, gold and fear: as termed by the enlightened Dr. J. on CNBC. (8/18/11). Remember, gold pays no dividend.

How do I define a former high? Look on a chart, on the web or in a financial publication: a new high erases prior high in price.

These dollar swings can last for months, and it's better to catch the train early rather than late.

Rarely does the dollar turn on the usual "noise," or meaningless chatter. Bank stocks do better as dollar rises.

Gold trades down when the dollar strengthens and up as the dollar weakens. In addition, Gold trades on physical supply and demand fundamentals. If gold rises from a weak base (look at its prior high and low; add together and divide by two). This median price, high (+) low divided by 2), represents a fair value of sorts. Prices which remain above the median price represent strength, as prices below the median represent weakness. Also, look at Money Flow of the GLD, an ETF that tracks the precious metal. Is Money Flow rising? Then gold is positive.

Another good surrogate is Barrick Gold (ABX) or Newmont Mining (NEM). However, the SPDR Gold Trust (GLD) recently hit a new high but its brother, Market Vectors Gold(GDX) failed to confirm by not hitting a new high, Barron's, P. 26, 9/21/09. That's why it's important to confirm.

Conversely, if gold is falling while bonds are rising then consider buying bonds. Historically, gold and the long bond (30 year Treasuries) move in opposite directions. In the 1970s bonds were losing value from rising inflation and the energy crisis. Gold soared. Some traders referred to bonds as "certificates of confiscation." MOST IMPORTANT: confirm ALL trades with the money flow index. As gold soars to new highs, the money flow index on Barrick Gold and/or Newmont Mining should also hit new highs.

We confirm by looking at the largest gold miners. But on occasion miners and bullion will diverge. But in a strong bull move hardly ever. Barrack and Newmont mining have been in the business for years, the Cadillac and Lincoln of the industry. These companies remained in business, have weathered deflations and severe recessions, wars, merger waves and will continue as global leaders. Stocks by their nature discount future growth so why not have the best discounting mechanism?

Sovereign or central banks buy or sell bullion as other investors. We are speaking billions over a predetermined period. These entities alone can move markets overnight. The good news is that these events are rare. In a strong trend, most banks and institutions will be on your side.

In general, negative 'real' rates are good for gold (the inflation rate subtracted from the short term interest rate, or the Inflation rate greater than the short rate). In the latter 1970s, gold soared as inflation soared.

# CHAPTER 32:
# A Second Look at Sector Funds -Add value to Your Portfolio

Recently I wrote a market letter advocating a better way to invest in mutual or ETF funds.

This novel tool is not the 'buy and hold' mantra of fund managers nor the seat of the pants trading described in those fast talking trading commercials you see on the television. Yes, I have been burned by buy and hold as well as trading like a nervous Nelly in earlier times. I figured that there had to be a better way. I firmly believe that the system described below will keep you in a fund longer, in other words "letting your profits run," but selling when excessive value is reached, kaput, the punch bowl removed. Really, this system is more akin to buy and hold while not being "buy and hold" in the true sense. I believe in trading with the trend, after all, that's where the money is.

Some of you may have mutual funds as your primary investment. That's OK, but over time as your knowledge of the market expands, and you should consider more risk, at first in small increments: common stocks. Common stocks appreciate and depreciate faster than funds; they move more quickly and will outperform the funds both in up and down markets. This is called beta. That is, if the S & P 500 is considered 1, and your favourite stock, as valued by your broker has a beta of 1.37, then your stock will, on average, move 1.37 times faster than the S & P.

Mutual funds need no beta (price rate of change) because of their inherent diversification. They're more conservative than stocks and safer. The Holistic Portfolio reconciles this and considers funds as an adjunct to your portfolio, especially the bond funds combined with cash. As a comparison, core stock should carry a low beta because of their mid-cap value status. However, don't compare stock and funds. I consider core stocks alpha stocks because they rise more slowly in up markets and fall less in down markets. Most dividend stocks carry a lower beta. Funds: mutual or ETF, move like alpha stocks. And mutual fund equity sectors won't perform as good as ETF's because you can buy or sell during the trading day. By contrast, mutual funds sell at settlement at end of trading day.

Sadly, mutual funds can't be traded intra-day. But this doesn't affect me because of my long term bond positions which provide more ballast to the portfolio. As a rule, I trade ETF's, like the Brazil or Singapore Funds when beneficial. Their beta price swings are less, on average than the S&P 500. Equity sector funds are the domain of ETF's because of the advantages described above. You can zero in on economic and nation sectors.

Exchange Traded Funds trade like stocks. Aside from paying a broker's commission, an ETF's beta resembles their mutual fund cousins. But the problem with them is that they reset their capital weighted portfolio at the end of the day which can impair returns. If your luck runs away, trading ETFs in a thin or sideways market may dampen your financial health.

There is another way to buy mutual funds. Play it safe. NEVER buy equity mutual funds in a trading range market. If the market, DJI or S&P"s high hasn't been breached and the low not breached on the downside, don't buy equity mutual funds. Eventually a range-bound market will give way to a bull or bear market. Once this happens, buy. Buy when weekly price closes above 10 week weighted moving average/10WMA>price. Look for the closing price greater than the ten- week average. Why?

# A SECOND LOOK AT SECTOR FUNDS

Because the 10 week average is the same as the 50 day moving average, a very important threshold. This threshold visible on a chart serves as a threshold for stocks and ETF's. If stock price sells down to the 10 week and recovers, it should bounce back up to original position. If not, consider selling.

For example, let's say you have a $10,000 portfolio. You want to buy into a fund that you've been tracking. Initially, go in with $250-$500. Play it close to the vest. Prior to your investment decision, you should have a positive picture (relative strength comparisons) on the overall market and sector. Questions: Has the market bottomed or traded down to a level considered oversold?

In other words, has your fund traded down from its high down to its 30 week moving average (200 day moving average)? Has it moved sideways along the bottom? These are classic signs a stock has bottomed. Buy closing price above 10 week moving average. As average changes, your fund should remain above it. As the average changes, you must reset your buy targets.

Wait for a breakout above its sideways channel (high minus low) over an extended period.

And if this occurs, buy. We buy small at first because we want to buy more later, the layered approach. Meaning, we buy in small increments on the way up. Rather than dump all your money into a fund, like betting on red or black, or odd or even at the casino; we buy in small increments. An unlike a casino, a stock or funds will move with the trend, taking its time, rather than caving to an all or nothing game in Vegas: a real loser.

Mutual funds, especially Vanguard because of their low cost, have been telling investors that index funds have many qualities. And this was true—in a buy and hold world. But because of market volatility, indexing doesn't work anymore. In a bull market institutions buy the indexes on the way up, or a basket of stocks in predetermined "buy programs." And likewise, sell on the way down. But the market doesn't go up forever. The funds will counter my argument because indexes have beaten money managers. This is true. So they will suggest that you should "buy bonds for safety." Good advice. But a bear market will arrive, on average once every four years, and in some cases, even bonds will lose value, especially if rates spike.

The Holistic Portfolio has an answer. Keep CASH AND STRONG CURRECNY BOND funds at forty to sixty percent AT ALL TIMES.

At the very beginning of this book I wrote: If you can't beat the market with half of your money than you have no business losing the rest of it.

Another truth that your index fund company won't tell you is that in a vicious bear market a regular balanced fund ( stocks, bonds and cash) will beat an index fund of stocks. An index fund will beat you on the way up and will fall more on the way down. ALL funds fall in a bear market…except CASH and treasuries.

I've developed a way to win in stable markets. Granted, an index fund will outperform in a strong bull market. Mostly, the market will drift higher or lower, sometimes without rhyme or reason, trend-less over an extended period.

I look at sector funds compared to a benchmark. Sector funds are a way to add value to your portfolio. How? Because at any given time a sector funds(value, growth, foreign, financial services, energy/natural resources, health, technology, bonds, etc.) may be doing better than its benchmark: the Dreyfus Peoples 500 of the Dreyfus Family of Funds.

The Peoples 500 is patterned after the S & P 500, the benchmark for stocks. In short, if your sector fund, say technology outperforms the Peoples Index, good. How do we determine this? We Divide the weekly close of the Dreyfus Technology Fund by the Peoples 500, as denominator, or: Dreyfus Technology/Dreyfus 500= x. Do this on a weekly closing basis.

Weekly closes eliminate the noise of day to day price swings.

Let's say that the Invesco Endeavour Fund closes at 8 on Friday and the Dreyfus 500 closes at 24, for a value of .333(8/24) for week 1. In the following week the Endeavour Fund closes at 8.50 and the Dreyfus 500 closes at 24.25, for a value of .3505(8.5/24.25). This means that the Endeavour Fund is gaining ground on the index. I track this input over a variety of sectors. The good news is that once a fund outperforms an index its momentum will continue for awhile. The broad market may be going nowhere, but you're making money. As in any new strategy, I advise starting small and building up larger positions later.

Now for some buy and sell rules:

(1) Buy at a new high, sector divided by an index base, or add to position in increasing smaller multiples:
$500 – $250 – $125, etc., three equal diminishing additions only.
(2) Over the weekend track closing prices of eight (8) sectors and make your buy decision by Monday.
Make sure your sector is strong Monday morning.
DO NOT TRADE ON FRIDAY IF VOLATILITY
IS HIGH (stocks moving up or down 100 points or more.
(3) Sell when value falls below market averages.

I should add that an on-line chart will help. Chart your sector (stock symbol). Compare it with the S & P 500. Is your sector trending higher? Run Bollinger Bands (indicator menu) and make sure price of fund remains within the band, not overvalued.

Sector investing involves keeping a weekly log(weekly closes) of at least eight sector funds INCLUDING the Dreyfus Peoples' 500 Fund weekly close. Eight sector funds can cut across different mutual funds. More than eight may become tedious.

Actually, a good weekend newspaper should contain all the prices you need, otherwise you can go online. I go to Yahoo.com/stocks/chart/historical quotes and type in stock symbol and dates: Monday -Friday arriving at the week's activity. Buy or sell on rules given above.

For example, I track four Invesco funds: Asia Pacific, Gold, Financial/Endeavour Services and Energy and four Dreyfus funds: International Bond, Strategic Value, Natural Resources and Technology

# HOLISTIC INVESTING IN A RISK-AVERSE WORLD

Growth funds. The Dreyfus Peoples 500 is a good surrogate for the S. & P 500 Index. Below is a format you can use:

## Sector Fund Analysis
### Sector vs. Dreyfus 500
### Week ended:

| Week M-Thur | High | Low | Close | 3 Week Low | New High | Ratio |
|---|---|---|---|---|---|---|
|  |  |  |  |  |  |  |
| Peoples 500 |  |  |  |  |  |  |
|  |  |  |  |  |  |  |
| Invesco Sectors |  |  |  |  |  |  |
|  |  |  |  |  |  |  |
| Dreyfus Sectors |  |  |  |  |  |  |
|  |  |  |  |  |  |  |
| A Visual history of Fund Sector Analysis: October, 2009: | | | | | | |
|  |  |  |  |  |  |  |
| Date Sector | High | Lo | Close | 3 Wk Lo | High | Ratio |
| Wk.10/5 Invesco Asia | 22.22 | 22.06 | 21.85 | Buy | Close near HI: Yes | .759 |
| "Gold | 7.70 | 7.35 | 7.35 | 7.35 |  | .251 |
| Finance | 7.74 | 7.40 | 7.40 | 7.40 |  | .253 |
| "Energy | 33.72 | 32.39 | 32.39 | 32.39 |  | 1.11 |
|  |  |  |  |  |  |  |
| DREYFUS 500 | 30.18 | 29.24 | 29.24 |  |  |  |
|  |  |  |  |  |  |  |
| Drey.Int'l Bd. | 16.15 | 16.05 | 16.05 | 16.05 |  | .549 |
| Nat'l. Resource | 21.83 | 20.92 | 20.92 | 20.92 |  | .715 |
| "Strtg. Value | 24.33 | 23.55 | 23.55 | 23.55 |  | .805 |
| "Tech. | 23.06 | 22.28 | 22.28 | 22.28 |  | .762 |
|  |  |  |  |  |  |  |

| Wk 10/12 Invesco Asia | 22.99 | 22.42 | 21.42 | | | .736 Hold |
|---|---|---|---|---|---|---|
| "Gold | 8.23 | 7.58 | 8.19 | 7.35 | | .270 |
| "Financial | 7.87 | 7.56 | 7.87 | 7.40 | | .258 |
| "Energy | 34.99 | 32.96 | 34.93 | 32.39 | | .106 |
| | | | | | | |
| DREYFUS 500 | 30.44 | 29.54 | 30.44 | | | |
| Drey Int'l Bd. | 16.45 | 16.24 | 16.31 | 16.05 | | .536 |
| "Nat'l Resource | 22.75 | 21.34 | 22.70 | 20.92 | Near High | .745 |
| "Strtg.Val. | 24.74 | 23.89 | 24.74 | 23.55 | Yes | .773 |
| "Tech. | 23.48 | 22.54 | 23.48 | 22.28 | | .732 |
| | | | | | | |
| Wk 10/19 Invesco Asia | 23.32 | 21.85 | 22.90 | | | .735 |
| "Gold | 8.35 | 8.21 | 8.21 | 7.58 | | .263 |
| "Financial | 8.15 | 7.86 | 8.13 | 7.40 | Near High | .261 |
| "Energy | 36.52 | 35.21 | 36.52 | 32.39 | Hold | 1.04 |
| | | | | | | |
| DREYFUS 500 | 31.15 | 30.49 | 31.15 | | | |
| | | | | | | |
| Drey.Int'l Bd | 16.51 | 16.36 | 16.46 | 16.05 | Low | .528 |
| "Nat'l Res. | 23.69 | 22.93 | 23.69 | 20.92 | Close at High Hold | .760 |
| "Strtg.Val. | 25.44 | 24.77 | 25.44 | 23.55 " | Yes | .817 |
| "Tech. | 23.99 | 23.55 | 23.91 | 22.28 | | .767 |

The illustration of Sector Fund Analysis determines buy, hold and sell rules. Relative Strength analysis on a chart web site (Bigcharts.com) will give you the same results of these funds.

This flies in the face of buy and hold, but after March of 2000 and October of 2007 the above would have beaten 'buy and hold.' BUT

REMEMBER. The above comparisons work best in a BULL MARKET. Bear Market: BONDS. Look at chart. Is price greater than 10 week moving-average. Good. The enigma of mutual fund investing is selling. WHEN do I sell?

Holding on for dear life can be very costly in a bear market. Selling or quitting does not mean giving up, or losing. It's about avoiding disaster and waiting to "play another day." This strategic decision is like regrouping for a future advance on the battlefield. The battle is not won by the biggest, as history has proven time after time. THE BATTLE IS WON BY THE SWIFTEST AND THE SMARTEST. Set limit Mental Sell by Friday's close.

The Holistic Portfolio has approximately 19.4% of capital in mutual funds. As I explained, when the market goes down, the funds will fall less. But when the market rises, your fund positions will add more value to your overall portfolio because of Sector Fund Analysis. The above system does address the SELL problem squarely. If your fund falls below its three (3) week low and/or underperforms S &P 500(Dreyfus 500), then exit trade. No questions asked. When buying, wait for a New High in your sector during a bull market, buying when your sector outperforms the Dreyfus 500. And let your profits run. Good luck.

# CHAPTER 33:
# Piquing the Apocryphal Pale - Beware the New Pharisees

The new Pharisee promises trading profits of 10,000 % if you pay a hefty tuition and take his course trading in fake money. Of course the program rests on control conditions of preordained outcomes as a learning tool. However, real day trading chart patterns, a basic tool of these programs become impacted by numerous real time events which have no predecessor. Breaking news, unique in nature, make up the emotional fuel which feeds the market, from stocks to soybeans, approaching an almost infinite variety of events and outcomes. Headline news: Europe concerns, the China central bank, Brazilian sugar or coffee output, terrorism, earnings, strikes and nationalizations by foreign governments, etc. make up a polyglot list of possibilities which affect markets on a daily basis. The old Pharisees sold snake oil to cure rheumatism from covered wagons.

Here is the latest epistle from Barron's: "Over the next 20 years, the U. S. Economy is likely to grow only 2% a year. This is down from the 3% or better since World War II"....... (Cover, "The Small Economy, October, 28, 2013.) This is the latest example from a most respected source. The above no doubt refers to our debt overhang but also from accelerated aging of the population and lower productivity gains in the future. Frankly, I don't see the next "Dreamliner" coming out of India or advanced energy technology hailing from China. Immigration reform can unlock more working age population in the United States, surely, not an option for India or China. Forget about Japan, where their economy is in advanced stages of aging. America will continue to outperform Europe, the world's largest economy. Time published an article in the early 2000 (5/22/2000) espousing the virtues of the Dow Jones Industrials hitting 50,000. Outrageous as this may seem, publishers and talk shows made a lot of noise over this fortuitous event as accepted truth. The market had topped in March of that year. The book's theme was that earnings would power the market and spur it to the new reality. Reality? Even after five years of double digit gains beginning in 1995 the Dow badly missed Dow 50,000 by a mile. By the millennium, the Dow was 40,000 points BELOW Dow 50,000.

Since then, the Dow rolled over, again, painfully dropping all the way down to the bear market bottom in October, 2002: the longest bear market since the Great Depression. Rightfully, the pundits laughed at Dow 50,000 later as a stale cocktail joke, probably the same pundits who sang the same hosannas after the book's publication. More than a few souls must had hinged their pocketbooks to the nonsense. No doubt those books on Dow 50,000 made their way to garage sales. Beware of the New Pharisee.

We live in a frenzied news society spewing out of the web and CNN by the minute. You as Holistic investor must cultivate a critical eye and ear to the noise. Yes, most of it is just useless and maybe three percent may affect your portfolio. Yes, buying gas and filling up your car is a good idea before a hurricane hits the Gulf coast or Libyan oil fields fall into unknown hands.

News runs by the minute, blaring away on tweets, cable news, talk radio and recapped later on the nightly news. I believe the lower you descend into the news food chain the worst it gets, the absolute worst being afternoon talk radio. Almost anything gets aired, stuff like the world is going to end(May, 2011) and Dow 50,000.

Cable ushered in the over-communicated society. Today, train engineers and airline pilots send (text) messages, including millions of drivers speeding along the interstate and freeways in rush hour. Thousands of lives lost needlessly. Living for the moment in the fast lane may be exciting only for a moment, maybe the last. Many others just want to stop the wheels and get off.

The 1960s and 1970s were all about 'being real,' a return to nature: Mean what you say. In college we had read Walt Whitman and Henry Thoreau. Along came the 1980s and all was swept away. The Decade of Greed as depicted by the movie Wall Street arrived in 1987, just in time for the Crash.

Yesterday was all about the culture of greed. Today technology is driving the culture. The New Mass Man has morphed into the New Mass Technocrat in the names of Bill Gates and the late Steve Jobs.

Meanwhile, obesity and illiteracy grow among the young, along with unemployment. Debt has gone down a little, a good sign, yet many remain pessimistic.

Yet I remain confident we'll pull out or our morass—but first we need an emotional face lift, like the Beatles in 1964. History moves in waves and rhythms. Think Joan of Arc, Winston Churchill, and JFK. They were able to rally their nations out of the dungeons of despair. We await a cosmic spark to roll America forward.

Let's not forget Madison Ave. Most of us watch television despite the web and smart phones. What may trend for the moment in cyber space will be ancient history tomorrow.

Do you really want to watch your favourite show on an I Phone? Maybe if you're stuck on an airplane. The men in grey flannel suits now open their shirt collars, extolling a new message. Ad men remain an influence, though their impact may diminish over time because of social media.

I get a kick out of watching Mad Men, about the advertising world of the 1960s. The bad old days of secretaries brewing coffee for the boss and wet pompadours of Happy Days are gone.

One time we sailors hailed a cab in New York's Grand Central to Penn Station, a short ride. We tipped the cabby a dollar. I'll always remember what the cabby said on that warm summer afternoon: "Hey guys, can you afford it?" Ha. Making just over 100 bucks a month on petty officer's pay was no picnic. They were the happy days.

Fast forward to the summer of 2008. The economy was reeling from the real estate mess while the market sank into a sinkhole. The election campaign reminded us of the new reality–lower expectations. No one expected the unexpected: an era of de-levering was about to begin, everyone paying down debt including state and local government. The consumer culture, as we knew it, was coming to an end. The market began belching the bile from decades of cheap money, un-regulation and its old time religion, greed. Not since 1929 had a financial meltdown blind-sided world financial capitals.

Unlike Black Tuesday, the Crash of 2008 was a global event unfolding by the second.

Money blipped electronically from the taps of keyboards in Hong Kong to London, panic breeding on panic. And unlike 1987, this financial crash ushered in a new age of unemployment, rising to 10%. Fate ordered the presidential candidates to Washington to confer with the Bush Administration. And making matters worse, all those millions of out-source jobs in the 2000s came back to bite those responsible: ah for the sake of cost.

The Holistic Portfolio dropped 9% from July 4th to Labor Day. Actually, the portfolio hit an intra-day high on June 23rd 2008 after a market top in October, 2007. By mid September, the market collapsed well into double-digit numbers. Nonetheless, no one can predict the day, not even the week of a calamity on Wall Street.

Financial crashes occur once every half century. Your portfolio may be down in paper value but if you have good core stocks as explained previously, you'll be back with a vengeance.

Take heart that America will rebound because of its innate creativity.

Nathan Rothhild, Europe's famous banker of the 19th century, was believed to have acted upon the following: it's believed he had spoken these famous words in the Age of Napoleon: 'Buy when there's blood on the streets.' As gruesome as this portends, it's true. I remember fund managers the Tuesday after Black Monday (10/20/87) buying in a feeding frenzy the day after the October 19th crash. Big buying opportunities don't come often. When they do, be ready. Let me express a motto that says all: In Omnia Paratus (Ready for all), from my alma mater.

Buying opportunities of stocks:

(1) When stock price chart displays tight pattern (no violent up-downs).
(2) Rising Free Cash Flow as a percent of Sales.
(3) PVG: Price Growth YTD greater than 2 times PE Ratio (price earnings ratio)
(4) Rising Weekly Money Flow Index confirmed by rising Slow Stochastic
(5) Weekly Close (closing price) above 10 week WMA (weighted moving average)

Consider above attributes after a major bear market bottom.

Risk taking gone wrong was a feature of a morning CNBC show. The report was about CALPERS, or the California Public Employees Retirement System. More than one-third of its multibillion value was lost in the events of the fall of 2008. Not only CALPERS had fallen victim but Ivy League universities also fell victim to the tsunami from their portfolio of exotic investments.

Falling endowments made matters worse by pinching operating budgets. It seems that the only survivors were those holding boring investments, plain vanilla stocks paying good dividends, bonds and cash.

In the fall of 2008, financials and their derivatives, commodities and real estate assets led the way down. And hard asset believers, gold and silver stocks, became non believers. A crash ushers in deflation from wiping out all those equity values. Office complexes, gas and oil drillers and other commodity stocks tied to the land tumbled. However, gold bullion and precious coins held on, after lying comatose for a decade. Yet the real value of coins, adjusted for inflation remained lower than the S & P 500. Coins pay no dividends. Common stocks pay dividends that will cushion downside risk. This is one of the principal reasons I advocate mid-cap value stocks with growth potential. Corporate bonds rated double A or better add value in a bear market.

Bullion pays no dividends and has storage fees while common stocks automatically adjust to inflation.

Who are the new Pharisees?: the subject of this chapter. I DEFINE THIS FORM OF ELECTRONIC AND DIGITAL BARKING AS ENGINEERED TRUTH BEFORE BEING BAPTISED BY REALITY.

Advertisers and politicians are its most frequent purveyors. And watch out for the BLOGGERS.

Politicians are also guilty of "spin." putting a good face on an embarrassment.

Ever hear the fast-talking automaton voice explaining interest rate charges or drug side effects (after the commercial)? Now you know what I mean. Of course it sounds like a blur—that's the idea. These blurs really detract from a product, dampening its credibility. And believe it, the longer the fast-talking buzz, the worse the product. For if an advertiser knocks himself out selling his snake oil, run to the nearest exit.

Remember when you were a kid? The New Jersey State Fair had its large freak show tent every year. A fast talking barker, if you will, would always bring in a crowd. After paying admission, we were herded inside for the show, the management making sure to fill up the tent.

Things haven't really changed, only the players and the technology. The medium, or way you get white noise from these hucksters of late night TV, not unlike those one size fits all blogs would trigger a dash for the remote. Thank God for the mute button. Do you really need all these facts? After awhile, the overload will begin kicking out the old nonsense.

Getting back to the state fair, I liked the military and industrial exhibits the best.. Even if those fat hogs in the farming exhibit were funny, the rides and the sausage sandwiches were the best.

This is another example of analyst buzz. After a 199 point gain on Monday, 10/29/09, a news show reported on the three best investment ideas of 2010: the "Power Play for Today" would tweak some eyebrows of the serious investor. Haven't you heard this before: "If we break below 1042 on the S & P...." Is the market going to tank, again? Probably not. What about: "A psychological effect to this…" Are traders seeing their shrinks?

So. That's what the market does. What about: "the dollar and the market will get it." Get what?

By the way, the market dropped over 200 points the following day. And, of course, continued higher later.

The lesson to be learned is this. Be wary of loose opinions from television and talk radio. Be MOST wary of bloggers. The chatter often contradicts each other. Be wary of some articles from newspapers and magazines. Often, its author may have an axe to grind, or an ideological agenda. Yes, some analysts and writers are good and deserve to be read. And the facts of an article may prove right and move an investment. Cultivate a critical mind set. Be comfortable with whose advice you accept.

I used to attend stockholder meetings and seminars with optimism. Sure, the management would report results to their advantage. It's their right and I can't blame them. They will take a positive spin from a down quarter, such as reporting on an improving book to bill ratio, improving cash flow, or launch of a stock repurchase program. These are good things. But if the stock continues to go down, then something else is wrong.

I found that the management team is one of the most powerful influences in a company's stock price. Everything may be in place, but if management isn't honest, why hang around?

How can you determine management's integrity? There's a couple of ways to this:

(1) Does management believe in the company? Are they holding material information? Of course this applies more to a small company. In large companies material information is a foot note in their annual report.

(2) Is management pro-active? Do they get ahead of problems? Is their website active with pronouncements? Are they really trying to get their story out?

(3) A rock-solid way to determine the integrity of management is the debt-to- equity ratio. Is it low? Is it less than one-third of capital? Good. The Lower long-term debt is to capital, including equity, the better. High debt can lead to share dilution. Bad.

If a company is always borrowing, sooner or later they will have to issue more shares to raise cash.

(4) Lastly, watch out for convertible securities. Convertible bonds or preferred stock can dilute common shares. Once a company proposes to issue these determine its scope, if excessive (from 25-50% of capital, head for the exits. I wouldn't advise selling tomorrow. Act, never react. A time will come when you should consider selling. It may be your luck that the stock may be in a temporary uptrend.

This concludes the chapter on identifying the new Pharisees. White noise is all about source.

If the source is credible, then its information may help. However, the standard sound bites are really no different that the stuff you read on most web pages, blogs, afternoon talk radio and late night TV commercials. Get the remote and flip the channel. Turn the dial of your car radio to avoid the same old, same old. Do yourself a favour.

However, I consider some advertising as art, or its close cousin. I love the GEICO commercials, a far cry from the early efforts before cable. I remember the late 'Hoss' Cartwright from Bonanza kicking that Chevy truck years ago. Now that was a vote for Chevrolet.

# CHAPTER 34:
# Avoid Commodity Products "A never ending Greek Tragedy"

The above quotation is from Peter Lynch, the former fund manager of the famous Fidelity Magellan Fund. He referred to flash memory chips and their continual price declines from market competition. Lower price means lower revenue. Falling product prices means a company will have to produce more if it wants to meet sales goals. It's like running faster just to stay even.

Commodity products aren't necessarily commodities, such as coal, timber, oil and gasoline.

A commodity can become incorporated into a product by containing food such as potato chips, bread, clothes, shoes, tobacco or wine. In addition, commodities distinguish themselves in price behaviour from services, like medical or software. Services are less affected from price declines.

Professional services keep rising in price.

Competitive pressures lowers price. If more manufactures enter a given industry, product price will decline. Another reason for price decline is because of globalization (lower costs from developing countries).

Remember a generation ago when cassette tapes were replaced by CD's replaced by DVD's replaced by Blue Ray's. Every time a new technology enters a market prices of existing technologies fall.

Studios and recording artists were paid full value for hit songs. Music Television, better known as MTV began to broadcast recordings and studio dance scenes. Overnight this morphed into a new dimension for Hollywood, later spawning entertainment channels and of course American Idol.

By the '90s, knock-off copies of CDs poured out of Asia in the millions for a fraction of their original value. The studios and artists sued for intellectual property rights which had taken years to settle–a prime example of commodity overload. Later, downloads from web sites into smart- phones changed the music business forever.

The entertainment industry has fought the down-loaders and won some important cases.

However, the Chinese continued to flood hundreds of millions of knock-off copies into the world including Elton John, The Beatles, The Rolling Stones, and "The Boss," Bruce Springsteen. It takes a very long time to settle global copyright infringement matters, the CD black market.

The automobile industry has become a commodity market of sorts. Brand name isn't what it used to be. Most foreign cars are made here and the designers and engineers are American.

Remember the early Korean cars? In a word: awful. These were cheap, unreliable and unsafe. I know. I hit one of them at an intersection, lucky for me no one sat in the passenger side. A red car cut in front of me, I swerved to the left and hit the rear panel, damaging the entire side. A friend of mine told me later that the Korean car was a "throw away car." In any event, even though the Korean cars have improved, domestic cars are hurt by the glut of foreign cars, including those better quality Japanese and German cars made here. Again, competition.

The U. S. market share has dropped drastically. G.M. and Chrysler had declared bankruptcy, not withstanding a weak economy.

# AVOID COMMODITY PRODUCTS "A NEVER ENDING GREEK TRAGEDY"

However, Ford has weathered the storm, its stock rising from roughly 2 to around 12 dollars a share (Ford had not received any government bailout because of better management). However, their debt position is precarious.

The most poignant example of the new commodity product is real estate, especially residential. Remember the residential 2 percent "teaser loans" at the height of the real estate bubble in 2005. At the time speculators were "flipping" houses bought low into a handsome profit a few days later. The government wanted everyone to own the American dream. The trouble was perception: real estate never goes down. Get in before the price goes higher.

Meanwhile, cheap money and foreign capital fuels the fires of easy credit. Builders scrambled into the fray by buying land, erecting more homes, shopping centers, office parks and condos.

Of course the music stopped. The market peaked in the summer of 2006; cracked in 2007; crashed in 2008. Today homes and commercial real estate have barely recovered, another generation baptized in the sins of Wall Street and the easy buck of Main Street. Beware. When anyone can get it, walk away from it. Life isn't meant to be easy.

Besides a housing glut, another cause of products falling into commodity hell is obsolescence.

Remember all those electronic gizmos of an earlier decade or two? Their value only resides in a collector's whim. TV's without remote have become worthless. And what about those clunker Ford Explorers: the most popular trade-in of the "cash for clunkers" program?

I remember a quotation from an accounting text book when in college: an automobile is on an irresistible march to the junk yard. The subject was about depreciation. In fact, any product except water will be marching off to an untimely demise. Obsolescence has become more rabid in a global economy because of lower costs and emerging market demand—a rising middle class.

In an earlier time, the 19th century up until the 2nd World War, product durability prevailed.

Cars and radios went to the repair shop, lawn mowers and washing machines hung around for years. The term "planned obsolescence" was coined in the 1950s. Detroit was blamed for making cars which would break down after a few years. I believe Hank Williams Jr. sang a song including in part that a Chevy should last about ten years. I see old Chevy trucks on the road all the time. The other day a guy at the gas station pulled in front of me with a 1972 Chevy truck.

GM currently advertises: "Chevy runs deep." Yes, we get the message.

Wear and tear, the depreciation of fixed assets is a businessman's best friend. Copyright and goodwill amortization is the same thing, the writing off an intangible asset. The IRS has shorten the life spans of fixed assets—the various methods of accelerated depreciation—to reflect faster write-offs. I used to write off my computer in 5-7 years, today their cost basis meets the ordinary expense category of one year because of low price and obsolescence.

Handheld calculators can be bought at the dollar store. Ten years ago a premium Texas Instrument handheld calculator would cost over two hundred dollars. Scientific innovation and offshore production in low wage countries have plunged these toys way down in price.

In 1971 services (information technology, medical), etc. had surpassed manufacturing as a larger slice of GDP. The Information Age was born. Today manufacturing accounts for around one-fifth of GDP. However, I think that will change: upwards.

Health care and IT remain at the forefront of the service economy. Mobile smartphones drive the information society. It used to be the PC. Google, with their new android system has gained traction. Google aims to go head-to-head with Apple. As for enterprise software, Google new operating system will make inroads into Microsoft's Windows 7. One wonders if the weak economy can absorb these wonderful products.

One final word. Technological marvels don't last long. But one must buy these gadgets to keep up. Enjoy the ride while it lasts, like a hit song. And yes, even Apple's best smartphone or Amazon's kindle

## AVOID COMMODITY PRODUCTS "A NEVER ENDING GREEK TRAGEDY"

reader will become just another commodity product. But watch out, Apple TV is coming. The beat goes on. The grim reaper of yesterday now gets a face lift from faster innovation.

A classic example of Joseph Shumpeter's 'Gail of Creative Destruction': obsolescence.

# CHAPTER 35:
# The Future of Holistic Investing Israel: A Powerhouse of Value

Why Israel, a small country with no resources surrounded by enemies? Because Israel has a nation's most important resource: knowledge, fostered by a culture driven by questioning its authority, and change, for its very existence: survival. Israel remains a culture tested in the cauldron of turmoil through the millennia as interpreted from the Talmud: centuries of rabbinic thought and Scriptural Writings.

Israel nurtures a peerless society reminding one of the Greek city-states of old. The nation had prospered because its people have answered in crisis and war, remembering their ancestors who lived and fought similar battles in their sliver of sand, arid and mountainous, sometimes at the mercy of their next door neighbor.

In the time of Joseph it was all about pestilence and food. As a boy, Joseph was tricked into slavery by his brothers because his father showered more attention on the younger son. Eventually Joseph's ingenuity reached the attention of Pharaoh who later allowed the Israelites to migrate to Egypt and avoid hunger. Many years later Moses led his people out of a different Egypt courting ruin from an uncompromising Pharaoh.

The centuries had proved hostile to the wandering nation fighting its way at every turn, Joshua defeating the Canaanites at the famous Battle of Jericho, an ancient city on the present day West Bank. Centuries later the Romans arrived under Augustus. Roman and Jewish Law prevailed side by side until about 65 A.D. at the time of the Jewish Uprising. In 70 A.D. the Romans decided to destroy the Temple in Jerusalem, brick by brick, according to the ID Channel (Investigative Discovery), Story of Jesus: Who Was He (9/4/11). Judea was no more, and a mass migration left for new settlements primarily in central and Eastern Europe where many remain despite the savage cruelties of W.W.II.

By mid Twentieth Century hundreds of thousands resettled Israel. A miracle transformation turned the dessert into orange groves, vegetable gardens and the seeds of light industry. Today, Israel has become a powerhouse of science, medicine, biotechnology and computer software.

Since 1948, this nation has taken its rightful place in a world reaching toward global solutions, a border-less world of trade and law. In fact, many of its citizens hail from places other than Europe. Immigration has helped Israel from a people wishing to start over to better oneself.

Despite Israel's border disputes and wars, the nation continues to grow stronger and better in a national cohesion and pride of work ethic. Visitors to the Holy Land will find this land, this people most welcoming as America was in the 19th century.

Start-up companies born in Israel, given a second chance in down periods, have become global leaders in their field: Teva Pharmaceuticals, Perrigo and Nice Systems of which I had owned. At present, I own Opko Health which was formerly Prolor Biotech. Just this week Opko sold Sorento, a testing company for $22m. (12/17/13). In 2009, Opko bought Sorento for much lower.

Start-up companies can become successful companies because failure in Israel isn't necessarily a bad thing. Knowledge gained from failure can bequeath dividends of profit down the road if put to better use. This phenomenon was artfully explained in Start -Up Nation by Dan Senor and Saul Singer, 12 (Twelve), Hachette Book Group, 2009. By comparison, in the United States real economic progress hadn't arrived until the onset of the railroad in the 1830s, some fifty years since the founding of the republic in 1787. After the Civil War an industrial transformation had taken hold, ushering in the telegraph, the telephone, oil discovery and later the automobile. By 1900 America had 100 million people, mostly from European immigrants itching to live a new life and to make a buck. Every nation has a growth cycle as America was the emerging economy of the nineteenth and early twentieth century.

Today Israel, Brazil, China and India are the emerging economies of the twenty-first century.

More Israeli companies are listed on the NASDAQ than European companies combined.

One of the more exciting stories of Israeli technological tenacity is Intel, the Silicon Valley giant as told in above book. By 1980 Intel's Haifa team designed the 8088 microchip, capable of 4.77 megahertz, transistors spinning at almost five times per second. On the heels of the breakthrough IBM designed the first PC for office and home. A few years later NEC and COMPAQ developed their own personal computers. By 1986 Intel's Israel's operation was making the 386 chip, smaller and faster than its predecessor. Some believed computer chips would become twice as fast and half its size every eighteen to twenty-four months (Gordon Moore, one of Intel's founders). By 2000, Moore's Law ran into a snag as chips indeed were becoming smaller, faster but also generating more heat. Overheated chips crashed computers as mine had a couple of years ago (a friend of mine installed a new powerful "mother board," and installed an additional fan—problem solved. However, laptops were another story. No fans. A power-curve problem ensued, the more power the more heat generated.

Meetings had taken place between the Israeli team and the engineers at Santa Clara. A novel solution was required. A race car analogy arose whereby if one can change gears slowing the engine can one run the car faster? Until then computer clock speed was the standard for more power. The problem demanded novel thinking. The Israeli team was going back and forth between Tel Aviv and California, brainstorming in heated sessions, attacked the "clock speed" sacred cow. At one point Intel wanted to cancel the partnership but Dov Frohman, the founder of Intel Israel, persevered. He created a new culture in addressing the problem: "fear of loss often proves more powerful than the hope of gain." He later went on to state that if you've weren't aware that people in your organization disagreed with you, then you're in trouble. Over time the Israelis showed that slowing down clock speed to 2.8 gigahertz (just over half of the reining Pentium chips for desktops at the time, 2003) had solved the problem. It paved the way for the Centrino chip—the breakthrough which would power future laptops. It sold for more than twice the price of desktops; however, portability was achieved without crashes from overheating. This new "architecture" opened the door for Intel with sales growth of 13 percent from 2003 to 2005.

By 2006 the Core 2 Duo replaced the Pentium, validating Israeli's concept of "right-turn" architecture, plus a new application called dual-core processing, at even faster chip speeds.

An unsung dividend can be noted from these breakthroughs. Intel's John Skinner figured that the company saved 22 million 100 watt bulbs, everyday, or an additional $2 billion in costs, similar to a "small number of coal-fired power plants or taking a few million cars off the road."

This gutted costs in most offices, a savings thanks to Israel's lead of bending the power curve.

The story of Israel was its struggle for survival. But the new story of Israel is one of technological innovation, an innovation nurtured from service in the military. It all begins at the age of seventeen, when all Israel youth, male and female, report to a recruiting station before reaching eighteen, when subject to draft. The Israel Defence Forces

(IDF) adhere to a democratic culture within unit command. A soldier will follow his superior into battle with full respect.

Personal responsibility allows for a "constructive failure" provided it leads to improvement. This Spartan like army allows a private to question his leader in battle.

Soldiers aren't identified by rank but respected by their attributes: what they do best. A very important element in the command structure is trust and leadership: will you follow your commander into the jaws of hell? This isn't to say that a unit sits around debating a plan before attacking. A commander would have already proven himself, otherwise his patrol wouldn't exist. After military service, personnel serve in the reserves for a number of years, many reenlisting even to maintain many years of friendship. Perhaps our Continental Army of the Revolution in 1776 can be considered a parallel to the IDF.

After the military many young Israelis travel abroad, making connections, working or just seeing a world very different from home. Many consider the learning experience helpful in rediscovering their career choices. Unlike their Jewish cousins in the states, a large number of Israelis get their education in the military from the many choices available, state-of-the-art technological programs. Some of these programs can be considered the MIT or the Ivy League of the nation, thanks to the nation's military demands. Maturity gained from a class-less military structure based on performance and respect is no small thing. In the West so-called "permanent students" have no meaning in Israel.

The elite intelligence units of the IDF are known as Talpiot, Mamram and Unit 8200. These military units select the best of Israel's youth who desire to serve. Born after the debacle of the 1973 Yom Kipper War, when Israel fell victim to a surprise attack, a program had begun to even the battle field, so to speak. Its youth learn modern battlefield technology, preparing the nation for the next battle. In fact, from these disciplines, start up companies like Compugen and NICE Systems had sprouted from elite IDF's alumni.

Every year, the top two percent or roughly 2,000 high school students take a battery of tests. About ten percent pass the math and physics components. Of these, the two hundred are given additional personality and aptitude testing, the successful trainees advancing to the Talpiot program. A university degree training program continues for forty-one months in advanced math and physics studies along with basic military training with the paratroopers. This brings to mind our Naval Academy or West Point. The cadets adapt to the needs of the IDF. Along the way intense training help the recruits to become leaders, especially in combat, serving them well later in life. The "Talpiots" are esteemed in Israeli society. In thirty years, only about 650 have graduated from the program, many becoming top academics and founders of global enterprises.

In addition, Israel graduates 45 percent of its population from university, among the highest in the world, according to the Organization for Economic Co-operation and Development (OECD).

Over the years the Israeli military have provided more than its share of founders and upper management in the nation's companies. I'll report on three of these, of which Perrigo remained one of the core stocks of THE HOLISTIC PORTFOLIO: Teva Pharmaceuticals and Nice Systems, Ltd. had been former core companies.

Teva Pharmaceuticals is Israel's largest company. Teva is the largest generic drug manufacturer in the world, operating principally in Europe and North America. In the last couple of years Teva had begun to establish distribution networks in Japan and China. However, this will require agreements with interested parties and their respective governments. Recently, Teva acquired Ratiopharm, Germany's second largest generic maker. This should generate an additional $400 mil. in cost savings from operating synergies over the next three years. Some statistics follow:

| Teva | Price Project | Gain(Loss)% | Annual Yr% 2011-5 |
|---|---|---|---|
| High: | 135 | 110 | 21% |
| Low: | 110 | 70 | 15% |

Source: Value Line Investment, April, 2010

Sales per share in 2011 were estimated around $19.65, $24.55 in the 2013-15 timeframe.

Concurrently, shares outstanding in 2011 were estimated to be 875-890 mil. by 2013-15. In other words, Teva bought in 15 million shares. Usually, a company grows shares along with sales over time. Dilution has tripped many a stock into a downward spiral, and an investor must be on guard against dilution. In addition, generic drug launches over this particular time period should see rapid increases, because many main-line drug company patents are schedule to expire. In April, 2010 Teva had 216 product applications awaiting FDA approval. Sales of these are estimated at $113 billion. Margin improvement is on target from the acquisition of Barr Pharmaceutica and from cost savings of some $500 mil. Teva will continue to expand its core business from acquisitions, and deepening penetration in global markets with low generic presence. It will continue to enlarge its branded products. Although today's price was trading around $40.00, Teva remains a good buy. Perrigo is an Israeli firm traded on the NASDAQ.

The company operates in three segments:

Consumer healthcare with private label over-the-counter drugs @ 82%; Rx produces prescription generic drugs @ 8% and API makes active pharmaceutical ingredients by contract @ 7 %.

A few statistics as above projected by Value Line Investment Survey, April, 2010.

| Perigo | Price Project | Gain(Loss)% | Annual Yr% 2013-15 |
|---|---|---|---|
| High | 90 | 50% | 11% |
| Low | 60 | 0 | 0 |

Today's stock price is around $101.00 a share (10/24/11). Sales per share in 2011 are est. to be $26.35 and by 2013-15 $33.50 per share. Common shares outstanding are estimated to be 91 mil in 2011 as compared with 88 mil. by the 2013-15 period.

This is good news. If sales are estimated to grow by $7.00/share while common shares are est. to decrease by three million then we have **NON-DILUTION**. When a company dilutes shares when sales fall this is considered its worst fate. Walmart accounted for 23% of FY '09 business, perhaps a negative because Walmart is known to squeeze costs out their suppliers: will the Chinese fill the void? I don't think so because Perigo makes the all important active ingredients, difficult for most pharmaceutical companies to do. Economics of scale bodes well for Perrigo as the supplier of choice. Anyway, quality of product is crucial. In this case, it would take years for the competition to ramp up for the global market.

As in a military contract, for instance, a company as sole producer of an Air Force contract would be at risk once the contract is pulled. By selling many products in different markets globally, diversification with scale matters.

In the 2nd Qtr. of 2010 Rx sales climbed by 38% because of over-the-counter business and margin expansions. Recently, the company launched its private label version of Miralax, and is awaiting FDA approval for Mucinex. New products are expected to boost revenues by $120 mil.

Recently, the company announced an acquisition of PBM Holdings, a store-brand infant formula manufacturer in an $808 mil. all cash deal that should add more to the bottom line in its store- branded products. Also, the company recently acquired Orion Labs, a leading OTC (over-the- counter) supplier in Australia and New Zealand. The company's stock closed at 60.58 on 4/23/10.

My last Israeli cyclical stock was Nice Systems Ltd. We live in a very dangerous world, both foreign and domestic. Hackers constantly break into the Pentagon from Eastern Europe and China. Fire-walls and other computer measures are upgraded daily, re-coded and reloaded.

In the days leading up to Pearl Harbour, the Japanese code was broken. We knew their naval forces were out there in the Pacific, as confirmed by submarines. By knowing the positions of the Japanese fleet, we were able to act first owning the element of surprise. General information is good, sufficient, but may not prevent an attack.

## THE FUTURE OF HOLISTIC INVESTING ISRAEL

By the Battle of Midway, our intelligence was able to infiltrate a false "laundry list" of unimportant items into general radio traffic accepted by an enemy radio operator. This ruse pinpointed an impending Japanese attack at Midway. We knew their carriers were closing while the Japanese didn't know the location of our carriers. We blind-sided them and sank three of their four carriers the first day. The battle won.

Security and intelligence means survival. Important as they are for the military, corporations rely on high tech surveillance too. Corporate "spying" has been around since before the First World War. Patent and process protection demands vigilance. Today, the global economy demands more corporate security.

A team of Israeli Talipots founded Nice, now protecting eighty-five of the Forbes 100 companies. Over the years an open secret was that Israel had the best security in the world.

Little wonder being that this nation survives on the edge of existence surrounded by enemies.

Nice is the leader of call-monitoring- pattern recognition in communications as applied to content and behavioral culture. Let's begin by surveying some financials.

Nice Systems provides solutions enabling users to extract "insight from interactions" on transactions and surveillance according to Standard and Poors, April, 2010. Its programs enable users to capture, manage and analyze "unstructured interactions." Listed below are some data:

| Nice Systems | 12 Months | 5 Year Growth |
|---|---|---|
| Sales | $583.1 mil. | 18.2% |
| Income | 42.8 mil. | 14.9% |
| Gross Margin | 59.38% | |
| Shares Outsd. | 62 mil. | |
| Earnings/sh. | $.69 | |
| 52 week High: | 34.3, Low: 21.19 | |
| Instit. Holdings: | 47.8% | S & P rating: Moderate Buy, 4/21/10 |

Below is some recent news:

Actimize, a Nice product, outperforms a key testing criteria in real-time "Fraud Prevention Benchmark." The top ten global banks confirm with high volume usage—PR wire.

In March of 2010 the company entered into a multi-million deal with Tele-performance Group, a leading UK out-source firm by adding Nice Smart Center. The system deploys interactive transactions of call recordings, managing and analyzing content. Tele-performance will deploy the system in thirteen sites throughout Europe. This is designed to "extract hidden insights" and apply them to harness a base of customer dynamics, generating value.

The stock traded at 32.39, 4/21/10.

This ends the discussion of Israeli companies as candidates to become your core holdings.

I mentioned earlier, your core position should be between three to five stocks. My other core holdings at the time were Baytex Energy Trust, a Canadian corporation in the oil and natural gas business. The stock pays a handsome dividend, paying over 10% when I entered over a year ago.

Core stocks should pay higher than average dividends, think reinvestment, because these companies are QUALITY COMPANIES which will continue to grow into the future. Most companies known for their dividends seem to have sub-par growth. On every dip down to its 30 week moving average, buy additional shares.

This concludes the chapter on the future of Holistic Investing. Ultra Europe, Singapore and Canada ETFs join Israel. Think strong currency global and invest global. WE DO THIS IN A RISK-AVERSE WAY. Also, you can buy a fundamental strong company in a nation with a strong currency like Swiss, German or Swedish firms in American ADRs (American Depository Receipts. I continue to seek investments in countries whose currencies are safe. Investing in nations with weak currencies means losing value on currency conversion. When translated into dollars a loss may occur if the dollar is stronger.

Always compare stock or fund of any nation against the almighty dollar. If a nation's currency is stronger than the dollar, buy into funds of that nation. If not, buy global bond funds or gold stocks as hedge against a weak dollar.

One of the futures of Holistic Investing rests on the future of a nation's currency. However, most common stocks won't be bought because of low accounting standards. Instead, consider their ETF's represented in emerging markets: Pacific area, European small stocks or Latin America funds as their economies expand.

As for common stocks, look into American Depository Receipts of Israel, Canada, Singapore, Brazil and Germany. Of course, treat these companies like any U. S. company if listed in Value Line Investment Survey.

My next chapter will discuss an alternate way to buy additional shares, because core stocks remain your best bet to make serious money into the future. Core stocks mean more time in market. Most important: the market, always, will dance to different beats over time, seemingly leaving your core stocks in second or third place: GOOD. Keep the faith and wait for your stock to fall even more. BUY MORE SHARES. Eventually, your stock will return and kick back into gear leaving the market in the dust. My Israeli and Canadian energy stocks will be around for the long-haul.

# CHAPTER 36:
# Wrapping it all up: Part 1: The Value 3 Portfolio: Content Drives Value

The structure of your portfolio armed with above principles will define your new tomorrow.

At the very least, if I called attention to the nuances of investing in your best core stock paying above average dividends, then my job is complete. Also, look at market sectors which can add value to your bottom line by way of mutual funds.

And last, if you protect your portfolio with mutual Bond Funds of strong currencies and Cash, 40-60% of your portfolio, then I've done my job. And in times of extreme overvaluation, buy into Index Option puts.

Confidence and improving performance will renew your investment outlook. This is what this book is about. For what good is any new method or system if it doesn't work? Holistic Investing works. The big idea is to invest with ½ THE RISK. Work with the other half of your portfolio. In the Appendix a new program is explained to approach Cyclical/Special Situation Stocks. This is within the principles of Holistic Investing. **PVG Momentum Rank.** This tool identifies value-driven growth companies of the Russell 2000 about to *lift-off* into a new trend.

There will be times when all hell is breaking loose, and the urge to sell is your only choice. Remember, in an equity sell-off ALL stocks fall. But in a Cubby Bear Market of which stocks correct 5-7½% most stocks will return to their former highs.

Today the market has fallen 250 points on a bad jobs number (9/2/11). All stocks fall. The good news is that this doesn't happen every trading day and sanity does return. And one should be prepared for this temporary madness. For instance, I have nearly forty percent invested in the Dreyfus International Bond and Intermediate Income Funds as a hedge. In addition, a good core stock is an all weather stock regardless of market volatility, a value driven growth stock paying above market dividends. Core Stocks are the first to rise when the carnage is over.

In the deep bear market of 2008-9, a once in a lifetime event, stocks like Baytex Energy and Crosstex Pipelines held value and have returned from the debacle of the housing bubble. I bought these two stocks when paying double-digit dividends. For instance, stocks of companies became value-less as in the Tech Bubble of 2000. No sales. Mid-cap value companies, such as Master Limited Partnerships (MLP) pay 7-10% dividends. These value companies weather bear downturns.

Perigo, Lorillard round out my core stocks as I write this. Earlier, I bought Herbalife as a cyclical-special situation stock. I later sold the company at a profit after questions on their booking of revenues. I hold long-term if a company continues to outperform the S & P 500.

Common stocks, both core and special situation (cyclical stocks) make up approximately one-half of the HOLISTIC Portfolio. The other half is comprised of mutual bond funds, Cash including strong currency Bond Funds. Yes, cash at .5% interest isn't competitive but it can provide a temporary haven. Some day cash will pay around 5-6%. But by simply having Cash as a cushion, the surplus liquidity will allow you to buy a promising candidate when needed.

## WRAPPING IT ALL UP: PART 1: THE VALUE 3 PORTFOLIO

Cash provides ballast to your portfolio when the marked turns sour. In a bull market your Portfolio should be Cash/Bond funds, 40%; Common Stocks, 40% and Sector Fund(s)/Index Options 20%. During bear markets it should read: 60-20-20% (high-dividend Core stocks).

The Value 3 Portfolio:

| | |
|---|---|
| Cash & Currency ETF's | 25-60% |
| Common Stocks/Ind. Options | 50-20% |
| Mutual Sector Bond Funds | 25-20% |

Holistic Investing is about the big picture, getting the most value from safer alternatives.

The received wisdom of 60% stocks and 40% bonds has had mixed results. In a market decline most stocks will tumble. The bonds may have to do double duty in playing catch up. With cash and bonds nearly 80% in a bear market, the Holistic Portfolio offers better protection.

For decades the financial industry, banks and insurances companies had preached diversification for good reason. For example, the common benchmark between stocks and bonds was 60-40%, i.e., 60% stocks to 40% bonds. Today, my portfolio reads: 60% stocks, 30% bonds and 10% gold. This works in times of a weak dollar. Eventually, the dollar will strengthen and wipe out those gold investors.

Most bear markets in my experience begin from the beginning of a recession or efforts to cool an over-heated economy by raising interest rates. BOTH stocks and bonds fall in value. However, CASH benefits from higher rates, especially money market funds. Back when money market rates were above 5%, most of my adult life, one-half of portfolios grew from interest income while the remainder treaded water during a market bottom.

Mutual funds have been around since the 1940s and some earlier. Many funds had begun in the 1950s and 1960s. For instance, the flagship Dreyfus Fund had begun in 1947, a great time in the American economy: G.I.'s returning home from the War, beginning families, buying homes and continuing college on the G.I. Bill. The Levittown model homes were built out in Long Island and suburban Philadelphia selling around $10,000. Today, many of these properties are unrecognizable, with huge oak trees and renewed homes. In fact, I worked in one of the homes, preparing tax returns in my senior year of college. I would meet clients in the evening.

I currently track 4 Dreyfus bond funds and one index fund, the Treasury Bond Fund depended upon relative performance. The funds:

| | | |
|---|---|---|
| DRGBX | Dreyfus | Treasury Bond Fund (Bear Market, Stocks) |
| GPGAX | " | GNMA (Ginnie Mae) "not as volatile |
| DRITX | " | Intermediate Term Income " |
| DIBAX | " | International Bond Fund (local currency) |
| PETBX | " | Municipal Bond Opportunity Fund: All Weather |

The above Dreyfus Funds perform with their respective markets sectors, waxing and waning over the market cycle. The GNMA Fund had performed relatively well in 2011. Its beta remained lower than treasury bonds and is capable of getting an added boost from a healthy mortgage market. The intermediate-term income fund also is less volatile than the long treasury as these bonds are shorter in duration. International Bonds historically do well in a bear market. These investments include German Bunds, Japanese Bonds but their other Europe holdings of Eastern Europe haven't done that great during the current Europe EU crisis (August—October, 2011).

The Dreyfus Municipal bond funds have done very well in 2011 to date. Municipalities around the nation are beginning to get a firmer grip on local finances.

I compare above these bond funds to the Dreyfus Treasury Bond Fund, DRGBX. Never compare bonds to stocks, i.e., bond fund/stock

## WRAPPING IT ALL UP: PART 1: THE VALUE 3 PORTFOLIO

fund for example. However, because of funding problems in Puerto Rico and Detroit in 2013 one must exercise due diligence.

DRITX divided by the DRGBX. Like apples to apples. Both are bonds however of a different stripe. You also want to compare, for instance, the DIBAX/DRGBX or the International Bond Fund to the Treasury Bond Fund.

In any event, bonds, especially Treasuries are your best bet during a CRASH or during periods of declining inflation, deflation. EVEN IF TREASURIES ARE FATED TO RISE BECAUSE OF THE U.S. DEBT SURPLUS, bonds will continue to HEDGE your portfolio against the gyrations of the stock market. Also, International Bonds are great if the dollar is weak and bonds priced in markets of STABLE CURRENCY/Euro-zone as of this reading.

Always invest in the STRONG CURRENCY nation. Similarly, a STRONG DOLLAR is good for Treasuries, as in the 1980s and 1990s. Let's move on to index options.

Index Options are employed for hedging purposes only. Buy puts or sell calls slightly out of the money, lower premium value. I wouldn't even consider buying index options for speculation. They work better as SHORT-TERM HEDGES. I track the following index options representing primary sectors of the market: ACRA Natural Gas (XNG, CBOE Russell 2000 (RUT), KC Bank (BKX) and Phila.Sox (SOX), semiconductors. Buy just after expiration of old contract. Remember, as time in contract progresses, a "wasting value" will occur so ACT within contract before expiration.

The above indices provide the volatility necessary to make strike prices in market downturns. Major market indices such as the S & P 500 play important roles as hedging for the large institutions. These are very liquid meaning price points will be met on trade execution.

Natural gas has become an important component of the energy complex. The Russell 2000 has become a bellwether for small cap stocks. The KBT Bank Index has become a surrogate for financial stocks and for the banking industry. Phila. SOX Index remains a good indicator of technology stocks.

These fall sooner and harder during market corrections than their broad market cousins. The greater the volatility the greater the decline. Low volatility means OPTION DECAY (wasting value) or slower price movement over time. Index options expire monthly, and the nearer it approaches expiration, the less its inherent value.. I view Futures and Index Options as the raw nerve of the market.

Options can provide insurance against a segment of your portfolio. This cost is very small compared to overall portfolio value. These instruments, handled with consideration and analysis, can cost say $200-400. Even if your option isn't working out, you can exercise it prior to expiration. And if successful, you can roll a position into the following month seeking even greater returns. I would invest no more than $500 on a portfolio of $20,000 or less. Of course this is an arbitrary number. BUY PUTS ONLY. Your calls really are your common stocks and ETF's. Rule on puts:

Buy puts, ONLY WHEN, a second LOWER TOP appears and fails on Index Option chart of weekly data. Make sure Momentum Indicator of price decline rolls over pointing the way down.

Before I leave this topic I like to share some pointers on how I trade index options.

Most markets move from a top or bottom by making double tops or bottoms as discussed on pages 77-79. Also, you need Bollinger Bands (Big Charts.com) as discussed on pages 69 and 78.

Buying puts or Selling calls (Bearish): Look for option price to move above upper Bollinger Band (+2) and dip below on a weekly close. Next, look for another LOWER HIGH the following week or so and prepare to buy put(s) at Friday's close. Since option price is OVERVALUED, according to Bollinger Bands, a lower high following an extreme (emotional high) signals bearishness.

Accordingly, look for weakness in the S & P 500 as confirmation.

# WRAPPING IT ALL UP: PART 1: THE VALUE 3 PORTFOLIO

Getting Started:

Beginner:

If you're one of those who want to take responsibility for your investment decisions then I have good news: welcome. Beginning anything new means learning the language and rules, whether it's a new job, boating, camping, or investing. An open mind is essential. In investing: RISK is the element one must understand before funding any new investment.

REWARD becomes potential reward from taking this risk. RISK and REWARD are those two keys underlying investments, from the billionaire to the beginner. The idea is to understand and build up CONFIDENCE before advancing. As stated is this book, investing isn't easy; take it seriously, and a few victories can build confidence when buying in small increments. But beware of overconfidence. It could mess up your day to say the least. Go in small, understand why and keep a log as to the reasons for buying or selling. Later, once you fully understand a breakout, breakdowns and sector rotation, etc. you can relax more. In most cases, a stock or fund will rise to top after tracing out two legs on a chart, with minor pullbacks in between. Once it tops out, it usually moves sideways with less momentum dipping slightly lower. A day will come when it will fall, sometimes ugly, and eventually reach a bottom, bumping along week after week, before moving back up. Do some research or scouting if you will, like an army in battle. Is your stock or fund gaining momentum? Are its attributes turning positive (better than S & P 500, strong sector)?

I would advise you to begin with mutual funds because funds are more diversified and price volatility is lessened. Stock or bond mutual funds would do. In general the economy should be growing, especially after a downturn. The best time to get into stock mutual funds is at the beginning of an economic recovery. Along these lines, I would prefer The Dreyfus Fund as your first vehicle, or a general purpose fund like Vanguard's Windsor Fund or Fidelity's Magellan Fund. For now, avoid the sector funds as discussed above. Just get a feel for the market by noting the price changes daily; however, weekly price information is more reliable and a better tool for spotting trends (weekly high, low and close).

Become a member of Marketwatch.com or Yahoo Finance.com and build a chart of your stock, weekly price information of bar charts to determine price direction or trend. Go to a good library and take out a book on chart investing. Read up on stock charts.

It's essential to display Bollinger Bands as suggested, to display overbought (+2) or oversold (-2) standard deviations when higher or -2 standard deviations when lower. Marketwatch (Bigcharts) and Yahoo Finance web sites offer these services for free. Keep reading charts and take advantage of this free service. Join an investment club if available.

I remember John Bollinger in the early days of FNN back in the 1980s. CNBC was the successor network. In general, funds or stocks would hit the upper Bollinger Band (+2) and keep on moving higher for awhile, only to pull back to make another run to the top, and often, the fund or stock will run out of steam and fall.

Conversely, a fund or stock falling would often dip below the lower band (-2), only to rally and fall back. A giveaway would be if the stock or fund falls again but not as low, and rallies from a higher bottom. This would be a good time to buy. Moral: Never buy a stock without consulting its chart first.

And never buy a falling dagger (stock in free fall) prior to a bottom.

There are a number of web-sites which display charts of stocks, funds, etc. Become familiar with these as well as reading the fund brochures and financial section of the media.. After a period, maybe some months or even a couple of years, it's time to consider buying common stocks. Most important: Only buy what you understand and feel comfortable with: period.

This is really an old adage. Would you consider buying "a cloud computer" company or a "flash memory" chip maker if you're unfamiliar with the terminology? We live in an age where new words, meanings, tech terms, are being invented almost every day. Become familiar with them.

# WRAPPING IT ALL UP: PART 1: THE VALUE 3 PORTFOLIO

The most important thing is this: your initiation into the stock market may indeed be a worthwhile endeavour. During this time of growth as in any new skill, setbacks become necessary before you can move forward. Welcome them, learn the mechanics, correct those pesky problems and move forward, onward.

Seasoned Investor:
Fundamental Analysis:
Although not a prerequisite, look for market sectors with a tailwind to its back. BLEND WITH THE TREND; don't fight the tape. Barron's displays a section called Industry Groups located near the back of the weekly. Various stock sectors (industry groups) are ranked. Look for the YTD (year-to-date) rankings, especially the top five rankings.

These rankings, i.e., biotech, travel & tourism, oil services, specialty chemical, etc., don't really change all that much. For instance, at the time, May, 2011, the pipeline group had held the top spot for months. Actually, I acted on this some months before and bought Crosstex, XTEX, an oil and gas pipeline transmitting natural gas to various distributors in the Delta Region of the south. The stock paid double-digit dividends.

The yield at time of purchase was ten percent. I placed a limit buy at 16 and it traded as high as 18+ prior to a recent pullback. The stock traded down to a sideways pattern for awhile because of the Mississippi Flood, a time to add to my position.

Be on the lookout for mid-cap value stocks which pay above average dividends. Remember, getting on first base is everything. As a Holistic—Value investor, I've combined the best of both worlds. By waiting for a pullback, you buy at an even greater value. But in a bull market your target stock may not pullback for awhile. That's why I would look at another company, similar, called Enterprise Products. This company transmits and processes natural gas in the Gulf Coast Region.

Some investors have held on to Microsoft for many years because of their franchise value. The software company had piled up accumulated earnings and paid a one-time dividend, only to trade at essentially the same price in all those years. This is A Value trap. Beware. Value Traps can't keep pace with the S & P 500.

One of my most important tools is my **PVG Momentum Rank**. This consists of Year-to-date) (YTD) price growth percent (whole number) divided by PE. Growth divided by / PE. If answer is 2 or better I continue.

For example, a stock with a low PE of say 10 with only 7% growth, a true value stock, would fail because 7 divided by 10 is less than 1. In most cases, a stock with a rating of .7 has a problem, especially if the S & P 500 has grown more than 7 percent.

Also, look at historical data such as % Return on Equity, should be double-digits and 5 year % sales growth, again, double-digit is preferable. In addition, look for % institutional ownership at 33% to 50%, relatively undiscovered. Ownership greater than 66.67% or two-thirds of float should be a flag; however, many stocks heavily owned (weaker hands) continue to rise because of hype and promises (analyst pronouncements). Over-owned stocks suffer when the music stops—massive dumping on the way down. In any case, think of an exit strategy.

I used to look at insider sales but discovered this data isn't timely. By the time the owners are unloading to uninformed buyers at the top, it won't become public until after the fact. I still consider an old measure of the 1980s, or working capital divided by long-term debt, or WC/Ltd (working capital divided by long-term debt) greater than 2. A solvent company paying an above average dividend can weather an economic downturn. Also, don't forget rising free cash as a % of sales.

TechnicalAnalysis

Situation or Cyclical stocks benefit from technical chart patterns. My favourite three indicators are Money Flow, Slow Stochastic and Momentum, in this order. A slow stochastic is 15 K periods interacting with 5 D periods. However, most web charts factor in their own parameters.

# WRAPPING IT ALL UP: PART 1: THE VALUE 3 PORTFOLIO

MoneyFlow is what I call a **Conviction** Indicator confirming trend. This is most important. For instance, this indicator may keep on rising at the top of a price range. Good news, even though the Stochastic K has crossed under D, overbought. This contradiction may be noted because MoneyFlow is more forward looking. The stock may drop but with a rising MoneyFlow, the stock tends to move higher. On chart, look for a double top whereby second top lower than original. This presents a classic sell signal.

The Slow Stochastic is what I call the **Direction** Indicator. This is more important after a market bottoms or tops, at turning points. For instance, if K crosses above D in oversold territory from a higher low be prepared to buy. As stated, MoneyFlow can be rising along with stock price, but the Stochastic may signal from a higher low. This is a buy confirmation. Remember, weekly data rules.

Conversely, if K crosses above D from a higher low even if Money Flow is off its high, not trending down, buy. The only time I wouldn't take this signal is if Money Flow is about to make a new low.

Momentum is what I call the **Thrust** Indicator. It's reliable if price spikes above its 10 or 52 week moving average on a weekly close, after stock has traced out a bottom. Here, MoneyFlow would be down as well as the Slow Stochastic. If you buy from a positive volume spike, buy 25 shares or less. If it proves out and stock rises, they'll be plenty of chances to buy additional shares on the way up.

Momentum works better when price spikes well above its 10 or 52 week average after a top. If it spikes down from a top the stock will fall hard. Get out.

Pattern Recognition:
Perhaps good readers of patterns should work for the CIA. Apart from the usual triangles, diamonds which most books on technical analysis provide, there is a couple of others which I'll walk a mile for: Double tops and Double bottoms. Yes there's symmetry in chart analysis. Most trading vehicles patterns, from hogs to beans, to Index

Options to common stocks and futures run in pattern similar to each other.

These signals are very important. Even if above oscillators are neutral or contrary, these patterns work out only from extreme tops or bottoms. Conversely, after falling to a bottom, stock rallies to a minor top, falls again but makes a higher bottom, stabilizes, and moves up again.

Inside or Outside Weeks: these patterns are particularly important if price trades at extremes, the top or bottom of chart. If price range (high to low) remains inside the prior week, sell if price at top, buy if at bottom. However, don't bet the ranch. Also, if price range is greater than prior week, higher high and lower low than previous week: sell if near top, especially is price closes at low and/or buy at bottom if price closes at high.

I've discovered that a **Candlestick Cross Pattern** (fine line) can be very helpful. I've been using these for the last couple of years. Since the days of Japanese rice traders of the Sixteenth century, these patterns have been very helpful. There are books on candlesticks at major libraries and online. I recommend reading up on this. I believe there's one candlestick pattern which often, sometimes not, depicts CHANGE OF TREND especially at major turning points of tops and bottoms. Look for a + (cross) pattern around the 10 week average on chart. Some crosses are filled in, not so fine and they don't seem to work as well. In this case, volume doesn't seem to make any difference.

Limit Trades: The ONLY way to trade.

Act, don't React. Don't panic. Try to buy a stock (doesn't apply to mutual funds) at Limit Price. At market price will probably overpay on the buy side and undersell on the sell side. Set strict limits when trading. In other words, when buying, wait for a pullback, usually a retracement to the 10 week moving average provided that Money Flow isn't collapsing, fundamentals good, etc.

For instance, if stock is currently at 15 wait for a pullback to the 9-12 range before entering this trade. If this doesn't happen than stock may not be worth your while. If it dips to 12 ½ and continues to go back up, the stock will probably make a new high. Consider buying. Some stocks trade in a normal range with a beta of 1(equal to the stock market). Beta of 1.5, say a Tech stock with reliable fundamentals may be a better candidate. Health and utility stocks don't move as much as other groups. Your group may be out of favour now. Why bother. Move on because your favourite groups may be in the dog house for years: financials since 2008.

I'm not saying don't buy banks or insurance companies, but isn't it easier to wait until they move up. In the meantime there's a bucket full of stocks to consider. Remember: Is your stock moving with the rally?

Doing better than the S & P 500? Good. Look for an entry point at a limit price.

# CHAPTER 37:
# Wrapping It All Up: Part 2
# 15 Lessons Learned

### 1. GET ON BASE: BUILD CONFIDENCE

You heard of the saying: hit the ground running. Truth endows this thought. Be an active player. Think about this: you go to bat, ground out or worse, called out on strikes. Back to the dugout shaking your head, thinking: got to eat more carrots.

Investing is like stepping up to the plate. Start small, buying a stock with an above average track record. Buy a few shares at the right price. Now your stock belongs to the market, hoping that its sector or the company comes through. Any one of these components will move the stock in short order. Suppose it goes up a few points. Now you're on base, maybe in scoring position. Oops, it falls back a little, not much. OK. It may mount another advance soon. The company reports good guidance with stronger sales. Great. Perhaps prices move higher before the news. This means the stock is closely followed. Now for the Ah-Ah moment–your stock moves on to an all time high.

I painted an ideal scenario. I've recommended throughout this book that you buy from a bottoming pattern. Since your stock has fallen to a low, MOST OF THE RISK HAS BEEN REMOVED. Rather than buy a stock anytime, WAIT for a bottom. Let the stock move sideways and bump along the bottom prior to its breakout. As in athletics, hockey, basketball, etc., after a surge of scoring a time will come for the streak to end, running out of steam, before another spurt up. It's the same with investments. Always keep your goal in mind, and all the power to you.

All of this wouldn't have worked if your stock, or the runner in the baseball analogy, wasn't in position to score. A good omen is that your investment begins moving early. You didn't swing for the fences. The guy who did down the street had struck out or lost his capital. Many individual investors buy a stock on a whim and wake up every morning with a stock that can't get out of its own way. Sadly, their portfolio may be mired in the mud for a long time.

My getting on base analogy doesn't mean you over trade. And of course you may have a few strikeouts (sector turns sour, an analyst downgrade, etc.) If necessary, get out and take a small tactical loss. However, in most cases, the setback is temporary. Clue: companies which generate tons of cash like Lorrilard and Perrigo with rising Free Cash as a percent of Sales will keep you on the right side of the curve. Beginning on a sound foot goes a very long way to investment success. Arm yourself with better knowledge. Do your homework:

Overall market, sector and stock: does it all fit. Go get 'em.

## 2. WHAT MARKET TIME IS IT?

Before you enter the market, know if the stock market is in a bull market or bear market. Often, bull or bear markets will correct, go down for a spell if bullish or up for awhile if bearish. Of course this begs the question: How would I know if stocks are riding a bull market?

Often, by the time you commit to buy a stock the media would have scores of analysts and mavens announce their opinions ad nauseam. Some will rely on fundamental studies, i.e., a pricey PE ratio, the market fully valued, a weaker economy, stronger dollar, The Fed ending QE2 (quantitative easing) and a host of others.

Also, don't rely solely on traditional technical studies: The Advance-Decline Line, Volatility Index, S & P Support at 1250 or

## WRAPPING IT ALL UP: PART 2 15 LESSONS LEARNED

the Dow Support at 11,750 or Dow Transports vs. Industrials. In short, Fundamental analysis often cancels Technical Studies leaving the investor confused. What do you do? Create your own market barometer.

Over the years I've tried a number of studies, some good in some markets and others bad in other markets. A Man for all Seasons so to speak. We aim for an indicator which works in All Market environments. IT'S MORE IMPORTANT TO CATCH MARKETS AT TURNING POINTS. I don't mean major market moves lasting for months on end. I spoke of the usefulness of the MoneyFlow Index, Momentum and Stochastic Indicator working in tandem. Yes, these have worked for me. However, during the latter stages of market declines or advances these may give false signals, fake outs, after which the market will continue on its merry way. In a sense, eliminate the noise of false readings as much as possible.

I've developed the Accumulative Up-Down Indicator which works especially well at market tops and bottoms. However, your stock must beat the S & P 500. Most proprietary indicators work around market tops or bottoms. However, you really don't need these because there's really a more simple and accurate way to chart this. Look for Double Tops and Double Bottoms which foretell and end of the old trend and beginning of the new respectively. Key: if the second top of a market rally is lower than first top: sell on weekly close BELOW its 10 week average. Conversely, if the second bottom of a market decline is higher than first bottom: buy on weekly close ABOVE its 10 week average.

I've also developed an Index Option Momentum Indicator. Index Options are cousins to Futures and are traded principally in Chicago, the derivative capital market of the world. For ages farmers and food companies have hedge their crops, airlines hedged their future fuel purchases and so on throughout the global economy. I view options as the raw nerve of capital markets, trading pits belching emotion, putting it mildly, arriving toward the closing bell to the joys and sorrows of its participants from Tokyo to New York.

I chose four indices which I believe represent the economy by sectors: AMEX Natural Gas, XNG; CBOE Russell 2000 (small cap stocks), RUT; Phil. Banks, BKX and Phil. SOX (semiconductors), In other words, Energy (natural gas), Small Stocks (small business the backbone of America), Banks, both large and small, and Computer Chips.

The Formula: closing weekly prices of XNG, RUT, BKX, SOX multiplied by each other, then take the cube root of multiplicand ='s equals value for week. Plot weekly values on your computer, at least 30 weeks for a start, and overlay a 5 week weighed moving average over a 13 week weighted moving average, plotted in separate indicator window: **Index Options Momentum Indicator** will cross over or under moving averages when buying or selling.

You should wait for the Indicator to cross above both 5-13 weighted moving averages when buying and sell when Indicator crosses below 5 week moving average. By the time it crosses both averages on the downside it may be too late.

I have an early version of Meta Stock for Windows from Equis International. Their address:

Equis International, Inc.
90 South 400 West, Suite 620
Salt Lake City, UT 84107
Tel. 801-265-9996, 800-882-3040

3. LIMIT ORDERS: The Foundation of Stock Market Profits.

These protect you against yourself. I can't count the number of times in my investment career that I wanted to buy a "barnburner" stock now, only to see it sink later. Emotions play a major role in stock market selection, especially execution. A consistent winner on the playing field and in the cyber world of investing is to filter out the noise, "animal spirits." LIMIT ORDERS are the answer.

Remember what I said earlier: BE FOCUSED. Wait for random daily price to meet your price target. Market players, fund managers, speculators, large block traders and foreign interests drive

# WRAPPING IT ALL UP: PART 2 15 LESSONS LEARNED

prices up or down to extremes in some instances. Count on it. By waiting for your price to meet a predefined level is smart. A limit buy at a lower price or sell at a higher price it the way to play. It gives you an edge over a fund manager of billions of dollars. Set your limit, and let the nerds with their smart phones chase the latest craze. I learned in a Chicago trading seminar that all gaps are filled, sooner or later (prices which leap up or down beyond previous week's trading range return to former level). Don't be whipsawed. Set your price limit and enjoy a morning coffee at your favourite cafe. NEVER BUY OR SELL AT MARKET. Would you buy a new car at the sticker price?

4. VOLUME IS YOUR FRIEND: Respect it

Market volume can give away a stock's position in time. However, I consider weekly volume more important. A stock spikes up or down daily, but its overall weekly volume may tell a different story. Weekly volume may still sit above or below its 52 week's average. Look for a weekly volume spike above 52 week average if previous volume had been weak. This tells a better story if weekly close at or near high.

Volume triggers turning points. Often, a stock will just run out of steam at a market top. Stocks that rise on weaker volume is like an old steam locomotive gasping for more steam. Weaker volume is a no-no at or near a price top. Look out. Similarly, a stock riding down on expanding volume means correction. When buying, look for a stock with better than average volume in the early stages of an upswing. Make sure stock is at or near bottom of trading range. When selling, look for weaker volume at or near top of range.

Volume Spikes at the bottom of a trading range is good news. Be prepared to buy.

This surge of volume can signal a price rise later. "Price follows Volume," a tried and true saying of Joe Grandville, famous market guru of the 1970s and 1980s.

5. SEPARATE WHITE NOISE from Real News:

White Noise discussed in earlier chapters is the bane of thousands of investors, even professionals. Discard it. Rumours, opinions or analyst's views have forced some investors to take to the hills, stock up on canned food. And when the rumours or opinions prove false, where are the perpetrators? Why they crawled back into the woodwork. Hold on. Most of these pronouncements don't amount to much and will be cancelled out by other pronouncements. I rely more and more on my data. Reading credible articles from impeccable sources (NY Times, Barron's) may not pan out.

Respect the facts. News considered real: Free Cash Flow growth, expanding market share and sales. Stock dilution, reverse stock splits and corporate mismanagement are what you don't need. If a company keeps issuing shares BEYOND executive bonus plans, watch out. Issuing corporate debt in a low interest rate environment is normal. But if a company issues stock at every chance, get out. Stock dilution helps no one. Conversely, company buybacks are great, however if sales fail to grow much, take notice. Remember, SALES GROWTH IS BETTER THAN EARNING GROWTH. Earnings emerge from sales, a true measure of a company's demand. DEMAND IS EVERYTHING. Witness Apple and its I-Phone.

Often, white noise can mask a firm's weak earnings. Companies can buy back shares to support earnings/share. Microsoft has been accused of doing this to support its earnings. Sales growth is a better measure of organic growth. The famous Price-to-Sales Ratio, a measure of value reflects this view.

Look for companies with strong five year double-digit sales growth while keeping a lid on shares growth. Sales are very difficult to hide. At times, earnings are subject to accounting manipulations (creative accounting). Worse, earnings issues will surface in a falling stock. The mechanizations of earnings by sleigh-of-hand make good case studies. Product demand and honest management is the antidote. Look for a strong track record in sales.

## 6. SECTOR ROTATION:

Bear markets begin from a change of macroeconomics: recession fears, a hike in interest rates or geo-political events. Lately, because of a continuing sovereign debt problem in Europe, a Lehman type event remains foremost in institutional circles. In 2011 nearly a day had not passed without some mention of French or Italian banks. This overhang reminds investors to commit to essentials: consumer staples, utilities and bonds.

A pullback within an ongoing bull market can begin from sector rotation.

A change from financials for instance to consumer staples or commodities (energy, food, metals, etc.) can make sense in uncertain times. Industries must dance to the tune of the economy. Market perception has favoured the above groups in selloffs.

An important economic concept is inelastic demand. Water will fill the same demand whatever the price. Products or goods like gasoline are more elastic (price change triggers quantity change: the cheaper, the more consumers buy) because drivers will shop around for a better price.

Service companies like utilities and medical services are basically inelastic because price won't budge in the face of falling demand. On the other end of the spectrum commodities and food companies will reduce price to increase sales. Another way to gage elastic products of companies are the multitude of sales and promotions issued. Grocery stores and restaurants forever issue coupons. Prices lowered to increase traffic.

In most cases, a rising sector will outperform for a few weeks, 3-8 weeks before another sector replaces it. For instance, the Pipeline subsector (oil and gas) remained in the top five for weeks on end, some five months. It continues to occupy this spot, number four (9-19-11). Earlier, pipelines remained number one over the summer. LOOK FOR SECTORS (really sub-sectors) occupying the TOP 5: their stocks may be under accumulation. The strength of the dollar hurts exporter sectors such as energy and commodities. As of this writing, Airlines and

Travel have remained in the Top 5 for most of 2013, 12-9-13. Airlines and Travel benefit from a strong dollar (discretionary spending).

Financial stocks do better as the dollar rises; conversely, commodities and energy stocks fall. A weak dollar will push precious metals higher and a strong dollar will do the same for financials and bonds. A weak Euro/dollar weakens European stocks and benefits U.S. bonds. In principle, a nation with a strong currency attracts foreign capital such as America did in the 1980s. The emerging economies have played this role. Moral: keep an eye on the dollar. Be in the Right Church and the Right Pew so to speak. My Core Stocks as of 12/18/13 are Insurance: Retirement (AEL), a Bank Holding company (FNF), a Biotech (GILD), and a Real Estate and Tobacco conglomerate (VGR). These benefit from a strong dollar.

I believe Stock Prices are affected by the following:

The Market: 60% The Company: 20% The Sector (Group): 20%

In a Crash all stocks fall. Yet in periods of market stability, an entire sector can move more rapidly than the market. High-end retailers can gain even if consumer spending is weak. The Leisure and Travel industries have done well in economic downturns. The Wealth Effect? But a complete company's fundamental analysis pleads for due diligence even if a company's sector is favourable. Weed out bad apples. Start by looking at the services mention earlier, Value Line and Standard & Poors. THE MOST IMPORTANT DUE DILIGENCE IS AN HONEST MANAGEMENT. Get this right.

Another way to screen management integrity is insider ownership. Look for large positions of management, at least 10% INSIDER OWNERSHIP (most large firms won't meet this standard but some smaller companies will). WALK IF MANAGEMENT DOESN'T PUT THEIR MONEY WHERE THEIR MOUTH IS.

### 7. THE BIG PICTURE: THE POWER OF CHARTS

A chart is a big picture in time. A tight chart is a better picture. A tight chart is one which doesn't have many violent up-down swings, like a ping-pong ball bouncing around. An ideal tight chart has dips and hills with an upward projection. This chart makes a succession of new highs after a dip.

Before anything else discussed above, consult a chart. Do you find price gaps? Gaps are weekly price ranges completely higher or lower than preceding week. As a rule, all gaps fill on the way up or down. Look for charts where price ranges overlap in a tight pattern. As explained in Chapter 10: if a stock can't move within a reasonable time, then it's time to move on. Don't get trapped because the clock is ticking against you. Look at a chart as if looking at a coil. Sooner or later the coil will spring from a tight chart. This means that the high and lows of your ideal chart have definable ups and downs. A TIGHT CHART like a good puppy has definable outcomes.

If your stock is on the way to new highs, a pattern will trace out this picture. Look for a series of plateaus, a high, another series of random up and downs, another new high, etc. I have found these tight chart patterns produce results. Look for them. Aside from a $2^{nd}$ Wave Stochastic, previous explained, rising momentum and rising money flow I've found that price of stock remaining above its 10 week weighted moving average (10WMA) as excellent confirmation.

Conversely, the best signal on the sell side is the REVERSE OF THE ABOVE.: a 2nd Lower Stochastic high with Momentum and Money-flow Falling. Be prepared to exit this Cyclical Stock. Core stocks may be held because of their longer term duration AND YTD>S & P 500.

### 8. WELCOME CORRECTIONS:

Real money is made when buying additional shares of Core stocks after a correction of 5-10%. I spoke of Cubby Bear markets in an earlier chapter. Believe it or not, smart professionals make more money during these temporary pullbacks. A good stock will always return to its old high. It's unfortunate that a roaring bull market draws in the unsuspecting public who buy shares away from the smart money.

I remember a work colleague of mine, Willfert Skillman, or Skilly, my boss when I began work with the NJ Office of State Auditors. Working in downtown Trenton, Skilly invested in a closed-end fund called

National Aviation. The closed-end fund barely moved but it paid a very good dividend. At the time the market was buffeted by higher rates and rising inflation at the beginning of Viet Nam in 1966-7. The market had taken a dive beginning in February, 1966 until October of that year.

National Aviation fell little if any but its dividend added additional shares for its holders.

Skilly kept his cool as others were climbing the wall from deteriorating stock prices. When a new bull market arrived the following year, Skilly would consol us on the merits of his strategy one afternoon while returning home from the Freehold Raceway. With its limited number of shares (closed- end funds don't dilute shares) existing shares take on a greater value because of dividend reinvestment. The shares are poised to grow even more from the next bull market. I may add that this is particularly true if dividends don't represent a return of capital.

I spoke about a similar situation when my parents held Computer Sciences in the 1970s.

At the time stocks were down from the bear market of 1973-4. The stock hit a low of around 7.

My mom was upset and thought about selling. Cliff, my step-dad, said maybe it will go back up again. It so happened that the company was expanding in California upgrading their software on medicare-medicaid claims. We lived in Alameda and knew that Computer Sciences signed a contract with the state. So Cliff said, "Why not buy more?" My mom agreed. They more than doubled their money a few years later.

The moral: Buy more shares of a growing company when its shares are cheaper.

### 9. BECOME STOIC: PEACE AT THE CENTER

A stoic mind is a clear mind. The stoics were a Greek school of philosophy that showed an indifference to grief, joy, pleasure and pain. Of course in today's frenetic world this is impossible.

The western culture encourages an outpouring of emotion; otherwise, repression of feeling can lead to deep seated neurosis.

Investing and trading demands clarity and concentration. Preoccupation with a cell call or CNBC with its burbles of information, some contradictions, tend to take your eye off the ball. I do my work in my den, interrupted by the dogs or an incoming call. At times I tune in to a soft-rock station. My mom once told me about a diet misstep: Once on the lips, forever on the hips. Stay focused, do your research and investing in private. DON'T BRAG ABOUT YOUR WINS OR FRET OVER YOUR LOSSES IN PUBLIC. It's none of their business. All of us must live a private life to maintain sanity. Cherish it.

You may find this lesson controversial, but remember, Holistic Investing isn't business as usual. We Zero Base conventional wisdom and consider new thoughts more consistent with new realities. Yes, reality, materially and philosophically evolves as we sleep. Time-worn principles may remain, yet some have eroded from the impact of technology. We must move, grow, or die. A new set of principles will always supplant the old, bending nature and perhaps yielding new species, organizations and institutions. Adapt, wither or die. The principles of Holism deal with wholes or integrated systems rather than any of its parts.

Enlightened doctors and scientists have practiced Holistic medicine for decades. In the East, holistic medicine has been around for millennia. We are finally catching up to the wisdom of China and India. Instead of killing all the cells, let's target the bad guys before the good ones become infected. Improve your diet and sleep and your immune system will benefit. Just taking pills is no longer the answer.

Holistic investing directs you to look at the big picture first. Just buying and selling good stocks may not be enough. Good stocks working in concert with good funds and occasional index options with plenty of BONDS/ CASH carry more weight.

A time will come when you'll hit the mother lode from a great trade. Your portfolio will thank you. Guess what, the market gods have a way of taking everything back soon afterwards. Set a Limit Sell after a New High!

**DON'T LOSE PRIOR PROFITS.** Don't fight the same battle again. Remember: reinvest profits from short-term trades back to cash and losses into your best core stock. Resist the urge to tell your friends about "hitting the big one." Why? Because all may be lost the next day. Cool down, keep your head. Even telling your girlfriend about your new fortune may boomerang soon afterwards. **FATE HAS A WAY OF TAKING BACK.** What comes around go around. Be one step ahead of fate and shut up, keep it to yourself, and she'll hug you when you put a nice ring on her finger. She'll appreciate this more.

Zeno was a Greek philosopher around 308 B.C. He held that all things, materials and relations are governed by natural laws, and a wise man should seek virtue obtained through reason. By remaining indifferent to the external world of passions and emotions, one can overcome himself. If not, those feelings can get the better of you and unravel your world. Of course in today's world this is impractical outside a monastery. **A COOL INVESTOR IS A WINNING INVESTOR.**

I remember when living in the Bay Area. Reports of a person jumping off the Golden Gate Bridge had occurred about once a month. Keep your distance from fools, fast talking barkers, and astrologers. Keep your head. If indeed you make your fortune from a great trade, don't take it to heart. A portfolio requires constant work, researching, trading. The market throughout American history has moved approximately 3 steps up with 2 steps down. You may hit a soft patch now and then. Don't worry. Your day will come again. Call it investment Karma. Better yet, call it

Holistic Investing applied.

### 10. WAVE POWER OR THE POWER OF TRENDS

You heard the bromide timing is everything. It is. Timing is the ability to catch a powerful force at its very beginning. Timing is also the ability to catch a tail wind, surf the wave just before it breaks.

Fortunes have been made or protected from buying commodities or currencies such as orange juice futures just before the freeze. In the early 1970s, those who bought wheat made a killing from the killer drought affecting the Russian wheat crop. And those who tasted the ill fated winds in the fall of 1987 saved their fortunes from the crash. Numerous other examples abound where investors knew or had some lucky feeling that a major event was about to strike.

I spoke to you about my visit to San Francisco during October, 1987 celebrating my parents' 38th anniversary. While reading Investor's Business Daily, Thursday morning, the 15th, I ran across an article on Richard Russell, keeper of the famed, Dow Theory. I remember reading the article while enjoying a morning coffee on Fisherman's Wharf. The Theory gave a sell signal and I had taken heart. I called the mutual fund and sold all shares of clients, parents and myself. At the time I managed client retirements in mutual funds. Hardly anyone had remembered Friday's market activity. But everyone did remember Monday, October 19, 1987, a crash similar to an October crash 58 years earlier.

Today we remember September 15, 2008. At the time, the October, 1987 collapse was the worst since that fateful October Crash of October, 1929, a fateful era that would take a quarter of a century to correct. Wall Street doesn't ring any bells when it's time to get out.

A market letter I wrote recently analyzed the Crash of 2008: Anatomy of a Crash:

## New Lows (Barron's)

| Date | Copper | Investment Advisors | Dreyfus 500 |
|---|---|---|---|
| 1/25/08 | 301 | 933 | 36.9 |
| 3/24/08 | " | 732 | 35.97 |
| 6/16/08 | " | 718 | " |
| 7/21/08 | " | 585 | 34.5 |
| 10/13/08 | 257 | 392 | 25.65 |
| 11/3/08 | 162 | 353 | 24.22 |
| 12/26/08 | 125 | 237 | 21.53 |

Clearly, the price of copper hardly moved until after the summer of 2008. Meanwhile, Investment Advisors fell hard by a resounding 294% and the Dreyfus 500, proxy for the S & P 500 fell by 42%. Clearly, the Investment Advisors were the canary in the cave, the barking dog before the storm. Investment advisors are the large brokerage houses who are ubiquitous to Wall Street. They advertise big time on the money channels. Since the recovery of 2009, the Advisors have been doing better but haven't fully recovered. Yet in late 2013 they did.

Enjoying the wind at your back is the same as being in the RIGHT SECTOR at the RIGHT TIME. Not many chances come along when major turning points occur. But market sectors do rotate with frequent regularity. Take advantage of these.

## 11. 'THE COSMOS SPEAKS IN PATTERNS'

The ancient Greek Philosopher, Heraclitus, as described in Roger von Oech's wonderful book (Expect The Unexpected, The Free Press, 2001) truly was one of the great thinkers of Western Civilization.

College professors, for good reason, write or teach the big three of philosophy: Socrates, Plato and Aristotle. But little mention is paid to Heraclitus.

One of my courses in my senior year at Rider was just this. I enjoyed reading the dialogues of The Republic and Aristotle's grammar, except on a Phi Sig blow out weekend. Even if Heraclitus was less important than Plato and Aristotle, his insights into human nature are worth your while.

These include the following:

'You cannot walk into the same river twice' and 'Knowing many things doesn't teach insight' are two of the many thought provoking pronouncements in Roger von Oech's book. Heraclitus brings philosophy down to the gut level. Find a pattern, page 24 goes into Fibonacci (an Italian mathematician) numbers, considered by some as turning points of the stock market. For example,

2001(1) Fibonacci number(s): 2002(1+1); 2003 (1+2); 2005(2+3); 2008(3+5); 2013(5+8); etc.

The market did turn in February, 2001 (Bear) into a multi-year bear bottoming into late 2002. And again, the market did turn in 2008 (Bear) and again, the market did turn up in 2013 (Bull). The economy did improve in 2003 after a long recession. The market and economy reaccelerated in 2005 creating the Real Estate Bubble. The market did crash in 2008, dragging the economy into The Great Recession.

In technical studies, I see **patterns**: Inside and Outside weeks, and Candlestick Crosses (+), important technical turning points setting up trades. Volume patterns are also important, especially declining volume trends into a stock or market's topping. Sell if at +2 Bollinger Band) and so on.

I've told story of my experience many years earlier as Yeoman 3/ class aboard the Coast Guard Cutter Castle Rock. While patrolling the North Atlantic we began a pool as to who would guess the number of radio aerial contacts. I won $40 by arriving at the correct number of radio communications with commercial and military aircraft over a 20 day period on station. Curious crew and officers inquired about my guess or method as it turned out. I explained that I've revisited my high school algebra and devised a ratio-proportion analysis from the number of contacts after 5 days, the last day to join the pool. I believe I was about four to five off the number. I also learned plenty about locks on ships. Never use a combination lock. But this time the 40 bucks remained in my pocket.

12. BE FLEXIBLE: Growth vs. Value, Small Cap vs. Large Cap, Technical vs. Fundamental. Human nature has survived since the dawn of Cro-Magnon when he discovered leverage by swinging a club and fire by cooking his catch and keeping warm in his cave. In millenniums since, we've constructed super cities and have sent rockets to Saturn and beyond. Surviving in the stock market isn't that much different in principle. Cultivate new beliefs, values, systems, science

including math, physics and even a book by a noted author, George Soros, The Alchemy of Finance: Reading the Mind of the Market, Simon and Schuster, 1987. I found the book interesting, and indeed the book refined my fundamental feel for the market.

Another book which came out in the early 1990s was about the coming growth explosion in the economy: The Great Boom Ahead. The author correctly forecasted the boom in the latter 1990s which begat five years of double-digit gains in the stock market. However, by mid 2000, the bursting of the Tech Bubble blew everything away. The gig was up.

Small start-ups with 0 earnings had risen to nose bleed levels, only to crash back down to earth.

The tech bubble went bust, and as we speak, consistent with another bubble in real estate, many fortunes will be lost. Unfortunately, we'll be paying for our sins for a long time. Bulls make money; bears make money; pigs make nothing.

Don't subscribe to the reining conventional wisdom, labels, ideologies, or whatever received wisdom you read on the web, hear from a talk show, or even read from a book. **Cultivate Critical Thinking.** Trust but verify your facts. It wins the day, today and tomorrow.

Captain your own ship.

I try to believe in the best advice available. Even in bad advice, maybe a small gem of it can work for you. Be open minded. Save yourself grief. I remember a saying by the 33rd President:

"It's what you learn after you know it all that really counts." Harry Truman.

Don't be afraid to court new ideas; take that lesser fork in the road sometimes, it may lead to riches. Cultivate your imagination because it rules the world, not mass, energy or the speed of light squared or even the latest App on your I-Phone. Cultivate a laser beam focus, of a quiet tension of Buddhist philosophy. Yes sir, if it works for you, great, and nothing else matters.

13. **FAVOR COMPANIES WITH MONOPOLY POWER:** Look for an Inelastic Demand Curve. For awhile, some competitive firms

have monopoly power. What is monopoly power? Monopoly power is the ability for a firm's product to attract little if any competition. Remember the cabbage patch doll craze back in the 1970s. Its company battled in a competitive market while its product soared to unseen demand. Market Demand rules at the end of the day. Apple as a company was doing OK. However, when it introduced the I-phone demand soared to stratospheric levels. And because of the I-phone, I-pad and other innovations the stock sits at much higher price levels.

A firm with an inelastic demand curve is a firm that sells its product at a set price regardless of demand, from 0 to 100,000 units at $10.00 per hundred gallon of water for example. Utility companies, such as power and water companies have been allowed by states to charge a set rate to cover investment costs. Price remains the same unaffected by market conditions. For instance your local pizza shop will advertise specials from time to time by cutting price. Gasoline prices will rise and fall according to market conditions. However, your water company will sell all its tap water.

No promotions or specials required. The water company's demand curve is inelastic. In fact, there's no curve: it's a straight line. Why, because we need water to live.

In reality, an inelastic demand curve will not slope slightly down to the right along its X or horizontal axis. Price remains fixed at most levels of output. Another example is a block sale by a defence contractor by lowering price at greater units of output. Elastic demand relies on lower price to sell more. Its demand curve flows from NW to SE at lower price Y price falls along its vertical or Y axis at greater X or horizontal output.

Many corporations with elastic demand will issue "quantity discounts" to sell a greater volume.

Its demand curve will slope downward to the right as greater units are sold. Commodity companies, food, chemicals and raw material firms offer "quantity discounts" to move their inventory. But most service companies can sell service packages at a contract price per job, even at greater volume: Inelastic demand. This means little or no downward sloping demand curve to meet the last widget sold. Inelastic demand companies are more profitable in terms of gross margin.

Companies with established "brand names" like McDonalds charge a set price on a meal order.

They compete in a monopolistic competitive climate. Ford and GM, along with their foreign competitors trade in the same monopolistic competitive climate. True monopolies, like your local utility enjoy a protective price regardless of usage set by public utilities commissions. Yet I don't like to invest in utility companies despite their monopoly power because of regulation by state authorities and humongous capital expenditures. Are their dividends able to make up the difference? Yes, in a down market but once the tide turns, guess where I'll be headed?

In short, look for a competitive stock with monopoly power. Some of these firms have a higher barrier to entry ("a moat around the business") which exacts higher costs to enter industry for a potential competitor. Increasingly, I turn to companies with little competition, providing a service, paying a nice dividend, a mid-cap value company that performs like a growth company.

Examples of these were the following back in 2009: Baytex Energy (Canadian); Crosstex Energy LP(natural gas pipelines); Perrigo (generic drugs) and Lorillard(tobacco products). Knightbridge Tankers (Bermuda), Perigo (Israel, generic private label, compound ingredients) and Lorillard (tobacco) provide growing exports to emerging markets).

14. **BUILD YOUR PORTFOLIO FROM KNOWLEDGE**: This is a 'no brainer." As your knowledge and experience grow, so does your portfolio.

No one, especially those new to investing should buy stocks like tomatoes off a shelf. Do your research first. One should go about this from a cool, informed mind focused upon a price entry considered "fair valued." Rarely, does one buy an undervalued stock less than book value or with a Price-to-sales ratio under 1. By the time most stocks get down to aforesaid levels a company has a problem which may take years to work out. Your stock should have made a HIGH within the last six months. It should track the market and one shouldn't go out and buy financial stocks even if banks are doing well. In most cases, even if a stock had made a low the market will bring it back to old highs provided that the company has internal issues.

For those new to investing: welcome. Begin slowly because there's always plenty of fish (stocks or funds) to fry, or buy, on any given day. A multitude of brokers, market letters and TV programs will tout the latest Apple. As spoken in an earlier chapter on white noise, beware.

Your stock or fund should be a stock on the make: its time has arrived. Look for growing sales, growing free cash and order backlogs, a bottom with strong volume and stable price and temporarily out of favour. Look into Value Line, Standard & Poors, and Reuters, read up on your choices(always have two or three selections when doing this). Get a feel for the stock or fund and keep emotions aside. Wait for a breakout from market bottom above 10 week moving average.

Will your choice prosper in the coming economy? I believe so. I foresee:

A slow growth economy into mid decade until personal and government debt finally stabilizes. Remember President Clinton's second term when federal debt was repaid and the market rallied for five consecutive years of double-digit growth?

The answer is the rebirth of the energy and manufacturing sectors drive capital investments and exports. Growth of jobs will grow consumer spending. The American worker is the most productive in the world. Also, every manufacturing job creates at least 7-10 jobs downstream (small business shops, restaurants, service companies, suppliers, etc.). Meanwhile, we must REALLY become energy independent by substituting more NATURAL GAS into the equation. WE HAVE THE CAPACITY TO BECOME ENERGY INDEPENDENT. Finally, add to the above the REBIRTH OF THE REAL ESTATE SECTOR, the linchpin of the Great Recession. In return,

China and India need our technological knowhow, food and of course energy from our pipelines.

A number of Commercial and public vehicles have switched into natural gas from oil. More cars are destined to follow into natural gas. A huge number of trucks have already made the switch, cheaper and cleaner. Meanwhile, the number of gas- hybrid vehicles will grow. When this happens, and I believe it will, America will enter a second secular boom as in after W.W.II.

Bet on the new label in town: **MADE IN AMERICA**.

## 15. VALIDATE YOURSELF: TAKE OWNERSHIP:

Holistic is a health term. Its principles have applied to other disciplines. It is time it applies to investments. **You have to go through it to get through it.** My mom instilled an indelible lesson into me when in high school. I smoked in high school in front of my parents and she never said a word. They weren't too alarmed because they smoked also. In junior high I was hitching home from soccer practice when my dad and friend picked me up when hitchhiking. I forgot that a cigarette was behind my ear. Back then, about everybody smoked. I continued to smoke until 1971 when one night in Philly, a young black kid asked me for a cigarette on the way out of a bar. My friends and I couldn't believe that he was only about 10-12. I said, "aren't you kind of young to take this stuff up?" He smiled and looked at me, a look that I'll never forget. He said: "you smoke, don't you?" I took out my pack of Marlboro's and handed him one.

I said: "I'll stomp on my entire pack if you break your but in half." He broke it in half, and I promptly stomped on my pack of cigarettes. Since then, I've never had a cigarette and I hoped he kept his promise too.

My dad smoked for fifty-one years and died of lung cancer, probably knowing that he would have problems later. Before leaving for Florida, he would implore me to stop in North Carolina and pick up a couple of cartons on the way back. I would talk to him about the dangers, of course to no avail. I'd bring him his Tarryton 100s. I'm often haunted by this, but I figured that you have only one father, why hurt him?

A few weeks ago my wife was watching Ophra, her last week on ABC. She called me over when a clip from Dr. Oz aired, one of her regular guests. He was about to leave the national audience some final advice, a benediction of sorts:

(1) **Walk Briskly**. I walk our dogs every morning. Our Jenny, almost 17 1/2 went on to doggie heaven about two years ago. We acquired Gretchen, a Brussels Mix to take her place. The other two, Madison, a Cocker, 8 years and Jessie, a Jack Russell, 7 years keep me active, rain or shine. Get that oxygen into your lungs, good for the brain, and live longer. My activity level and chores have just bumped up.

(2) **Eat 50%** of your diet from what comes out of the ground. For years, I have eaten a salad for dinner; it's a religion. However, on weekends we have pizza or cookout. Greens have fiber. Good for circulation. Include Oatmeal and bee pollen with fresh fruit for breakfast. Think a yogurt protein shake for lunch. Keep it simple.

(3) **Be Passionate**. Validate yourself by becoming interested in a cause, hobby (the stock market) or a group. I love sailing but haven't sailed in a spell. I will pick it up soon. I joined the Coast Guard Auxiliary after 9/11 because I wanted to serve again. I joined the Guard just out of high school to beat the draft. A few months later I found myself aboard a weather ship out of Boston, The Castle Rock. These were the best years of my life. I remember my ship mates, and an epic Atlantic storm in February (we made the Navy Times and the Trentonian) after an aborted rescue search. We iced up between Greenland and Newfoundland trying to save an Icelandic trawler, Judi. Instead, we had to save ourselves because ocean spray turned into ice topside. We knocked off a couple hundred tons of ice with axes, baseball bats and screwdrivers, The search turned into a rescue for our own necks during the two day event in heavy swells, tying our lifelines to spars, poles, grabbing railings chipping ice with one hand and holding for dear life with the other. It got warmer. The Judi sank.

This is the end of my book, I hope the beginning of your new investment career. I hope Holistic Investing opens up a wide world for you, A NEW WAY TO INVEST. Holistic Investing can help you meet your income goals and create the edifice toward your journey to prosperity. In using a football analogy, the more productive your first downs, the more third down conversions you'll make.

Yes, investing is a journey, a journey worth taking to refund and build your retirement with less risk. Holistic Investing is designed to empower you and rely less on Wall Street. Risk -averse is very important in these times of 24/7 global events, both political and economic. We learned that the margin of error has narrowed since the disaster of September, 2008. Millions of retirement accounts and IRA's have yet to recover. AND RECOVER YOU WILL WITH MUCH LESS RISK.

YOU MUST INVEST TO RETURN TO SOLVENCY. My Holistic Value 3 Portfolio will help you return to solvency. Ride tomorrow's winners and cut your risk in half. Consider:

**Cash/Bond Mutual Funds**
**Common Stocks (Small to Mid-Cap PVG Value/Growth Companies**
**Sector Funds to add value and Index Option in Down Markets**

If I can leave you with one lasting image, it's this: I'll see you on first , together we'll steal second, and we'll score

Joseph F. Ippolito, MA, DpFP, RIA
December, 29, 2013

# Appendix: Holistic Investing

### Graph 1: **PRICE VALUE GROWTH MOMENTUM:**

PVG or Price Value Growth applies to Cyclical or Special Situation Stocks from the Russell 2000 data base. These are rapid growth small companies echoing the cutting edge of innovation. It's what makes America great.

To begin, PVG Momentum works best in a **Bull Market**. This is important because small company growth stocks should only be bought in a Bull Market. Core Stocks are Value Mid Cap high dividend companies, their buying signals covered in Parts B & C would suffice. DO NOT BUY CYCLICAL STOCKS IN A BEAR MARKET.

The principal parameters in the PVG Momentum System are the following:

Stochastic (Slow) Indicator: K & D waves: BigCharts.com (Marketwatch)

Price Momentum: BigCharts.com (Marketwatch)

The process begins when Stochastic Wave K (moving average) crosses ABOVE) wave D (K>D) from a HIGHER PRICE LEVEL on Chart.

Step 2 is to determine PVG (Year-to-date) Price Growth percent (%) **Divided** by PE ratio. The resultant Value is MULTIPLIED by Momentum expressed in 100s (if Momentum is 4 or 7 on Bigcharts.com) then Momentum is expressed as 400 or 700).

Step 3: PVG x Momentum or if PVG is 5 and Momentum 500 then result is 2500. Does this belong in your Top 3 Rank for the week?

Case #1 Federal Signal Corp (FSS)

In late Aug. 2013 FSS scored 3422 (PVG: 14.26 x Momentum of 240 for a score of 3422. AEL, another stock in portfolio was 3393. I decided to take a position in FSS. Stochastic K>D had occurred a couple weeks earlier (the 3$^{rd}$ time). FSS rose from 25% YTD to 100% by Nov. Notice that MoneyFlow was rising in sync. I sold FSS at a handsome profit in the market correction of Dec., 2013. Notice the declining Momentum and MoneyFlow beginning in mid Nov. Chart pg. 302

Case #2 Fidelity National Financial Incl. (FNF)

FNF appeared on the PVG radar scope in early Dec. 2013. The stock had a rather low rank of 745 but benefited from a powerful Stochastic Crossover K>D (the 3$^{rd}$ time as in FSS). At the time, FNF went from a price of 28+ to around 32+ or from 20% to 40% price growth in short order, mid Nov. to mid Dec., 2013. Notice the rising Momentum and MoneyFlow. Chart Pg. 303

Case #3 Graph of **PVG MOMENTUM RANK** dated 12/30/13 to 1/6/14:

This presents an example of a contradiction lost in the order of priorities. Just last night while watching *JFK* one of the characters, David Farrett explained to Kevin Kostner the following: *This is a mystery inside a riddle wrapped in an enigma.* Not to labor the point, the stock, AEL (American Equity Investments) is clearly the front ranked stock with the highest rank of 7350, But FNF (Fidelity National Financial) with a rank of only (1372) is rank higher than Gilead Sciences (3185), Hawaii Telecom (5296) and Micron Technology (3246). Why? Because FNF, although rather overvalued at 32+ in on the

# APPENDIX: HOLISTIC INVESTING

verge of a Stochastic 3rd Wave breakout. In short, the Stochastic Indicator, **direction**, rules. But make sure MoneyFlow and Momentum take 2nd and 3rd place, respectively. BE SURE to get the Stochastic K & D right before proceeding.

## PVG MOMENTUM RANK
### 2013-4

2013-4
12/30-1/6/14

| Date | Stock | | PVG | (x) | MO | Rank |
|---|---|---|---|---|---|---|
| | AEL | Stochastic 2nd W | 16.97 | | 433 | 7350(1) |
| | FNF | " | 2.29 | | 600 | 1372(2) |
| | GILD | Re-check | 2.89 | | 1100 | 3185 |
| | HCOM | | 19.25 | | 275 | 5926 |
| | MU | | 12.98 | | 250 | 3246 |

Notes: PVG ='s PE Ratio x YTD Price Growth: Bigcharts.com
Buy ='s Stochastic 2nd Waves K>D above original wave
Sell ='s Stochastic 2nd Waves K<D below " "
MOMENTUM & MONEY FLOW follow Waves Up or Down
MO ='s MOMENTUM per BigCharts.com in 100's
M.F. ='s Money Flow: Should be at High

### Graph 2: HOLISTIC PORTFOLIO PERFORMANCE
### 2007-2013

| | | |
|---|---|---|
| 2007: | 25.6% | Year to Date |
| 2008: | (16.3%) | " |
| 2009: | 12.1% | " |
| 2010: | 9.63% | " |
| 2011 | (.009%) | " |
| 2012 | 7.00% | " |
| 2013 | 28.5% | " |

Graph 3: Cash Flow (sh.) x (times) PE.
Example:
Lorilard(LO): Cash Flow(sh.)   $14.6
(x) PE                          8.12
(=)'s Potential Price:          118.5
Less Current Price:             108.83
Undervalued:                    9.72

Cash Flow (sh.) x PE (MFQ: most frequent quarter)
Example:
HLF Herbalife) Cash Flow        3.88
(x) PE (MFQ)                    17.40
(="s) Potential Price           67.51
Less current price              53.88
Undervalued                     13.63

Graph 4: Seasonal Investing

*Dreyfus Intermediate Income vs. Peoples 500 Index*

| Date Range | %DRITX (Income) | %PEOPX (Stocks) | Cash |
|---|---|---|---|
| Jan. 2- 26 | 50 | 0 | 50 |
| Jan 27-Feb 13 | 50 | 50 | 0 |
| Feb 14- Mar 7 | 0 | 50 | 50 |
| Mar 8- Apr 26 | 50 | 50 | 0 |
| Apr 27-Jul 12 | 50 | 0 | 50 |
| Jul 13- 31 | 50 | 0 | " |
| Aug 1-15 | 0 | 50 | " |
| Aug 31 Sep 9 | 50 | 50 | 0 |
| Sep 10- Oct 20 | 50 | 0 | 50 |
| Oct 21- Nov 29 | 0 | 50 | " |
| Dec 1-19 | 50 | 0 | " |
| Dec 20- 31 | 50 | 50 | 0 |

## APPENDIX: HOLISTIC INVESTING

DRITX is ticker symbol for Dreyfus Intermediate Term Income Fund composed primarily of treasuries and corporate bonds. The PEOPX or the People's 500 is patterned after the S & P 500 Index, a composite of 500 mid to large companies. In general, buy bond fund on down day of greater than (-) minus 100 Dow points and sell bond fund on market up day greater than 100 Dow points. Triple digit gains or losses usually mean a change of trend.

Above Seasonal chart works best when interest rates and dollar are stable. In environment of rising rates, both stocks and bonds underperform precious metals and emerging market stocks because of rising commodity prices. In times of EXTREME VOLATILITY ALL INVESTMENTS FALL except treasuries.

For instance, during 2001-2 and 2008 DRITX returned an annual average of 17% including reinvested dividends. Over the same period, stocks lost value from 2000-9, "The Lost Decade." At times, municipal bonds will outperform treasuries.

Graph 5: Index Options Momentum and Stock Charts:
A. Archer Daniels Midland (ADM), Chart Pg. 301
B. Baytex Energy (BTE), Chart Pg. 304
C. Perrigo (PRGO), Chart Pg. 305
D. Knightbridge Tankers (VLCCF), Chart Pg. 306

ADM: Notice the price and volume breakout from a cup-consolidation pattern in late Dec. 2010. Volume breakouts-breakdown usually begin from extreme top or bottom positions, (+2 or -2 respectively). Declining volume at the top in Late January-February, 2011, led to a subsequent price decline. Notice the double-tops. Sell declining volume at tops and advancing volume at bottoms. Notice the continuing downtrend of MoneyFlow over most of 2012.

BTE: I consider this a "dream chart" of a stock everyone should own.
Baytex Energy was a limited partnership which became a corporation. This typical core stock pays a nice dividend and continued to

outperform the market by rising some 60% into April, 2011 year to date. BTE converted to a corporate firm. Notice rising money-flow, the best indicator of a continuing uptrend. Notice the 3rd Wave Stochastic in early Dec., 2012/

PRGO: Perigo is a generic pharmaceutical that supplies active ingredients to other pharma companies. In Nov., 2010 an inside week (lower high and higher low) from previous week appeared—a good sign from a bottom. The stock continued higher into April, July and December, 2011. Notice PRGO's negative volume spike in early December signifying a sell. Even if chart turns bearish, hold on to this powerful core stock. Notice the big rise of Aug. thru Sept. 2012 on a 3rd Wave Stochastic in early August. Meanwhile, MoneyFlow was rising throughout most of the year.

VLCCF: Knightbridge Tankers logged a good 2009-10. However, in 2011 I sold the stock because the entire bulk shipping group continued to experience weakness from the global recession. However, the enclosed chart remains instructive from the patterns within.

Notice the inside week of mid December, 2010 after a pullback (Always buy after a pullback from a LIMIT PRICE). Again, a lower high-higher low pattern triggered a nice uptrend into late February. However, an outside week occurred the last week of the month at the top of its range, upper Bollinger Band. This signals a fall for VLCCF. Notice Candlestick "Cross" pattern in mid-June, 2011, foretelling another downtrend followed by another "Cross" in early Sept. foretelling a major uptrend. But **VLCCF CRASHED BELOW THE S & P 500** in mid May, 2012. The gig was up despite a bounce and failure in late July. It's difficult for a stock to regain the lead.

Inside-Outside Weeks are very important when stock is trading from an extreme high or low. Look for these when trading Cyclical or Special Situation stocks. Core stocks, however, shookuld be held because of its dividends and good growth potential.

# APPENDIX: HOLISTIC INVESTING

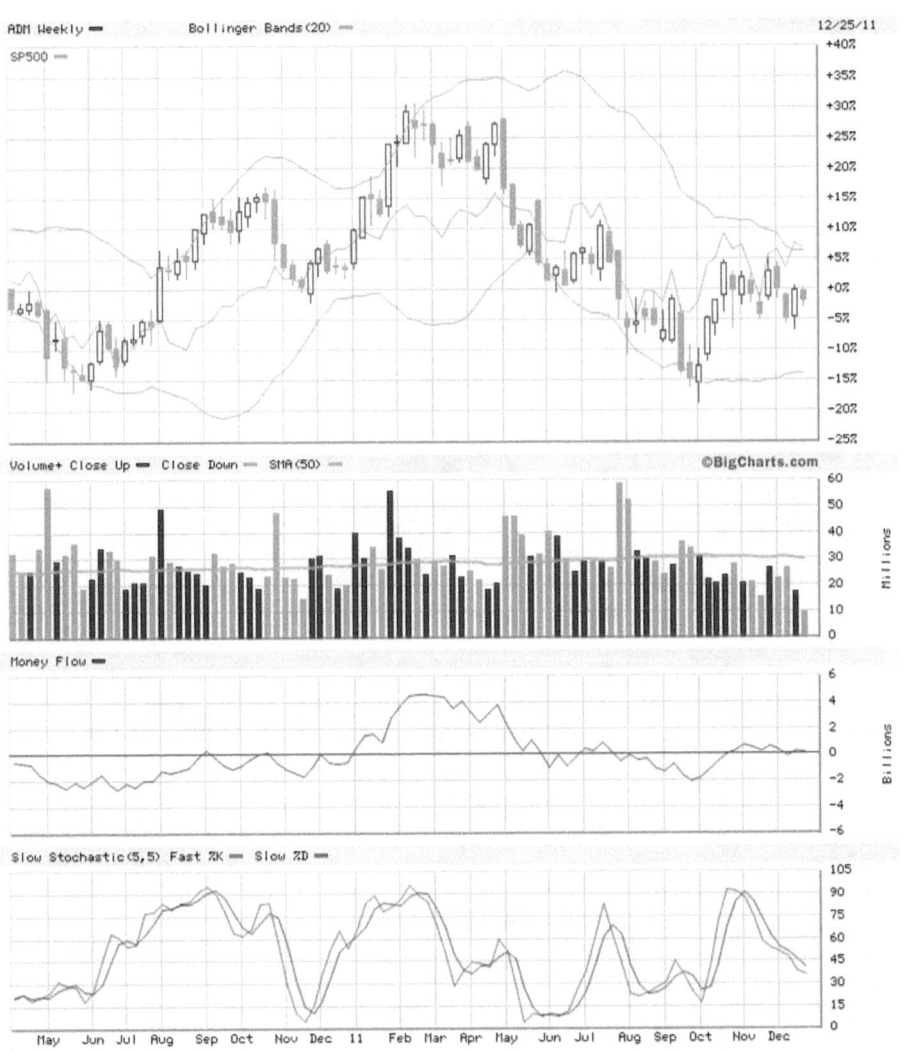

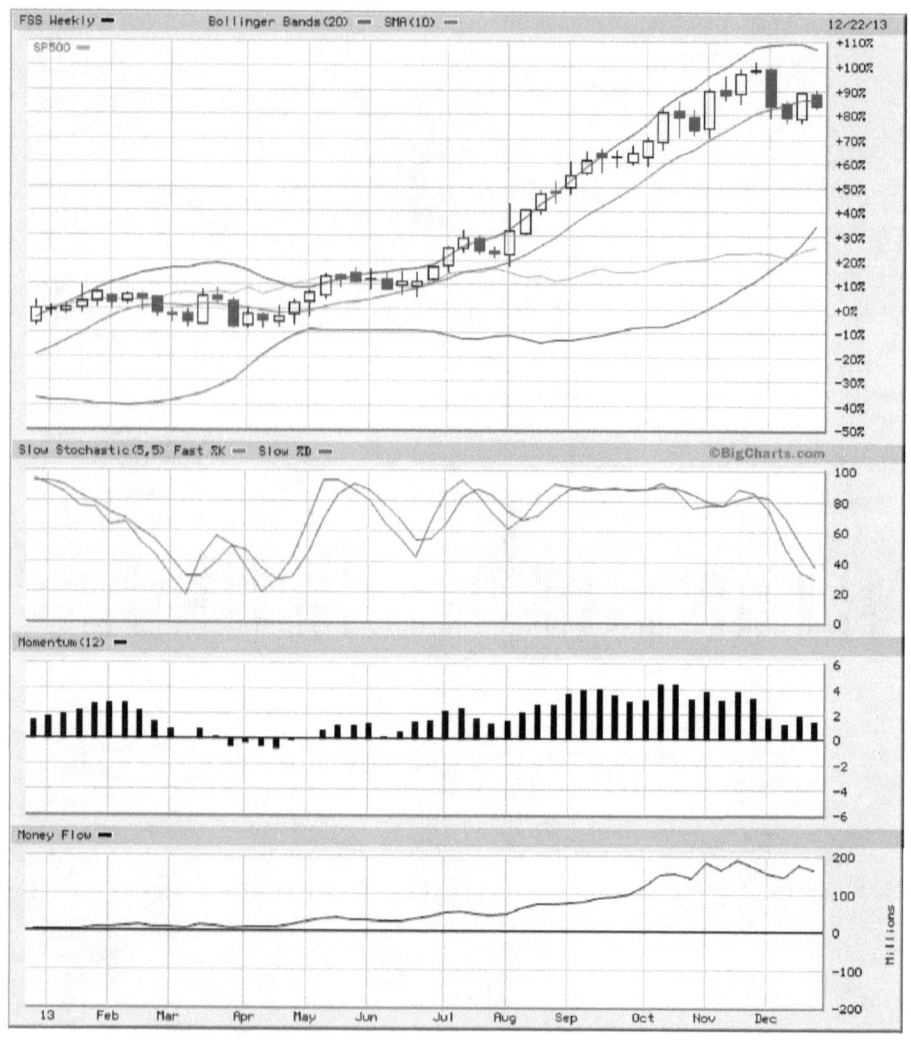

# APPENDIX: HOLISTIC INVESTING

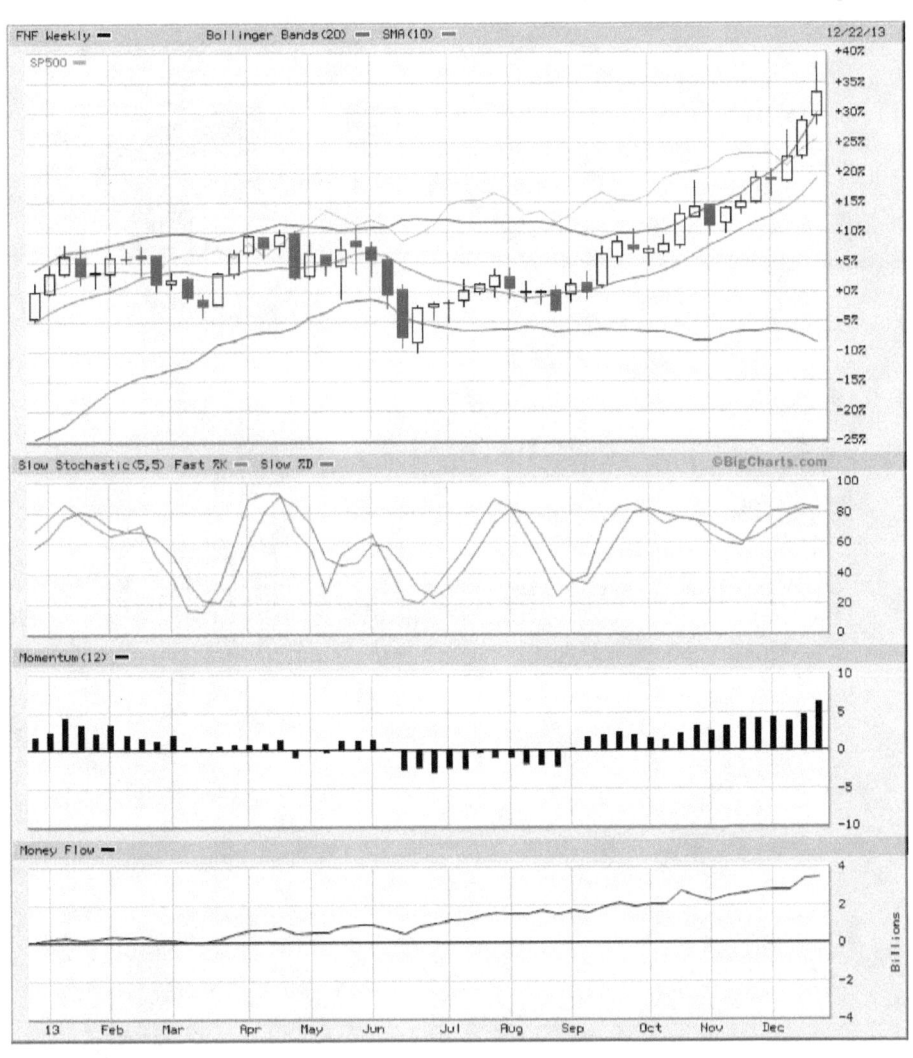

# HOLISTIC INVESTING IN A RISK-AVERSE WORLD

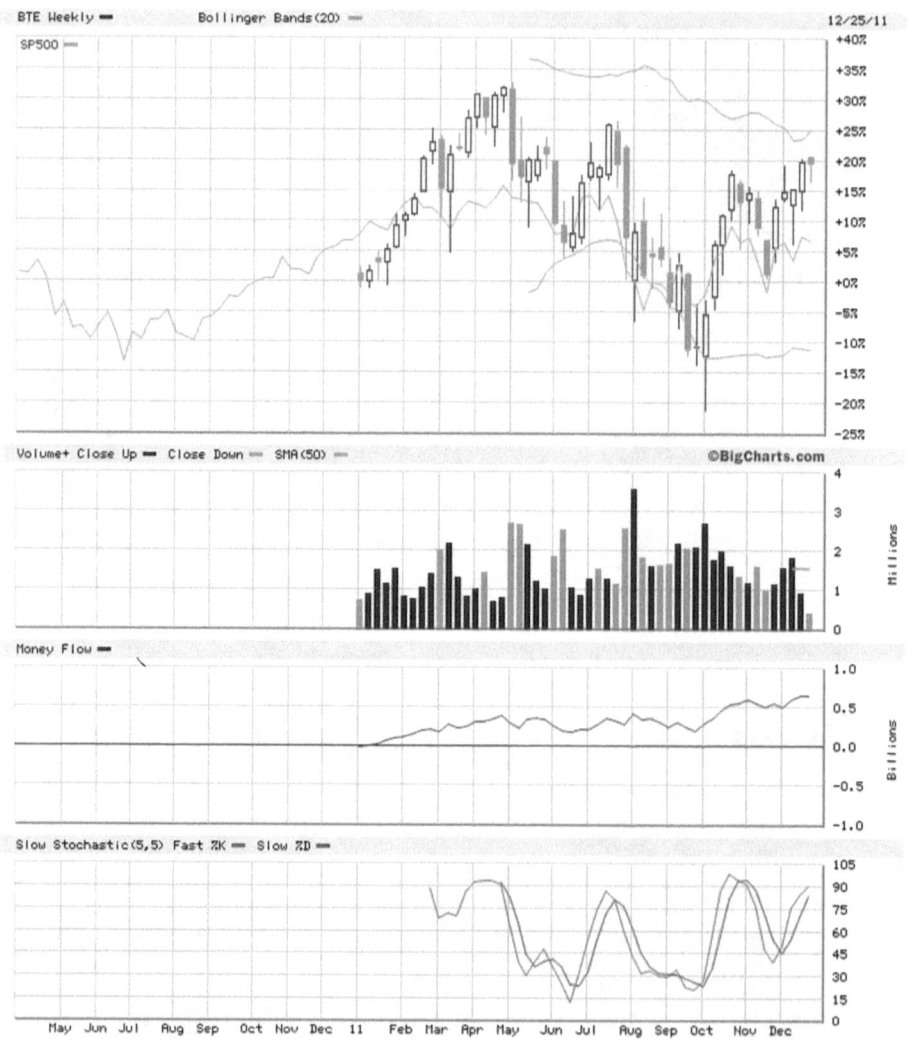

# APPENDIX: HOLISTIC INVESTING

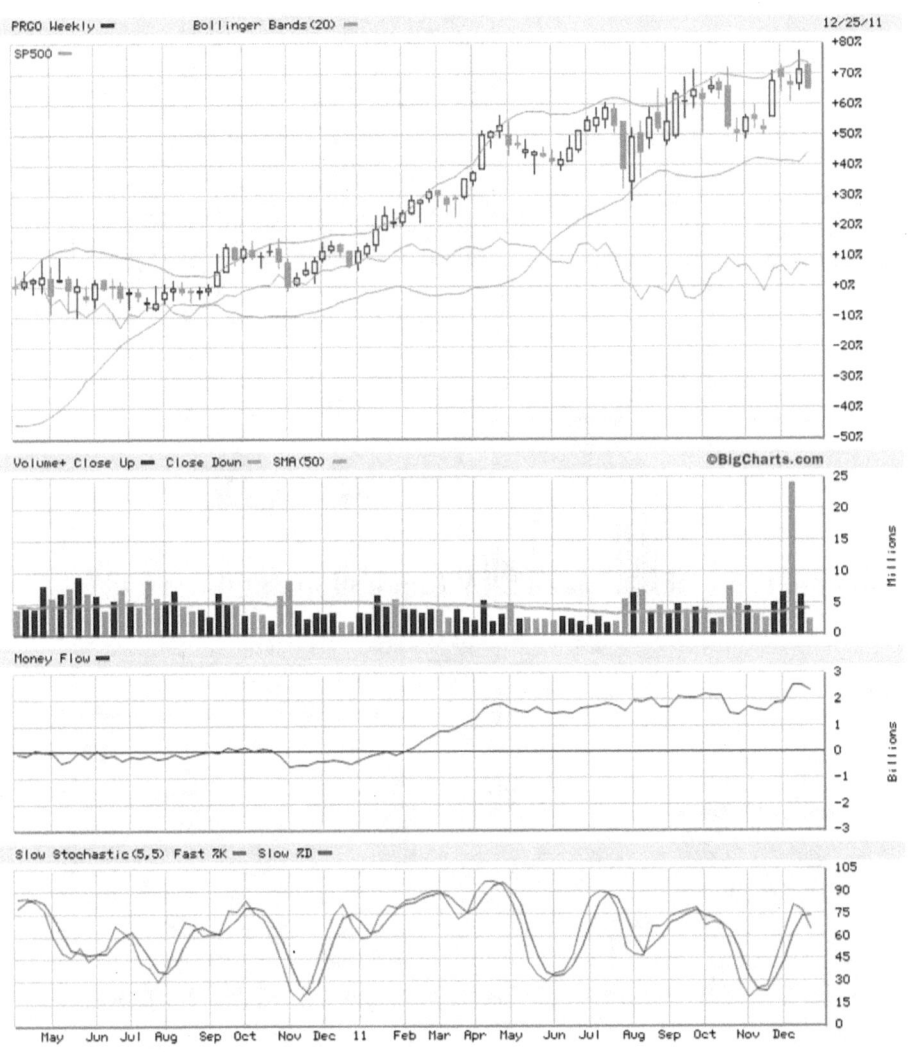

# HOLISTIC INVESTING IN A RISK-AVERSE WORLD

# Subject Index

Additional shares, 75-76, 78, 107, 121
Airlines, 32
Alpha Portfolio, 3
American Dream, 7
Anaconda Copper, 51
Animal Spirits, 75
Appeasement, Neville Chamberlain, 183
Analysis: Sector, 223-230
Apple Computer, 207-8
Asset Classes, 11
Astute investor, 219

Barriers to entry, 40
Barron's, Alan Abelson: humorous satire, 131
Battle: Investment Survival, Gerald Loeb, 155-7
Bear Market, multi-year, definition, 117-125

Beta: definition, Mutual Funds, 224
Beware of (ads: TV, Direct Mail), 129
Big Picture: 50-1, 151-7, 276
Big "Kahuna": market advance, 185
Black Box(Indicators), 57
Bollinger Bands: importance of, 69, 78, 262
Bonds: Chrysler, 33-4; Dreyfus, 186-8, overall, 209-12
Bottom Up: investing, 7
Brand names, corporate, 31-4
Breakouts, Breakdowns: 165; recovery (road to), 192
Bubbles (investment), 182
Burn rate (as applied to R & D), 63
Buying: Core Stocks, 95-9; Cyclical Stocks, 90
Buying Patterns (chart), 73-9; Opportunity: Stage 3, 125
Buffett, Warren, 144, 163
"Buzz" or gossip (beware), 38

Cash (King of 1980s), 62
Candlestick (Cross Pattern), 268, 298
Certificate of Deposit, CDs, 93
Chart patterns, 68-9
Cheap Money, 182, 241
Chinese: "Water Torture" (2000-2) bear market, 119, 190
Citigroup, 8, 159
Cohen, Stanley, CFP, NYU, 56
Commonwealth United: saga of, 27
Commodity products (beware of), 152, 219, 239-243
Company, love of, 13
Comparisons: S & P 500, 113, 131-3, 165-8, 193
Competition, 33, 39
Compound Interest, 84
Computer Sciences, story of, 44-5
Conventional Wisdom, analysts, 63
Core & Cyclical or Special Situation Stocks: 67-9, 90, 95-9, 102, 112-3
Core investments: outperforming, 86, 95-9
Corning, 33
Corporate Security, Israel, Nice Systems Ltd., 252-5
Crash of 2008, 5
Critical Mass, systemic, 107
Cubby Bear Correction: welcome, 111-5

DHA, Biotech, 206
Debt-to-share dilution (beware), 217
De-leveraging (debt draw-down), 7
Demand (market demand-pull), 152, 183
Derivatives, 235
Dilution, stock (beware), 217
De Niro, Robert, 215
Disinflation, bonds: welcome, 209-212
Diversification, 93, 96
Dividends, 6, 101, 106, 184, 235, 257
Dogs: love of, 145, 291
Dollar- Cost Averaging: benefits, Core Stocks, 191, 216
Double-Down, 210
Double Tops- Bottoms: patterns, 267
Due Diligence, 87
Dynamic-Static: concepts, 217-8
Dodd & Frank, Wall Street, 123

Earnings: minefield (beware), 17-21
Earnings Yield, 147
Economic Problem: Demand, 181
Economics: Cycle (10-year), 159-162, 181-3
Economics: "one-handed," President Truman, 50
Electric-Hybrid Cars: critical mass, 201
Emerging Markets (rise of middle class), 245-255
End of Prosperity: Time article, 8

# SUBJECT INDEX

Experts, market, 39
Exchange-Traded Funds, 224

FMC (Food Machinery & Chemical), lithium batteries, etc., 106
F. Lee Bailey, noted lawyer, 1970s, 45
Failed Order, process, 177-180
Fall of Trickle-Down Economics, 203-5
Fear, control of, 114
Final Thoughts: Part 2, 271
Financial Crashes, 177, 190, 234-5
Flexibility (Goal), 283
Focus: Importance of, 37-40, 275, 281-2
Follow the Money: The Haystack (sectors), 61-5, 139
Ford, GM, 32-3, 242
Foreign Stocks (avoid), 155
Franklin, Ben, 164
Free Cash Flow, definition (importance of), 69
Fundamental Analysis, 67-9
Future of (Holistic Investing), 245

G-7 Nations, 8
Gap: chart price(s), 261-2
Gen X, Y (values), 204
Getting: On Base (importance of), 269
Gifts: (Wall St. "story stocks," beware, 37
Going Concern (definition), 123, 216-7

Gold: attributes of, 171, 220
Good (desirable) stock: attributes of, 213
Grandville, Joe, volume studies, 56
Grant, Cary, 17
Growth/Value Investor, (contrasts), 168

Heraclitus: Greek philosopher, 284-5
Holding period: Core Stock, 90
Holistic Investing: 95-9, 108; Future of: 245
Housing Crisis ("bubble"), 159-162, Effects on Consumer Spending, 209-210
Human Capital, 50

Index Options: Uses, 90, 261-2
Indicators, 69, 266-8
Inelastic Demand: definition/usage, 275, 284
Inflation, 90-2, 173-4 (gold), 182, 199-200
Information (overload), 25-7
Inside Week charting), 78, 268
Insider Ownership, 266
Investor's Business Daily, 130
Investment Tools, 67-9, 266-8; Zones, 67-9
Innovation: Israel, 248
Israel, 241-255

309

Japanese Candle Sticks preferred charting), 78
Jobs, Steve, 25

Kennedy, Joe (father of JFK), 186
Key Reversal (charting): importance of, 78
Know Thyself, Greek Philosophers), 85
Kondratief (Long Wave economic), Russian economist, 160

Late night TV ( beware), 134, 205
Layered Method, definition, 225
Law of Probability: suspension of, (for a while), 163
Lehman Brothers, 7, 132
Limit Orders (Risk-Aversion), 74, 79, 179, 185; profits, 238
Loeb, Gerald: The Battle for Investment Survival, 155-7
Lynch, Peter: One Up on Wall Street, 163, 239

Macro View, 89
Management, company, 26, 63, 237-8
Managing Your Money, 177
Marginal Demand, 152
Market Dynamics, 4; Gods: taking back gains, 279
Math: gains/losses, examples; effects on psychology, 179, 198-9; duration, 248

Mass hysteria, 79
Media: Leave the market to, 143
Micro View: earnings, 19, 83
Monopoly Power: desirable, 287
Money Flow Indicator: confirmation of, 69, 76, 218, 266
Multi-Year Bear Market, 117
Myopic Vision (beware), 35
Myths, Name Brand Products, 31-4

Needles in Haystack (new concept), 61
New Issues (stocks), 37-8
NYSE: New York Stock Exchange, data, 68
Nice Systems (Israel), 252-4
Noise (market), false readings, 75

Obsolescence, 240-1
Options (hedging), 10; "raw nerve," 261-2
Outside/Inside Weeks (chart patterns), 268
Oversold (definition), 225

PCs, beginning of, Israel, 245
Pattern recognition, 266-8
Patton, George, American General, 75
Penny stocks ('pink sheet losers"), 51
Perrigo (company), Israel, 251-2
Phase, bull market, 123-4
Power of Mining Stocks (inflation), 171
Picture in Time, 55

## SUBJECT INDEX

Presidents: Kennedy, 49, 184, 187; Hoover, Truman, 182
Public Offerings, 37
Price (stock), 68

Railroads, 29-30, 247
Rainy Day (prepare for), 179
Random Walk Theory, 161; Randomness, 75
Raw Nerve of Market: Options, 90, 262
Real Estate Cycle, (Ideal long-wave), 161
Rebirth (bonds), 189
Reference, stock research, 130
Reinvestment Windows (Important), 98
Relative Strength, 255
Return on Equity (ROE), 69, 96
Retirement Gap, 2
Retracement Percentages, guidelines, 78
Return to (solvency), 287
Reverse Stock Split, Citigroup (beware)
Russell, Richard: Dow Theory, 57-8
Rising Value: Inflation, gold, 173-5
Risk: Economic, 6; Reduction, 144; Management, 168
Rothchild, 19th Century European banker, 43-4, 234
Rule of six, 120

Rust Belt, American Midwest: 1980s, 33; Rust Bowl, 92

Safe Haven, Treasuries,(T-Notes, Bonds), 121
Savers, 2
Seasonality: Stocks, 191
Seasoned Investor, 264-6
Second Wind, 108, 185
Sectors: Fund analysis, 64, 140, 179, 223-230; Investing (Crash), 178-180
Market Movements (contrary), 220; Cyclical Stocks; 73-9, 111-115; Volume, 79
Sell Stops, 77
Sideways: Market Bottom/ Top, 68, 225
Simplify: Investing, 74,105
Sinatra, Frank (That's Life...), 17, 108
Small Victories (build upon), 108
Snapple: advertising campaign, 39
Social Media, 232-3
Soros, George, 139, 163
S & P 500: Benchmark vs. Stock, 111
Stay The Course, future of, 215-6
Staying Power, 95, 98
Stock Buyout: "Buzz," 38
Stock Picker, story, 61-2; Buy-backs, 97
Story of Technology, Israel: Intel, 245
Stoic Investor (Become), 282

311

Strong Market: Rating Tool, 123-5
Switching Stocks, Core, 102
Systems: Market, 64

Tactics: Holistic Principles, 3
Talpiot, Israeli Leadership Program, 249-250
Tangible Common Stock, 213
Technical Analysis, 67-8, 266-8
Templeton, Sir John, 164
Teva Pharmceutical (TEVA), Israel, 250-252
Three Steps and a Rise, 191
Time (passage of), an Ally, 6, 98, 101
Time Value of Money, alternative perspective, 198-9
Tools of the Trade, 67-9
Top-Down or "Trickle-Down Economics," 5, 203; Crashing Down, 182-3
Trade Surplus: Asian, 140-1
Trading Seminar, Chicago, 57
Tsunami (financial stocks), 96
Turning Points: Volume, 275

Uncertainty, 58
Undervalued company, 105

Value 3 Portfolio: 3, 83, 259
Value Line Investment Survey, 134-5
Value Trap, 168
Volatility: Market, 108; Treasuries, 177-180, 260-2
Volcker, Paul (Fed Chair of 1980s), 92
Volume Spike: Test, 113-4, 267

Wealth of Nations, Adam Smith (1776), 160
Weekly Volume/Price data, 68
What Time is it? 49
When: (most difficult decision), selling, 73-7
Wide Moat Companies, 97
White Noise: definition, 25, 237
Work (your portfolio), 145
Working Capital, definition, 184
Working Technical & Fundamental Tools, 67
Wrapping It All Up, Parts 1 and 2: 257, 271

Yardstick (1): Management, 96-7
Yardstick (2): Charts: Moving Averages: 10 week (50 day), 30 week (200 day), 192-3
Yogi Berra, 209

Zero Base Data: Conventional Wisdom? 281
Zeno, Founder of Stoicism, 308 BC, Greek Philosopher, 282

# Biography

Joe began his career with Lebergern and Burns, CPA, Levittown, PA. He worked with small business on tax and payroll accounting. Later he worked for the NJ Inheritance Tax Bureau, Office of State Auditor, Health Department and finally the Dept. of Transportation, initially in Federal Grants. Later he was selected to begin the first Investment Recovery Program(surplus property sales to the private sector) working under the Director of Purchasing. His job was logistics: to organize material centers throughout the state while finding buyers, sometimes out of state. In September,1991 Joe retired early to begin his own company.

Joe attended Rider University and received a B. S. in Commerce in 1964. Later he attended the Graduate Faculty, The New School and received an M. A. in Economics,1982. Joe continued his education at New York University and earned a Diploma in Financial Planning in 1984.

In 1985 Joe became a Registered Investment Advisor and began *Financial Synergy*, managing investment funds for individual clients. He would continue to write a quarterly market letter, initially *The Strategic Investor* later to become *The Holistic Investor*. During this time, Joe has publish articles in local newspapers and *Barron's*. Later, Joe was interviewed by the *New York Times: The Bond Warriors: Three Voices of Experience*, January, 1999.